LEGENDARY LOCALS

OF

MCDOWELL COUNTY

WEST VIRGINIA

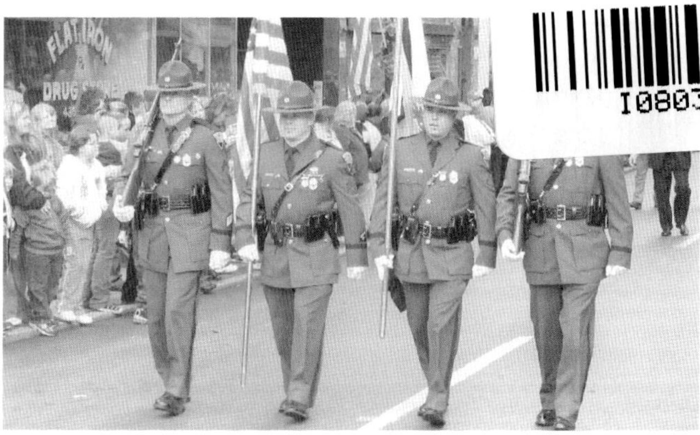

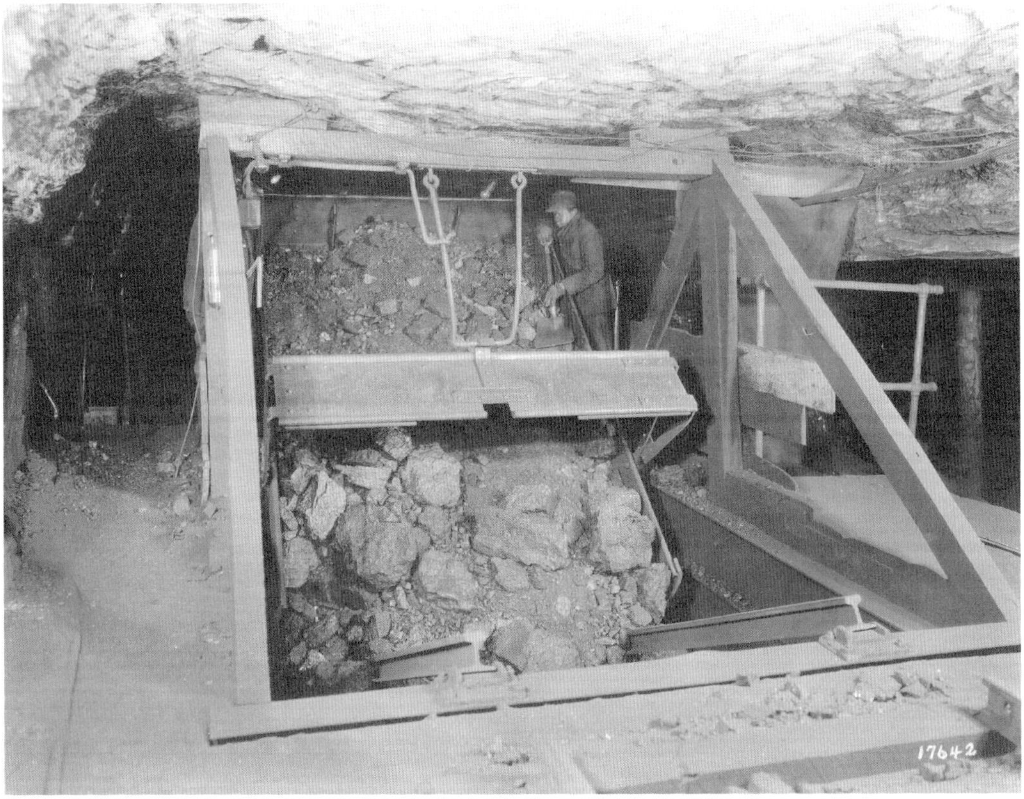

Can You Dig It?
An unidentified coal miner is shown here working at the Pond Creek Coal Company No. 1 Mine coal chute in Bartley, West Virginia. Coal from McDowell County fueled blast furnaces worldwide to forge the steel that formed the fabric of the Industrial Revolution. (Courtesy of the Eastern Regional Coal Archives.)

Page 1: Honor Guard
The West Virginia State Police Honor Guard members shown here were all stationed at the McDowell County detachment at some point in their careers. They are, from left to right, Cpl. Don Havens, Sgt. Chuck Tupper, Trooper First Class Charlie McKenzie, and Trooper Nate Workman. This photograph was taken on McDowell Street in Welch, West Virginia, during the 2007 Veterans Day Parade. Note keynote speaker (then governor, now US senator) Joe Manchin marching behind the honor guard. (Photograph by the author.)

LEGENDARY LOCALS

OF

MCDOWELL COUNTY

WEST VIRGINIA

WILLIAM R. "BILL" ARCHER

LEGENDARY LOCALS

ISBN 978-1-4671-0036-6

Legendary Locals is an imprint of Arcadia Publishing
Charleston, South Carolina

Printed in the United States of America

Library of Congress Control Number: 2012939425

For all general information, please contact Arcadia Publishing:
Telephone 843-853-2070
Fax 843-853-0044
E-mail sales@arcadiapublishing.com
For customer service and orders:
Toll-Free 1-888-313-2665

Visit us on the Internet at www.arcadiapublishing.com

Dedication

To my dear friend the late Dr. Thomas Clark Hatcher and to the people of McDowell County, who remain strong through unimaginable adversity.

On the Cover: From left to right:
(TOP ROW) David Lee Sackett, Bronze Star recipient (Courtesy of the US Military Academy, page 57); Booker T. Stephens, judge (Courtesy of Booker T. Stephens, page 98); Eddie Asbury, coal operator (Photograph by the author, page 110); Irene C. Berger, judge (Courtesy of Judge Irene C. Berger, page 79); Ed Shepard, Marine sniper (Photograph by the author, page 51).
(MIDDLE ROW) Elizabeth Simpson Drewry, state delegate (Courtesy of the Eastern Regional Coal Archives, page 69); James "Jimmy" Hampton, merchant and clown (Photograph by the author, page 107); Ellis Ray Williams, principal (Courtesy of Ellis Ray Williams, page 49); James Elwood Jones, coal baron (Courtesy of the Eastern Regional Coal Archives, page 25); Reba Honaker, mayor (Photograph by the author, page 101).
(BOTTOM ROW) Frederick J. Kimball, railroad president (Courtesy of the Eastern Regional Coal Archives, page 15); Sharon Sagety, volunteer (Photograph by the author, page 92); King Malachi "Mel" Street, musician (Courtesy of Melvin Grubb, page 78); Ergie Smith, basketball coach (Courtesy of Ergie Smith, page 71); Samuel A. Crozer, coal investor (Courtesy of Dorothy MacQueen, page 20).

CONTENTS

ACKNOWLEDGMENTS

During the past three decades, I have been honored to serve the people of McDowell County, West Virginia, as a newspaperman. Even when I was a total stranger to them, they welcomed me into their homes and businesses with a smile and asked me to come back when I could stay longer. I have received a great deal of help while compiling this project, and foremost among those who have helped me is my wife, Evonda Archer, who is a constant source of inspiration in everything I do, along with my friend and coworker, Ray Glover, who accepts the fact that I will push hard and does his level best to do all he can to help. I appreciate Shirley Ofsa for helping fill in the blanks of a mighty good story, Kenneth and Shirley Davidson for their friendship, Eddie Asbury for all he does for McDowell County, and Jack Caffrey for never giving up when others did. I want to thank Donna Morgan and everyone at the McDowell County Public Library in Welch, as well as Fran Caplan, director of the Robert Morris University Library in Coraopolis, Pennsylvania. I want to thank the entire Gianatto and Balasis families for their remarkable friendship, Judy McDaniel for continuing her mother Grace (Henderson) Haynes's commitment to preserving McDowell County history, and the late Early Smith for introducing me to the real folks who make Coalwood a special place. I would like to thank Ed Rotenberry for his passionate love of McDowell County history. I would like to thank Becky George of the Eastern Regional Coal Archives for going the extra mile to help me gain access to some important historic images. I also want to thank Anita Moody for all of her help, including the incredible image from High Rocks. I also appreciate the help of Christy Bailey, Barbara Blake, Karen Sword, Mel Grubb, the late Mike Hornick, Harold McBride, Tom Acosta, Markella Gianato, Jimmy Gianato, Ruth Surratt, Barbara Lewis, Gary Dove, Joe Monti, Ed Shepard, Jim Stafford, the Hassel T. Hicks family, Chris Shoemaker, Rick Barbero, Ellis Ray Williams, Glenn Friss, Karen Hogston, *Leatherneck* magazine, Patrick Corcoran, Dorothy MacQueen, Eric DiNovo, Michael Quick, Samantha Perry, Darryl Hudson, Charles H. "Bud" Gearheart Jr., Ergie Smith, the Reverend Tim Hairston, and the Reverend Dr. Earl Rogers.

INTRODUCTION

In a very real sense, the story of McDowell County, West Virginia, is the story of American freedom, although people who live in the economically challenged and job-starved southern West Virginia coalfields have borne the brunt of paying for those freedoms so that others might reap the benefits. Those enormous challenges have always been costly, and have served to temper the mettle that remains as the most enduring quality of the people who have called McDowell County home.

McDowell County and its people have lived in the global spotlight for a long time. About one-quarter of a century before the start of the American Revolution, several large companies took note of the county as they undertook explorations of what was then southwestern Virginia. In 1750, the second exploration of Dr. Thomas Walker, in the employ of the Loyal Company, reached McDowell County, and Walker reported the discovery of large coal deposits in the region. Walker and his associates, Ambrose Powell, William Tomlinson, Colby Crew, Henry Lawless, and John Hughes, discovered several outcroppings of coal along the Tug Fork of the Big Sandy River in the Flat Top Mountain region. John Peter Salley, who was commissioned to explore western Virginia by the governor of Virginia, wrote that the region contained "great plenty of coals," and Christopher Gist, who traveled along the Tug Fork in his 1751–1752 exploration for the Ohio Company, observed the "several kinds of timber and trees" in the region he explored.

When European settlers first started arriving in North America, many came to the New World in search of fortune, and many of those fortune seekers equated treasure with precious metals like gold and silver. However, in a short time, the effort to tap into North America's abundant wealth in natural resources supplanted the quest for gold. While Virginia's coastal and piedmont regions provided investors a quick cash crop—tobacco—the western mountains of the Old Dominion had a seemingly endless supply of hardwoods and the untapped wealth and power contained in sizeable coal deposits. Of course, at that time, the world didn't know how to harness that incredible energy source.

At the time of the American Revolution, the founding fathers were well aware of the riches buried beneath the mountains of southwestern Virginia, eastern Kentucky, and northeastern Tennessee. Thomas Jefferson, author of the Declaration of Independence, wrote about "the coal lands" of western Virginia in his 1785 book *Notes on the State of Virginia.* Other men who had a great deal to lose by signing Jefferson's Declaration also knew of the potential wealth locked within the mountains. Among those visionaries was Robert Morris, arguably the wealthiest man in America in 1776 when the war for independence broke out. Morris threw his entire fortune as well as his financial acumen behind the colonial cause, risking a comfortable life on the slim glimmer of hope that 13 separate colonies could become one nation under God. In return for his commitment, he received McDowell County, West Virginia.

Actually, McDowell County was at the heart of the 480,000-acre Wilson, Cary, Nicholas survey of the western Virginia coal lands, and just part of the enormous sections of land that Morris acquired during the post–Revolutionary War land speculation rush centered on the unsettled central Appalachian region. In all, from September 1, 1787, through March 25, 1795, Morris acquired 24 grants for huge tracts of land in what is now West Virginia as well as Virginia's (then) Kentucky Military District. In retrospect, looking at the grants he acquired, coal appeared to be the common denominator. His holdings went as far north as the West Fork River in the Farmington, West Virginia, area and as far west as the Green River valley in Kentucky. Truly, though, McDowell County was the heart of Morris's land speculation efforts.

Alas, Morris did not live long enough to see the benefits that his vast holdings might yield. His energetic investments didn't produce an immediate return, and by 1799, he was so financially overextended that Morris, the great "Financier of the American Revolution," landed in a debtor's prison in Philadelphia. Perhaps owing to his service to the nation and the support of friends like Pres. George Washington, who knew what his contribution to liberty had meant, Morris was released from prison due to health reasons in 1802. He died penniless on May 9, 1806, and was interred in the crypt of his father-in-law until his widow could arrange a proper burial for him some years later. Morris and Roger Sherman were the only two men to sign all three of the documents that formed the United States of America: the Declaration of Independence, the Articles of Confederation, and the Constitution.

The Philadelphia investment community didn't forget about Morris's extensive holdings. In 1834, Michel Bouvier, a Philadelphia builder/furniture manufacturer with ties to the court of Napoleon Bonaparte, served as the point man for an investment group that acquired Morris's fallow Wilson, Cary, Nicholas tract, but no commercial development came from that. The collapse of the agrarian-based economy of the South 30 years later inspired another man with ties to the Keystone State, Maj. Jedediah Hotchkiss, to resurrect Virginia's economy based on the mineral wealth of the southern West Virginia and southwestern Virginia coal lands.

Hotchkiss, a New York state native who taught school in the Lykens Valley of Pennsylvania before relocating to Staunton, Virginia, became renowned as Gen. Thomas "Stonewall" Jackson's mapmaker who charted the course for Jackson's famous Shenandoah Valley campaign. Hotchkiss saw post–Civil War Virginia in ruins, but instead of looking to the past he focused on the future, and worked to develop a new economy based on the industrial movement that was then in its infancy. Hotchkiss knew of the coalfields from his work as a field geologist in 1835 with William Barton Rogers, the first director of the Virginia Geographical Society. Hotchkiss also possessed a copy of Thomas Walker's notes of his 1751 discovery of the coal outcroppings along the Tug Fork of the Big Sandy River.

In 1873, Hotchkiss commissioned Isaiah A. Welch to survey the coal lands of the Tug River valley, and the survey uncovered the largest concentration of high-quality coal deposits in the world. From 1873 forward, Hotchkiss used his considerable energies to develop the southern West Virginia coalfields. From January 1880 until December 1884, Hotchkiss published a monthly newspaper out of Staunton, Virginia, called *The Virginias—A Mining, Industrial & Scientific Journal Devoted to the Development of Virginia and West Virginia*, which established a blueprint for the Industrial Revolution that transformed the United States into a global superpower in less than 40 years.

Hotchkiss knew about the coal firsthand, and as a publisher of a scientific journal, he was able to include information on Sir Henry Bessemer's success with his converter for making steel in 1856, and the discovery of the huge iron ore deposits in the Mesabi Range in Minnesota while *The Virginias* was in publication. The steel age had arrived, and the coke produced from the coal mined from the Pocahontas coal seams proved to be the global standard in metallurgical or steelmaking coke. Hotchkiss commissioned laboratory examinations of the coal and published the results.

The Philadelphia-based financial firm of E.W. Clark & Company was the first to buy into Hotchkiss's plan, and put a junior associate, Frederick J. Kimball, in charge of acquiring the Atlantic, Mississippi & Ohio Railway from its receivers for $8.6 million on February 10, 1881. Almost immediately, the new Norfolk & Western Railway began construction of a branch line from Radford, Virginia, to an outcropping of coal in Powell's Bottom, Tazewell County, Virginia—a town that would later be called Pocahontas.

Another Philadelphia businessman with Civil War profits to work with, Samuel A. Crozer of Upland (Chester), Pennsylvania, also took notice of the investment possibilities that Hotchkiss wrote about monthly. Crozer made a fortune in textile manufacturing during the war years, and invested some of the profits he made into developing the Crozer Iron & Steel Business in Roanoke, Virginia, in 1881. Ultimately, Crozer became the first major investor in the McDowell County coal property since Morris. Hotchkiss sent agents to purchase thousands of acres of land along Elkhorn Creek, a tributary of the Tug Fork. In 1884, Crozer bought the Elkhorn Creek bottom properties from Hotchkiss and formed the Crozer Coal & Coke Company. Crozer's entrance into the coalfields prompted the Clark investors to accelerate the construction of a tunnel through Coaldale Mountain in 1887–1888, run a spur line to Elkhorn, West Virginia, and open the McDowell County coalfields to development.

In 1888, with a tunnel open into McDowell, other industrialists became involved in the county's development. John Pierpont Morgan, and Judge Elbert Gary, his principal architect of the US Steel Corporation, worked with a southern West Virginia banker, Isaac T. Mann, to purchase coal property on the Tug Fork, and US Steel put its stamp on the future of the county. The US Steel mines in Gary Hollow on the Tug Fork enabled the company to grow into one of the nation's most prosperous businesses. The mine at Main Gary, West Virginia, produced coal until the mid-1980s. US Steel Mining's record of safety was unequalled when all of the Gary mines were operational.

However, mine safety has always been a major concern in the coalfields. Throughout the 20th century, coal mining has been among the deadliest occupations in the United States, with McDowell County experiencing many coal mine tragedies. Although not the worst disaster in terms of loss of life, the Jed Mine explosion remains one of the lingering legacies of coal mining in McDowell County. On March 26, 1912, a methane blast ignited coal "bug dust" in Jed Mine, resulting in the deaths of 81 miners. Many of the victims were foreign-born, and when no one came to claim their bodies, they were hastily buried in a potter's field that the gravediggers called "Little Egypt." In the community now known as Havaco, West Virginia, the potter's field remains 100 years later, unmarked, unattended, and essentially unknown to most people in McDowell County. Scars left by tragedies like the Jed Mine explosion aren't as obvious as scars left in the mountains by surface mines in the period before the Surface Mine Reclamation Act of 1977, but they remain part of the county's history.

While coal was king in McDowell County, timber was prince. William McClellan Ritter, a nephew of Robert Morris, arrived in southern West Virginia in 1890, and started working in a sawmill. Before the turn of the 20th century, the W.M. Ritter Lumber Company was incorporated in Welch and grew into one of the largest hardwood timber companies in the world before it was acquired by Georgia-Pacific. Ritter supplied crossties for the expanding railroads, mine props for the mines, and lumber to build the company barracks that would house coal miners and their families, with enough fine hardwoods left over to sell to domestic and foreign customers.

Yet, McDowell County's history isn't just one of industry. It's also a story of people. There were fewer than 500 families living in the county when the Virginia General Assembly established the county on February 28, 1858. The county was named for Virginia governor James McDowell of Rockbridge County, who supported the abolition of slavery after the 1831 Nat Turner Insurrection, which occurred during McDowell's first term as a delegate in the Virginia General Assembly.

Since there were no slaves living in the county when it was formed, it was known as "a free state," like many other counties in the South where there were no slaves. Hotchkiss published photographs of able-bodied, newly emancipated African American men who were ready to work in the blossoming coalfields. When industrial development came, a group of homegrown leaders liked the idea that these former slaves, as well as men who had lived through oppression in other lands, could find jobs in the coalfields. Those leaders started calling the county "The Free State of McDowell," and the slogan remains.

America has been called the "Melting Pot of Nations," and McDowell County exemplifies that expression as much or more than any other place in West Virginia. The coal communities that sprang up around every mine were segregated according to race and nationality by mine operators, but the men worked together, the women tended gardens together, and the children played together. Families of all nationalities, races, and creeds had very little, but in McDowell County, they had each other. When integration finally came to the county, sports teams excelled. The combined Northfork-Elkhorn high school boys basketball team won eight consecutive state titles—a feat that has not been equaled in the United States before or since.

The moniker, The Free State of McDowell, ultimately evolved to have a far greater meaning than its original intent. Coal mining was a hard and often deadly occupation. Railroad building was hard. Living on a steep mountainside was hard. Living through bitterly cold winters, deadly spring floods, and blistering hot summers was hard. Getting an education was hard. Survival on every level was hard, and as a result of all of these hardships, the people of McDowell County instinctively learned how to manage through tough times.

The United Mine Workers of America had a hard time penetrating the fortress of the organized mine operators, and one of the major moments in the effort to organize the UMWA came on August 1, 1921, when Sid Hatfield and Ed Chambers were gunned down on the front steps of the McDowell County Courthouse in Welch. The West Virginia Mine Wars that followed did not end until 1933, when Pres. Franklin Delano Roosevelt's New Deal gave labor unions the right to organize. The UMWA organized entire coalfields, and big-mine operators responded by placing even greater emphasis on the movement to increase mine mechanization to wrench coal from the bowels of the earth. In the next half-century, thousands of coal-mining jobs vanished from McDowell County as one coal miner could now do the work of 25 in 1900.

The people of the "Free State" knew that freedom came at a cost, and McDowell County has played a role in every major war that America has fought since the coalfields came into existence. Thousands of African American soldiers served in World War I, and had enough political clout at home to get the McDowell County Commission to build the first and only memorial in the United States dedicated to black soldiers who fought in World War I. In World War II, Lt. Sara Blanche Vance, of Iaeger, was the first woman from West Virginia to be killed in action; on May 21, 2002, in Operation Mountain Lion in Afghanistan, Sgt. Gene Arden Vance Jr. was the first West Virginia National Guardsman since World War II to be killed in action. Although he was born in Frankfurt, Germany, Sergeant Vance had close family ties to McDowell and Wyoming Counties.

While some McDowell County residents fought with weapons, thousands of miners waged war by extracting coal used to produce the steel that armored America's tanks and ships and powered the home front energy that contributed to the war effort. In 1932, the completion of an 18-mile drainage tunnel serving five huge coal operations made the Pocahontas Fuel Company capable of mining enough metallurgical coal to produce all the steel necessary to supply several armies. In the 1930s, Pocahontas coal went to rebuild the economy of southern Italy, Japan survived the global depression on discarded dust and slack from mines working the Pocahontas seams, and the US military used Pocahontas coal to build and power its war machine.

In the decades after World War II, mine mechanization and the arrival of huge mine companies changed the world for the people of McDowell County. Job losses and mine closings triggered a mass exodus from the coalfields starting in the 1960s that hasn't stopped yet. McDowell County's loss in terms of people power turned out to be the gain of communities worldwide, where McDowell expatriates bring a blend of talents including an ability to cooperate in a racially and culturally diverse workplace, an ability to respond to hardships of any kind, the ability to develop creative solutions for complex challenges, and the tenacity, strength, and dedication to achieve the impossible in the face of incredible odds.

That spirit—the "Free State" spirit that permeates McDowell County history—is not gone, and in fact, the seeds of new hope are in place that will no doubt bear fruit for generations to come. Before his death, US senator Robert C. Byrd used his political prowess to secure a federal prison for McDowell County that provides hundreds of jobs in the area and, with it, brings potential for a new kind of growth. Likewise, the Hatfield-McCoy Trail System is giving adventurous people a new way to experience the beauty of McDowell County's mountains, and local entrepreneurs are recognizing the potential and investing in the future.

One coal operator pointed out that as long as the world needs steel, there will be a market for McDowell County coal, and his statement is absolutely accurate. While other forms of energy may one day replace coal as a source of electricity for residential and commercial applications, the almost pure carbon contained in coke made from metallurgical coal is an essential ingredient in the production of steel. McDowell County, West Virginia, still has the world's best coking coals and, as a result, McDowell County remains very important to the world—whether the world knows it or not.

CHAPTER ONE

Speculation

Native Americans had little use for the geographical area that would become McDowell County. The mountains were too steep for even subsistence agriculture, and the narrow valleys were too uncertain in times of flash floods to establish communities. Hunting parties passed through the mountains of McDowell County, but there were several other, much better trails to use through less treacherous portions of the Appalachian mountain range. The Black Wolf Indians of the Shawnee Tribe tangled with Henry Harman and his two sons, George and Matthias, on November 12, 1788, on the Tug Fork of the Big Sandy River in the only recorded clash between Indians and pioneer settlers in McDowell County. The Harman family drove off the seven-member Black Wolf raiding party, and the county faced no more hostile Indians.

Even though the Harman family probably didn't know it, the land they defended was already owned by Robert Morris, the financier of the American Revolution who acquired most of McDowell County as well as other coal-bearing properties during the post–Revolutionary War land speculation rush. Over the next 224 years, the natural wealth of McDowell County would transform the world, and the county's people would make an impact on that changing world. Absentee ownership of the land and the extraordinary natural wealth on the surface as well as the mineral wealth buried beneath the soil would set the tone for the underlying theme that has been a constant throughout McDowell County history.

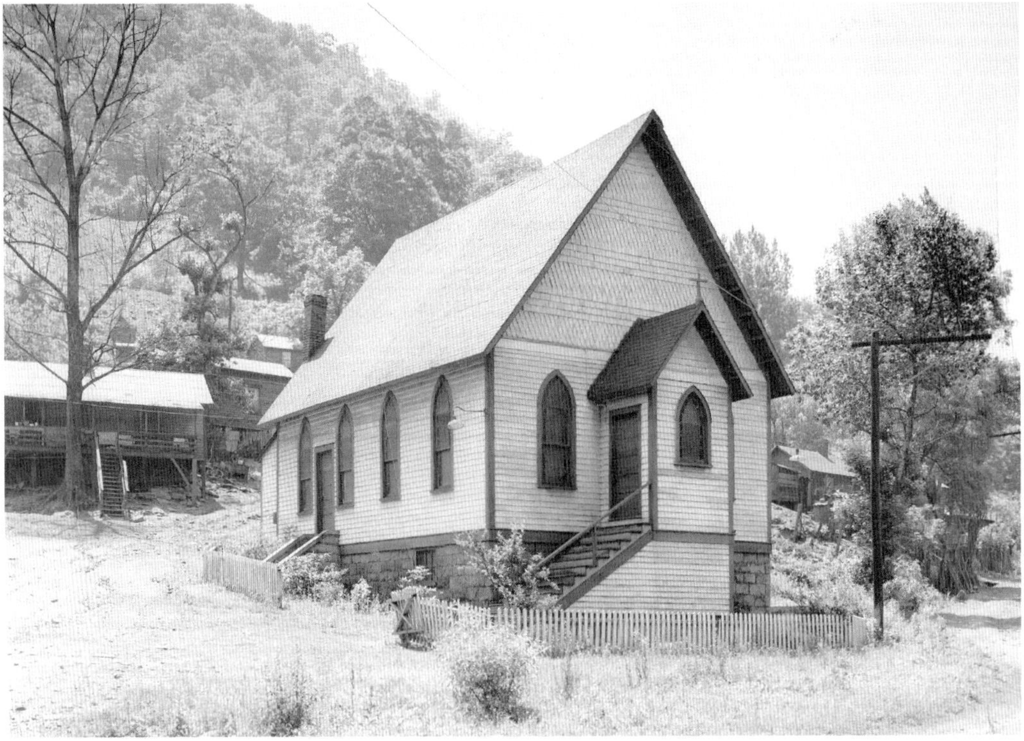

A Church in the Valley

Grace Episcopal Church in Eckman, West Virginia, was established on May 9, 1894. In 1899, Samuel Fisher Morris, a grandson of Robert Morris, along with his wife and seven other contributors, were instrumental in erecting the house of worship and providing its interior furnishings. (Courtesy of Shirley Ofsa.)

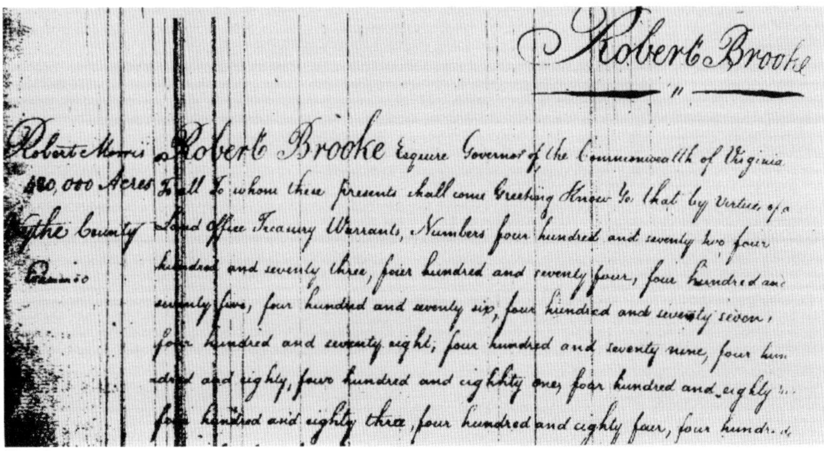

Robert Brooke

Robert Morris 480,000 Acres the County

Robert Brooke Esquire Governor of the Commonwealth of Virginia To all to whom these presents shall come Greeting Know Ye that by Virtue of a Land Office Treasury Warrants, Numbers four hundred and seventy two four hundred and seventy three, four hundred and seventy four, four hundred and seventy five, four hundred and seventy six, four hundred and seventy seven, four hundred and seventy eight; four hundred and seventy nine, four hundred and eighty, four hundred and eighty one, four hundred and eighty two, four hundred and eighty three, four hundred and eighty four, four hund...

The Price of Liberty

From September 1, 1787, through March 25, 1795, after the end of the American Revolution, Robert Morris invested in land in what was then western Virginia and Virginia's Kentucky Military District. Morris secured treasury warrants for 24 tracts of land in the region, including the 480,000-acre Wilson Cary Nicholas survey that included much of the territory that would become McDowell County. (Courtesy of the archives of the Virginia State Library, Richmond, Virginia.)

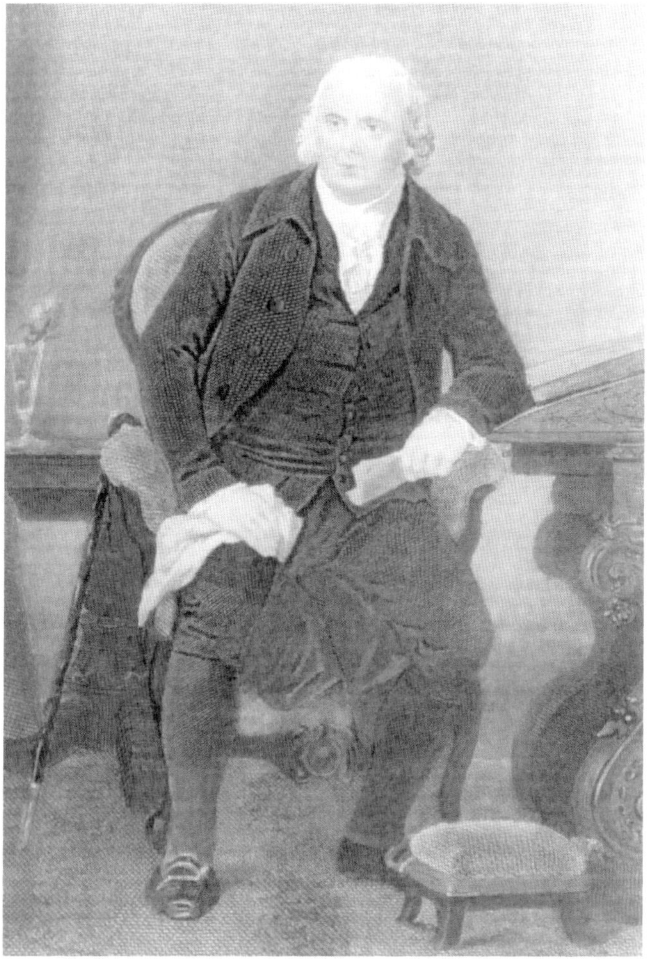

Financier of the American Way of Life

Robert Morris is perhaps one of the least known of America's founding fathers, but his legacy continues to have an impact on the course of US history. Morris and Roger Sherman were the only two men to sign all three of the documents that form the basis of American democracy: the Declaration of Independence, the Articles of Confederation, and US Constitution. At a time when the outcome of the American Revolution was still very much in question, Morris authored the plan for a national bank, which became the Bank of North America, and loaned $10,000 of his own money to the government so Gen. George Washington could equip his soldiers for the Battle of Trenton, New Jersey, a battle made famous by Washington's dramatic crossing of the Delaware River. At the end of the Revolution, Washington appointed Morris financial secretary, in which capacity he secured an international line of credit for the new nation. Morris declined Washington's appointment to be the first secretary of the treasury and recommended Alexander Hamilton for that position. Rather than cementing his position in the pantheon of founding fathers, Morris instead secured the nation's future by serving as a US senator from Pennsylvania and by purchasing huge tracts of land in Virginia's interior. Morris didn't buy just any land. Rather, the tracts he purchased were mostly underlain with untapped coal reserves. His extensive investments eventually led him to a Philadelphia debtor's prison in 1798. He was released in 1801 due to health reasons, and lived with his wife's family until his death on May 9, 1806. He was buried in his father-in-law's crypt until his wife could secure a burial crypt for him in the yard of Christ Church, Philadelphia. (Courtesy of Robert Morris University.)

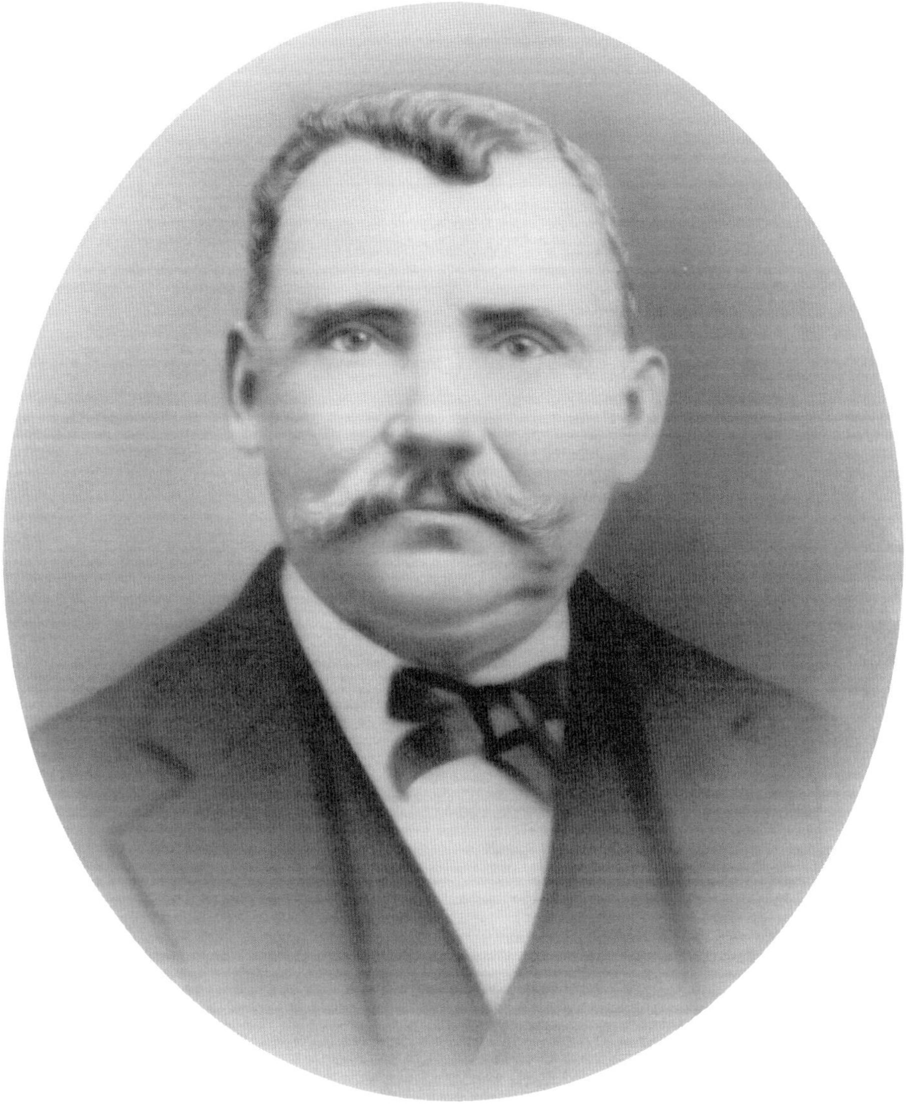

Coal Man

Jenkin Jones, shown here, was born at Glyn Neath, Wales, on September 25, 1839, into a family that had a long history of working in the Welsh coal mines. Jones started working in the mines as a boy, but left his native land in 1863 and came to the United States to work in the anthracite coal mines of eastern Pennsylvania. In 1872, he took a job in the iron ore mines of Clifton Forge, Virginia, and four years later, moved to the recently opened bituminous coal fields along the New River in Fayette County, West Virginia. After spending eight years in the New River coalfields, Jones went first to Mercer County in 1884 and then to Simmons, where he opened the Carswell Creek Mine. Jones followed the Pocahontas Number 3 coal seam as far north as he could, and at the same time, pushed the Norfolk & Western Railway to build a tunnel through Coaldale Mountain into McDowell County. That effort was rewarded in 1887 when the railroad built the Coaldale tunnel into McDowell County. Jones acquired some coal leases along the Tug Fork of the Big Sandy River and started mining coal in the vicinity of what is now the town of Anawalt, West Virginia. The town of Jenkinjones was named in his honor. (Courtesy of the Eastern Regional Coal Archives.)

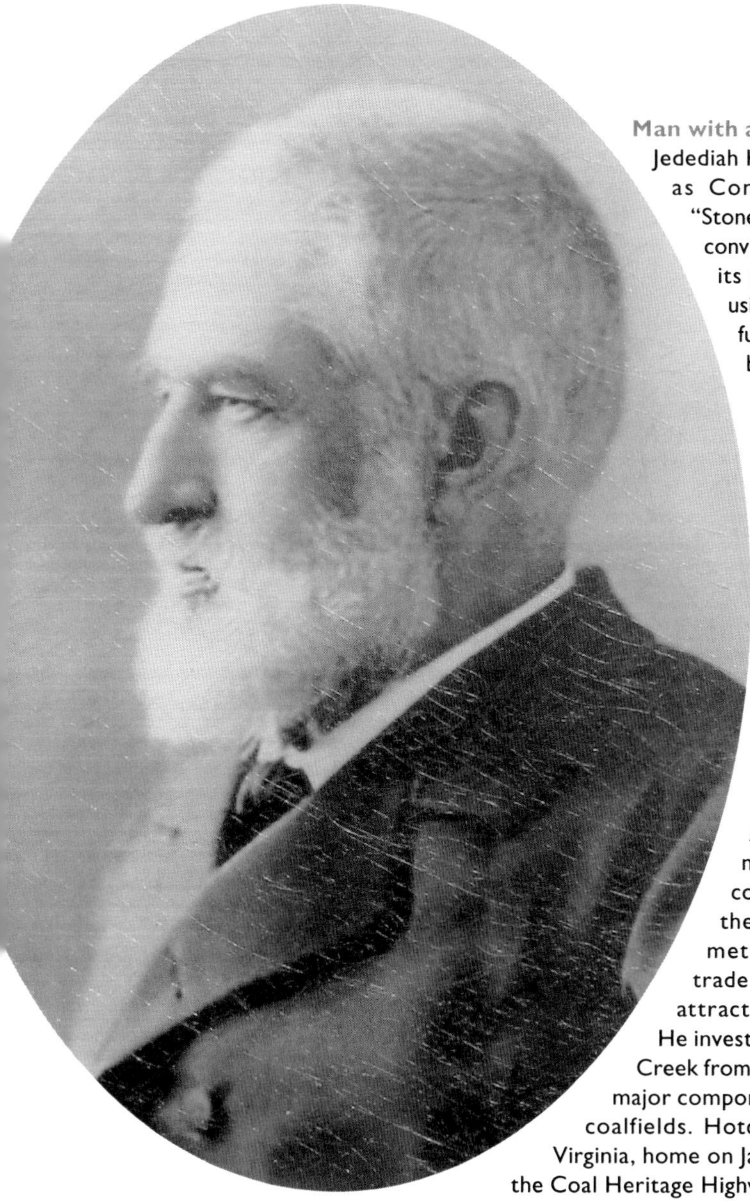

Man with a Plan

Jedediah Hotchkiss, famed in the South as Confederate general Thomas "Stonewall" Jackson's mapmaker, was convinced that Virginia could rebuild its post–Civil War economy by using its vast mineral resources to fuel the foundation of what would become known as the Industrial Revolution. Hotchkiss—a geologist by trade—used his organizational skills to develop national and international markets for the coal from McDowell County, and to help build the Norfolk–Newport News and Hampton Roads port city into one of the busiest ports in the United States. In 1873, Hotchkiss hired Isaiah A. Welch to conduct the first survey of the Pocahontas Coal Fields. After Welch's survey of the massive Pocahontas Number 3 coal seam, Hotchkiss promoted the use of McDowell County's metallurgical coal through his trade publication, *The Virginias*, to attract investors to the coalfields. He invested in coal lands along Elkhorn Creek from 1884 to 1889 to form the first major component of the McDowell County coalfields. Hotchkiss died at his Staunton, Virginia, home on January 17, 1899. (Courtesy of the Coal Heritage Highway Authority.)

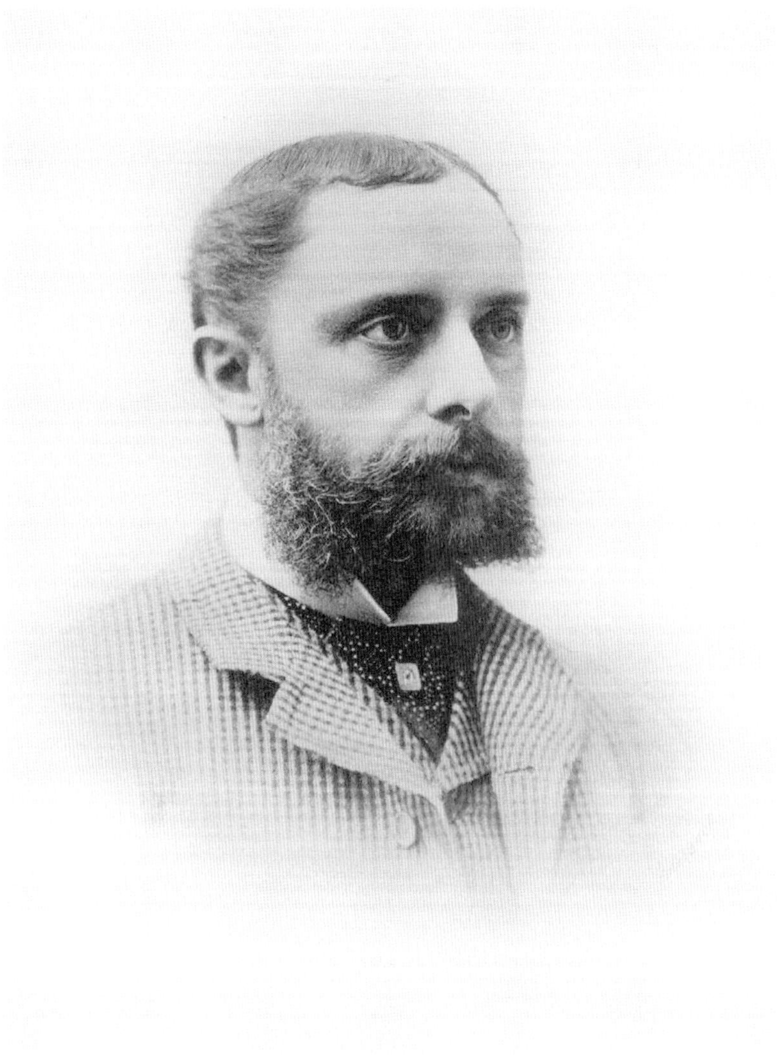

Railroad Genius

Frederick J. Kimball was the up-and-coming executive in the Philadelphia-based financial firm of E.W. Clark & Company who was selected to build the Norfolk & Western Railway out of the Atlantic, Mississippi & Ohio Railway that Clarence H. Clark purchased at a foreclosure sale at Roanoke, Virginia, in May 1881. Kimball, a civil engineer by trade who became a partner in the Clark firm in 1857, had been chosen to put the railroad together a year earlier, but while that effort wasn't successful, he formed relations in the European financial community with men like William Vivian during the railroad's formative years. Perhaps more than any other individual, Kimball put his stamp on the development of the N&W Railway as it pushed into the McDowell County coalfields and expanded westward to the Ohio River, connecting with the American heartland. He died on July 27, 1903. It is interesting to note that the McDowell County towns of Vivian and Kimball are side-by-side on the mainline of what is now the Norfolk Southern Railway. (Courtesy of the Eastern Regional Coal Archives.)

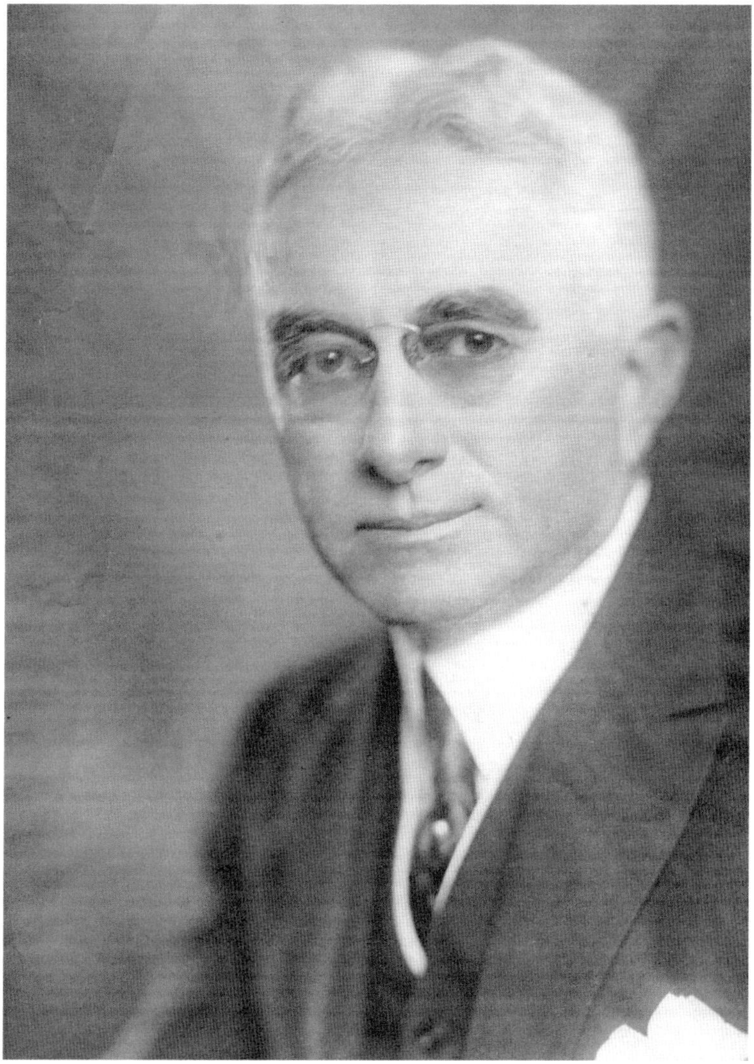

Family Matters
William McClellan Ritter, known as "Uncle Mac" to his family, came to southern West Virginia around 1890 from his home in Benton, Columbia County, Pennsylvania, after the timber reserves in that part of the state had been depleted. Ritter got his middle name from Gen. George B. McClellan, the Union Army general with whom his grandfather had served. After the war, McClellan served as president of the Ohio & Mississippi Railway, which fell into receivership and was acquired by the Clark Company and transformed into the Norfolk & Western Railway. Ritter's paternal ancestors came from a long line of eastern Pennsylvania lumbermen, and his mother, Elizabeth Morris Ritter, was a member of the Robert Morris family. After working a few years as a lumberman in Mercer County, West Virginia, he acquired the timber rights to some properties along the Tug Fork of the Big Sandy River and established the W.M. Ritter Lumber Company in Welch in 1894—the same year that city was chartered. Ritter Lumber grew rapidly to support the growth in the coal industry, and expanded into seven more states and grew into the largest hardwood manufacturing company in the world, owning more than 300,000 acres of land. He became one of the most powerful industrialists of his time, was a friend to five US presidents, and the company he built merged with Georgia-Pacific Lumber Company. Ritter died on May 21, 1952. (Courtesy of the Eastern Regional Coal Archives.)

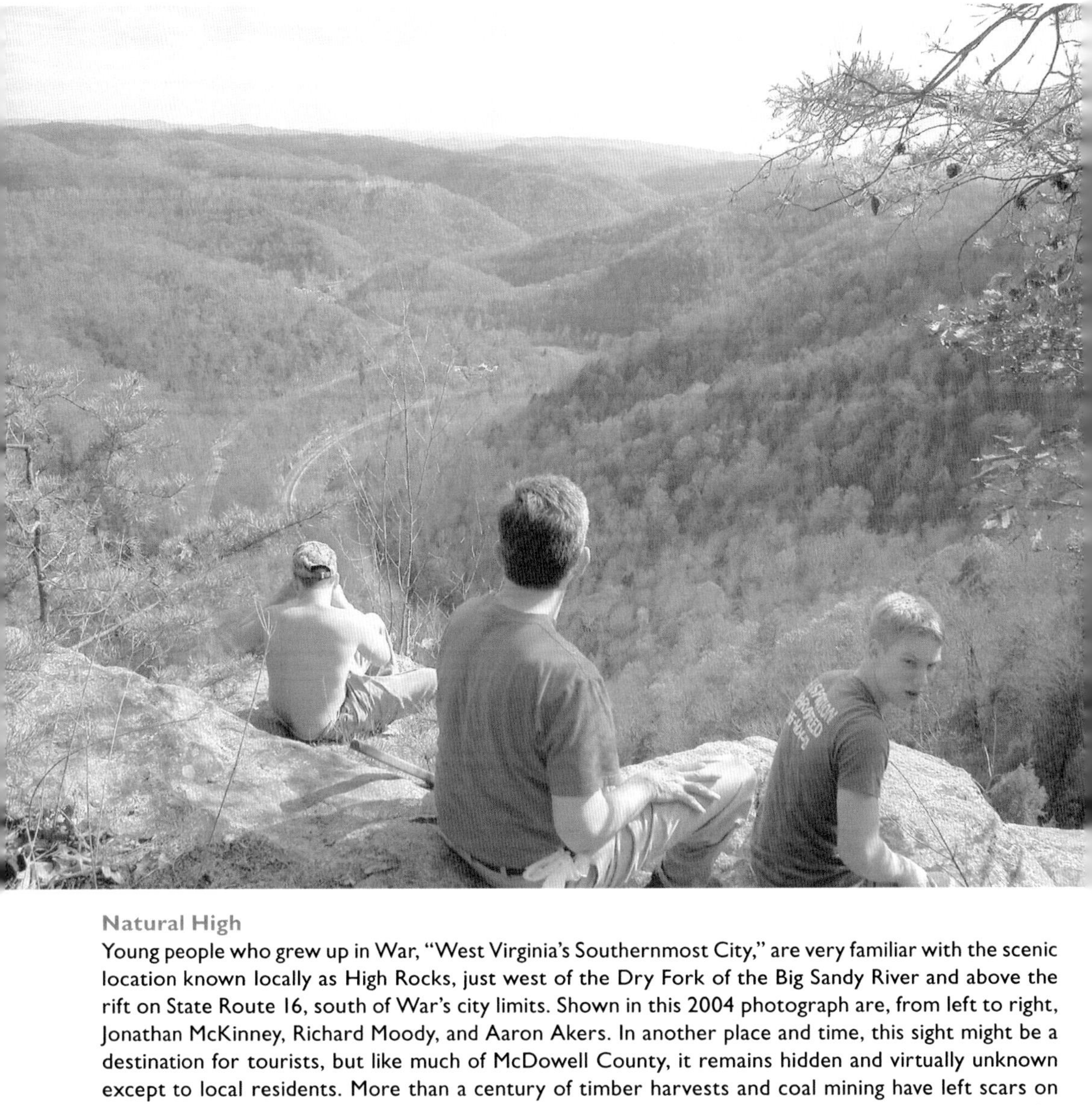

Natural High

Young people who grew up in War, "West Virginia's Southernmost City," are very familiar with the scenic location known locally as High Rocks, just west of the Dry Fork of the Big Sandy River and above the rift on State Route 16, south of War's city limits. Shown in this 2004 photograph are, from left to right, Jonathan McKinney, Richard Moody, and Aaron Akers. In another place and time, this sight might be a destination for tourists, but like much of McDowell County, it remains hidden and virtually unknown except to local residents. More than a century of timber harvests and coal mining have left scars on many of the mountains, but vistas like those that can be seen from High Rocks abound throughout the county. During his 1671 exploration into what was then western Virginia, Robert Fallon wrote in his journal that upon discovering the westward-tending valleys, "It was a pleasing tho' dreadful sight to see the mountains and hills piled one upon another." Fallon and Thomas Batts reached the New River Valley on September 13, 1671. (Photograph by Anita Moody.)

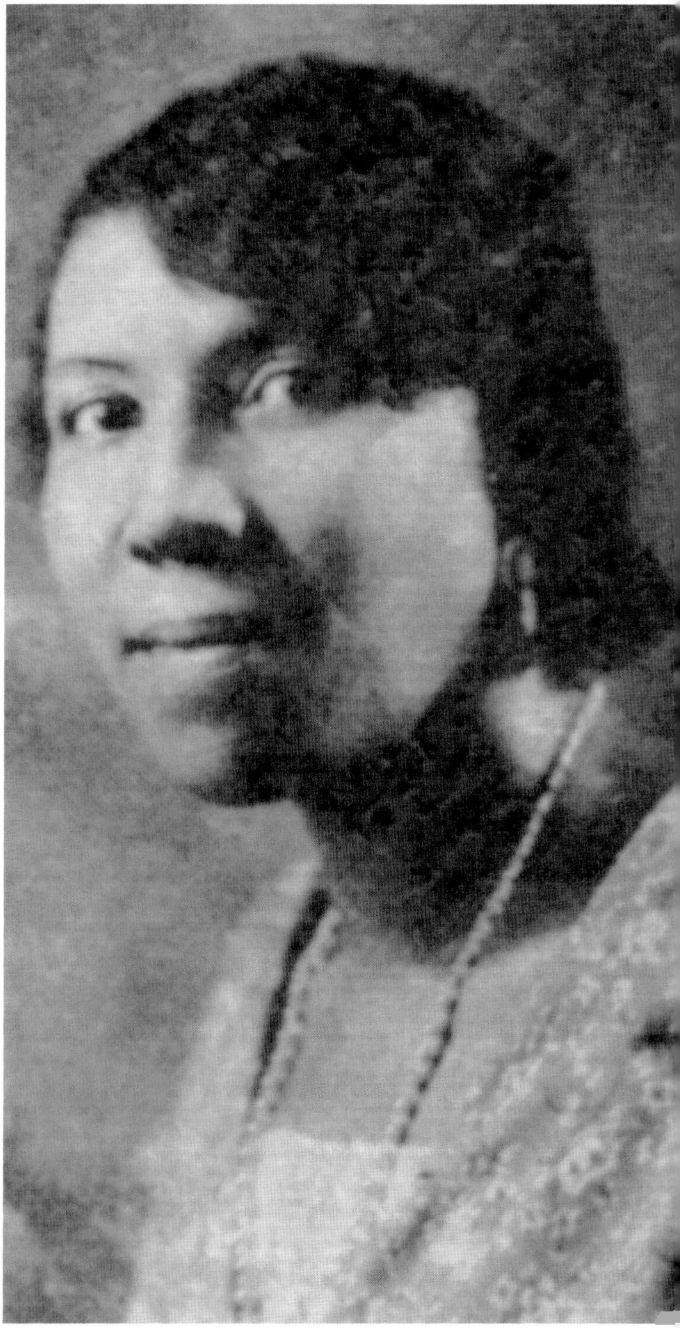

Going Back to Memphis
Memphis Tennessee Garrison was born in 1890 in Hollins, Virginia, but grew up in the coalfields of McDowell County. She was a child when her father died from injuries in a railroad accident, leaving her mother to raise her and her brother. Garrison drew her strength from watching her mother, a single parent, deal with hardships, and was inspired to join the civil rights movement because of the discrimination she saw around her. She attended Bluefield State College and earned her bachelor of science degree in elementary education in 1939. She taught in the segregated public schools of McDowell County, and gave her students a sense of culture and heritage. During the 12 years she taught in the county, she was instrumental in introducing her students to motivational speakers, including Olympic track and field gold medal winner Jesse Owens and Arctic explorer Matthew Henson, who was with Robert E. Peary when he reached the North Pole in 1909. As a result of her work, an entire generation of African American youth in the coalfields grew up believing they could achieve greatness. No less than four black generals call McDowell County home, as do athletes, musicians, educators, professionals, and others who went on to greater things. Garrison was the first female to serve as president of the West Virginia State Parent Teachers Association, organized the southern West Virginia branches of the National Association for the Advancement of Colored People, was appointed by Pres. Lyndon Johnson to serve on the National Citizen Committee for Community Relations, and was part of the first Human Rights Commission in West Virginia. (Courtesy of Barbara Lewis.)

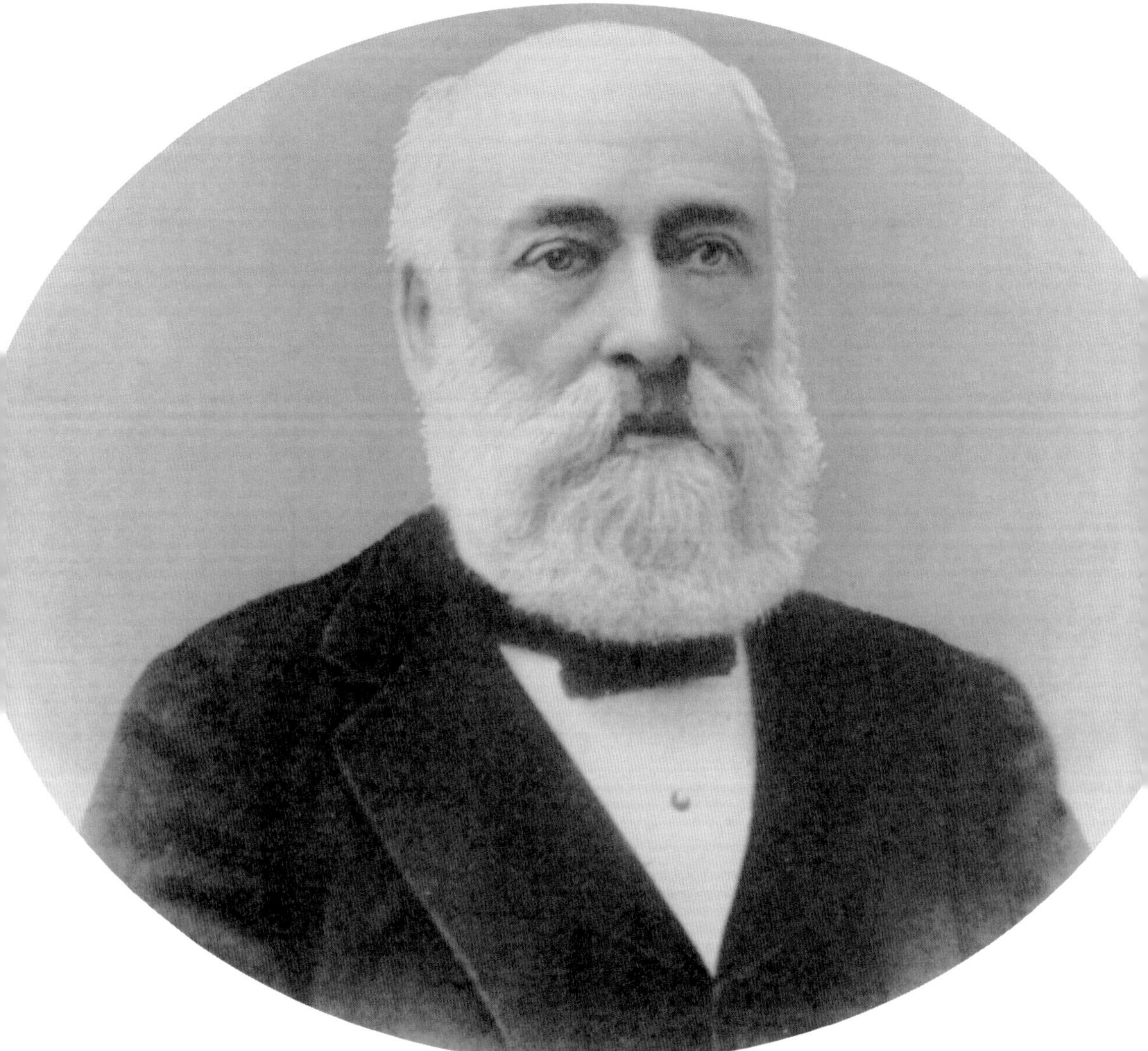

Coal Developments

Samuel A. Crozer was born on December 24, 1825, into a pious and industrious family living in the community of Upland, not far from Chester, Pennsylvania. The Crozer family textile business prospered during the years prior to the American Civil War, and the family invested profits into a hospital, college, and the Crozer Theological Seminary in Upland, the site of the first Dutch settlement in Pennsylvania prior to the arrival of William Penn's Quaker colonists. After the Civil War, Samuel Crozer became interested in the iron business in Roanoke, Virginia, and later in the coalfields of McDowell County. Crozer was active in developing the coalfields as early as 1884, when he sent men and equipment to assist in rescue efforts following the March 13, 1884, explosion that killed 114 coal miners at the East Mine in Pocahontas, Virginia. By the late 1880s, Crozer had acquired the coal leases to several parcels near Elkhorn Creek, from Crozer Bottom to Upland, and began mining operations in the county. It's interesting to note that the profits from Crozer's McDowell County coal operations helped bolster the family's eastern Pennsylvania interests, including the theological seminary. The Reverend Martin Luther King Jr. studied at Crozer Theological Seminary from 1948 to 1951, and, while there, became interested in Gandhi and the pursuit of achieving social change through nonviolent protests. (Courtesy of Dorothy MacQueen.)

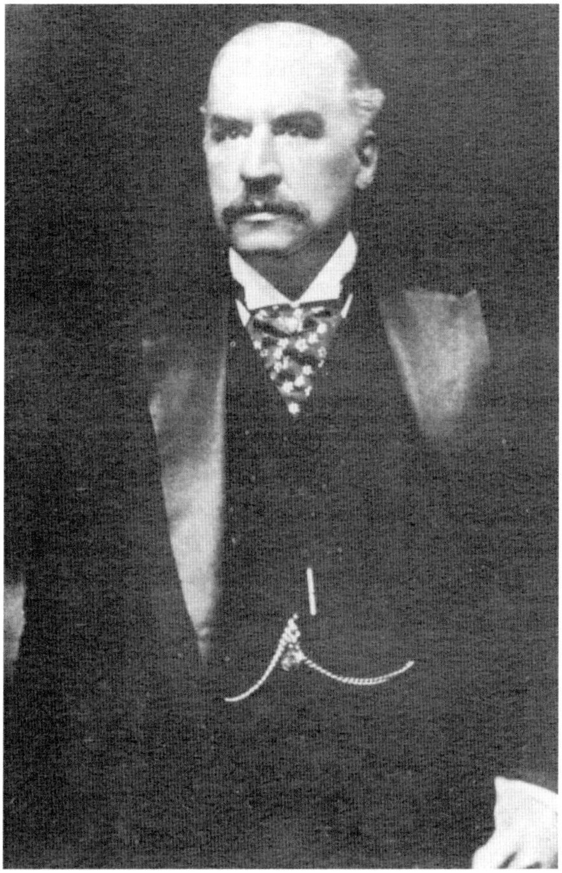

Steeler

American industrialist John Pierpont "J.P." Morgan recognized the important role that steel would play in transforming the United States from its agrarian roots into the industrial global superpower that it would become. In the first decade of the 20th century, the extent of the McDowell County metallurgical coalfields had become common knowledge, and Morgan knew he could combine the coal from West Virginia with the iron ore from the Mesabi Range in Minnesota at a central location to build a new steel empire on the foundation that Andrew Carnegie had laid. Morgan selected Judge Elbert Henry Gary to serve as the architect of his US Steel Corporation. Gary was practicing law in Chicago when Morgan brought him into the fold. It was easy to acquire the iron ore from Minnesota. However, with the Clark investment house and the Flat Top Coal Land Association controlling the development of the Pocahontas coalfields, Gary had to use a little guile to secure a large coal lease in McDowell County. In the spring of 1901, Gary worked with a Bramwell, West Virginia, banker, Isaac T. Mann, to broker a deal with Clark's field agents to acquire a 230,000-acre tract of property on the Tug Fork of the Big Sandy. When payment of the $10 million note came due, Gary stepped forward to seal the deal for a modest investment compared to the return that US Steel stood to realize. Unknown to the Flat Top association was that Mann and Gary had already purchased a 70,000-acre tract of land from W.M. Ritter for $3.5 million. By the end of 1901, the Norfolk & Western Railway interests purchased the 300,000-acre coal lands back from Gary and Mann, earning Morgan a $6.5 million profit. The 12-plus US Steel mines of Gary Hollow became some of the most productive coal mines in southern West Virginia. With US Steel Mining based in Gary, West Virginia, and a large portion of US Steel's steelmaking factories in Gary, Indiana, the company changed the course of American history as the nation headed into the Industrial Age. (Courtesy of Barbara Blake.)

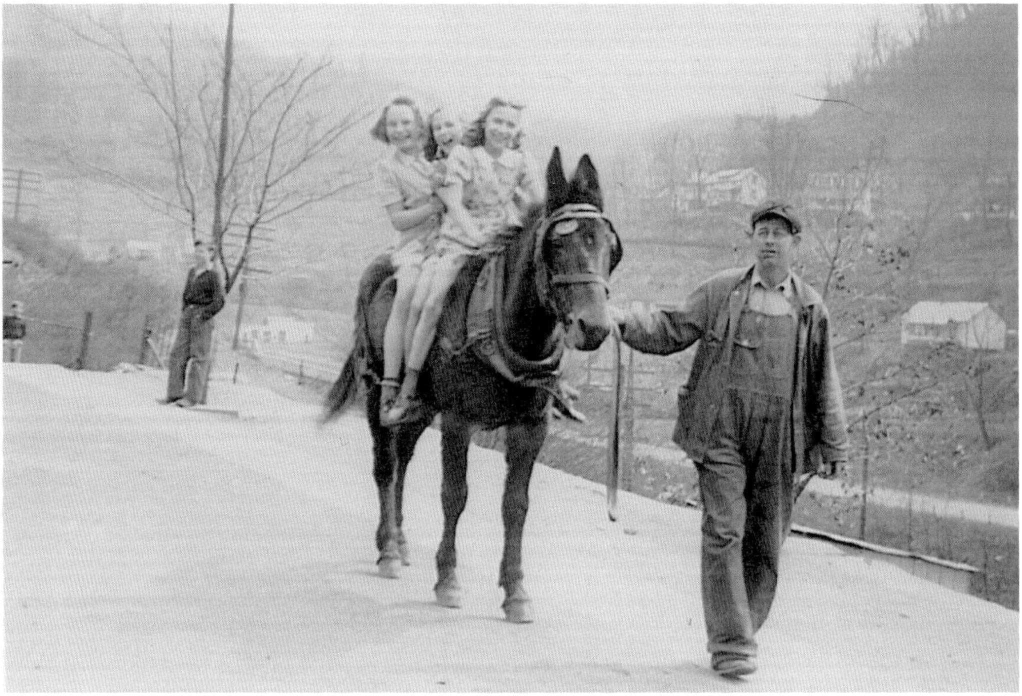

Mule Power
An unidentified custodian of the old Switchback School leads a mule carrying Trula Stophel (front) and two unidentified friends to the school on Elkhown Creek in McDowell County. Mules were important for underground coal haulage during the early 20th century. (Courtesy of Shirley Ofsa.)

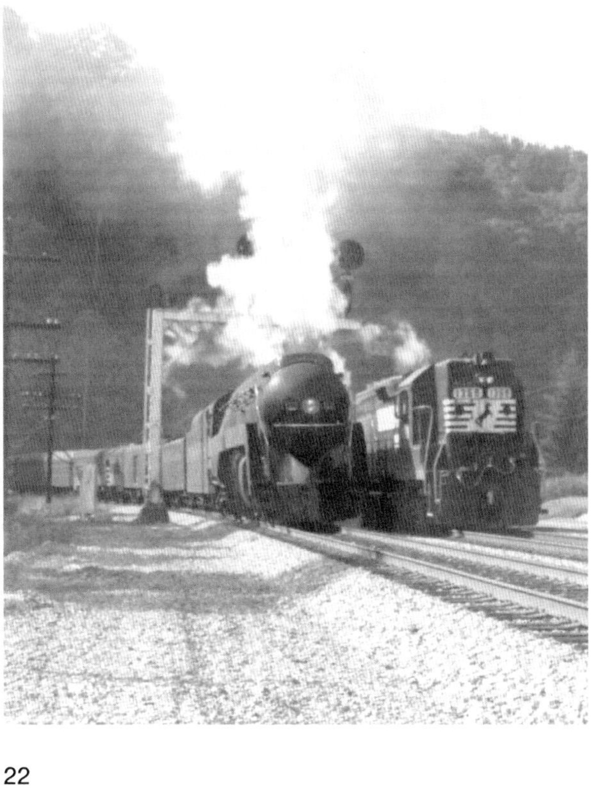

Steam Power
The J-Class 611 locomotive (left), shown here during a 1989 excursion through McDowell County, provided the power to transport passenger trains between Norfolk, Virginia, and Cincinnati, Ohio, during the late 1940s and through most of the 1950s. The steam locomotives were rendered obsolete with the arrival of diesel locomotives. (Photograph by the author.)

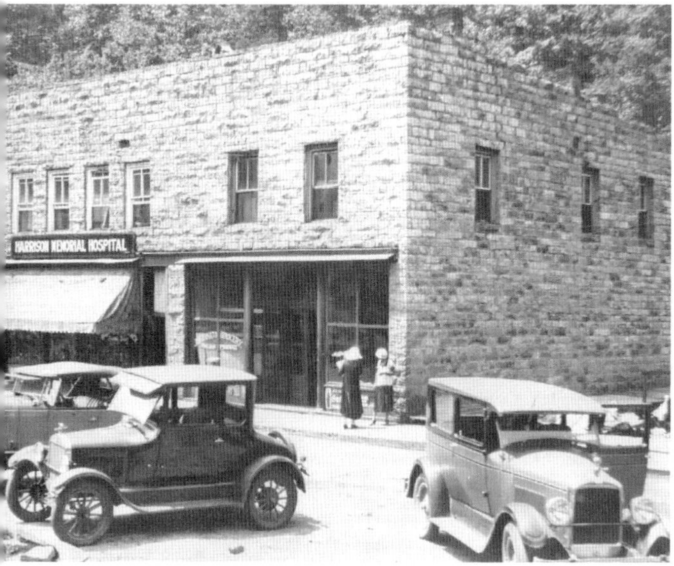

So Happy Together
The Gianato family's grocery store in Kimball, West Virginia, was located in the right half of this building, and Harrison Memorial Hospital occupied the left side. Harrison Memorial was a black-owned hospital that served African American families in the region. The Gianato family emigrated from Italy and served people of all races in their store. (Courtesy of Ken Davidson.)

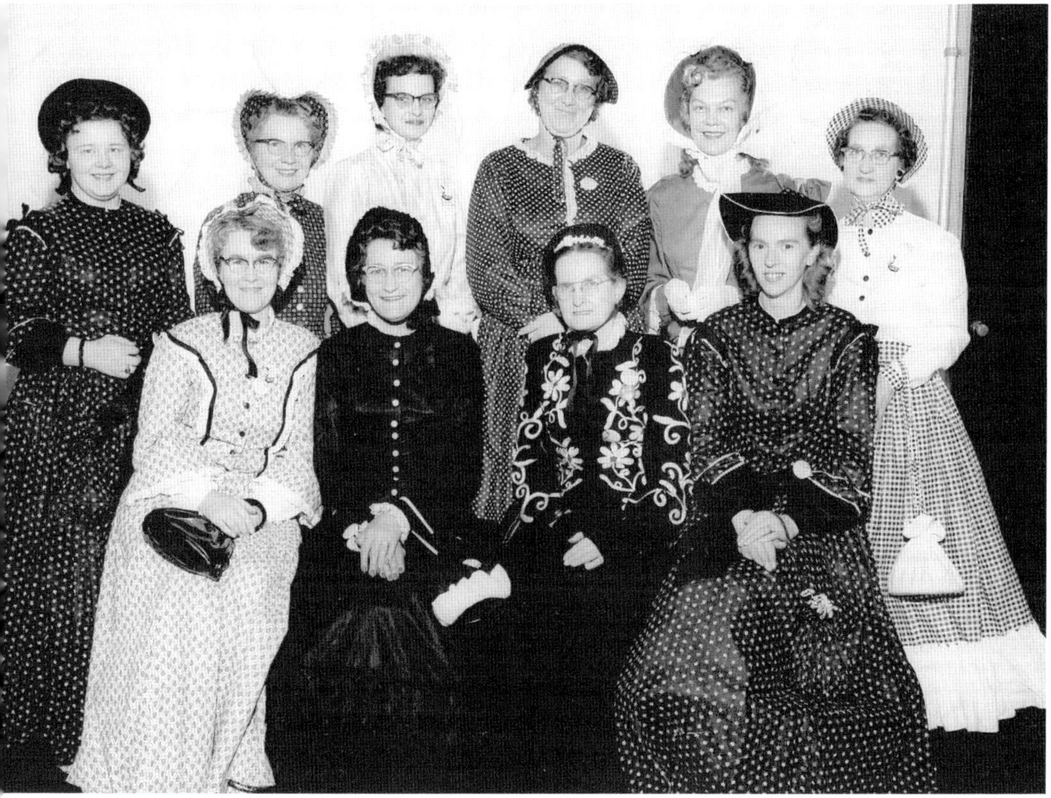

Powhatan Centennial Belles
The Powhatan, West Virginia, Centennial Belles are shown here in 1958 celebrating McDowell County's centennial. The participants are, from left to right, (first row) Anna Sheets, Rachel Pennington, Neo Wall, and Betty Stalnaker; (second row) Jeannie Williams, Mrs. Hornby Norris, Margaret Dixon, Mrs. Sam Curry, Libby Wade, and Mrs. Ed Williams. (Courtesy of Shirley Ofsa.)

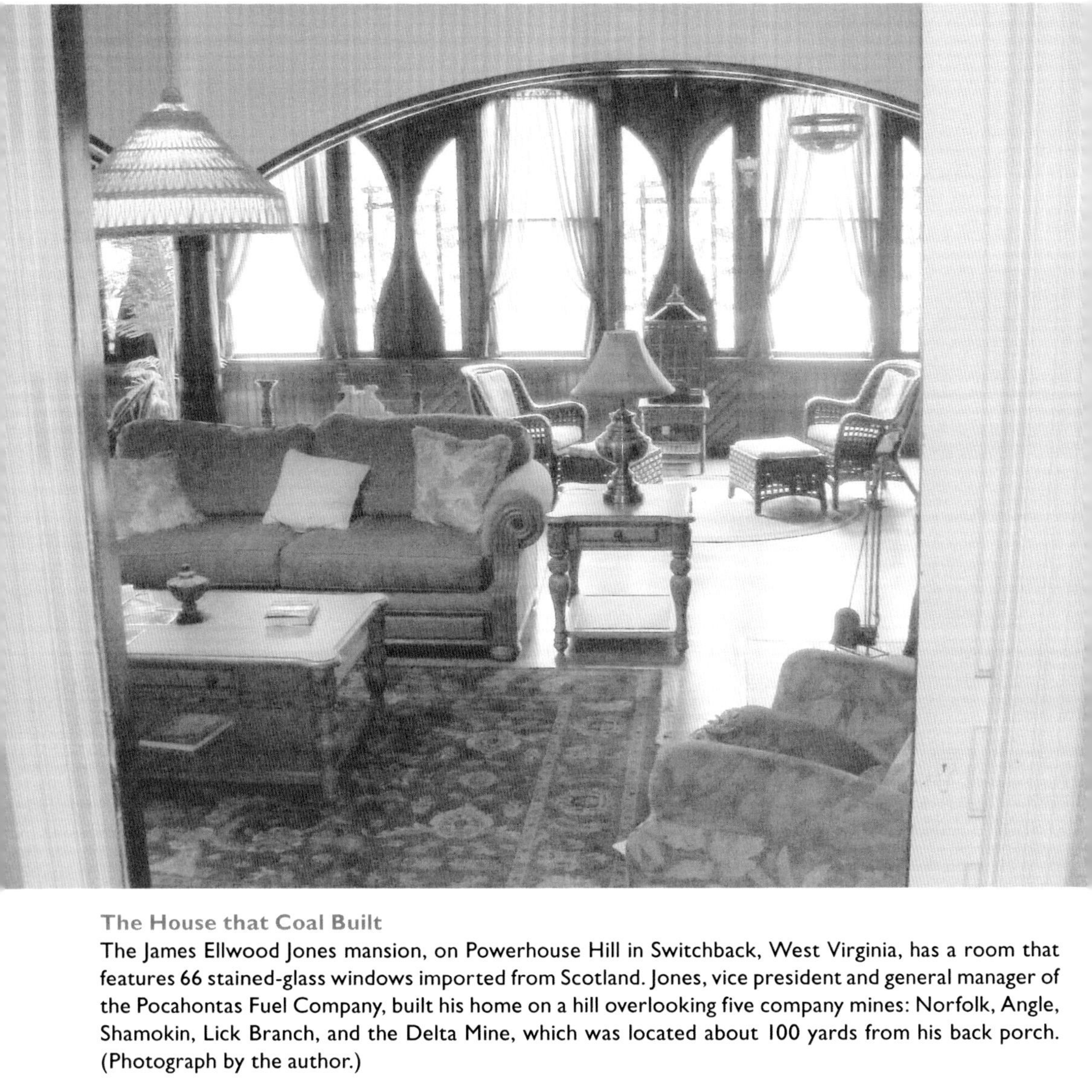

The House that Coal Built

The James Ellwood Jones mansion, on Powerhouse Hill in Switchback, West Virginia, has a room that features 66 stained-glass windows imported from Scotland. Jones, vice president and general manager of the Pocahontas Fuel Company, built his home on a hill overlooking five company mines: Norfolk, Angle, Shamokin, Lick Branch, and the Delta Mine, which was located about 100 yards from his back porch. (Photograph by the author.)

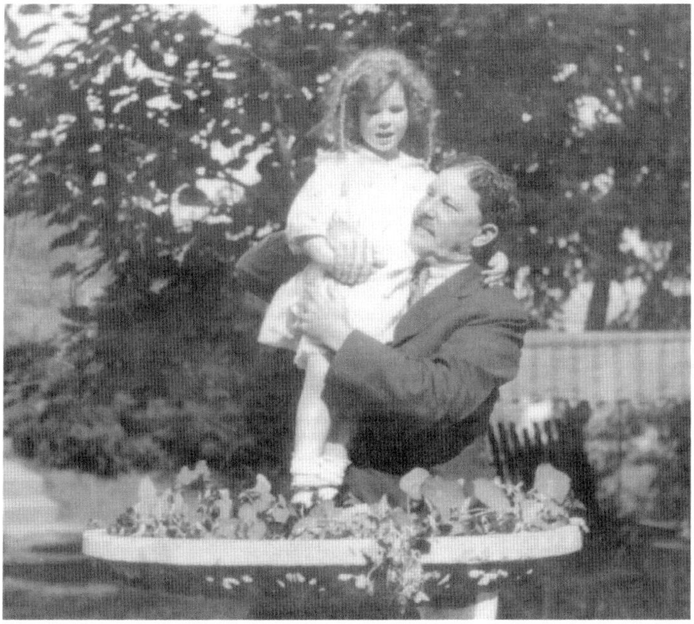

Home and Garden

In addition to the incredible beauty of the interior of the Jones Mansion in Switchback, the exterior of the home featured formal terraced gardens, rare ornamental trees, and a large outdoor pool for goldfish. James Ellwood Jones is shown here holding his daughter, Nancy. (Courtesy of Judy McDaniel.)

King of the Hill

James Ellwood Jones was born in 1874 in Trevertown, Pennsylvania, about nine years after his father, Jenkin Jones, had moved from coal country in Wales to work in the anthracite coal mines of eastern Pennsylvania. James Jones was very young when the family relocated to Fayette County, West Virginia, and then to Mercer County, West Virginia. While he grew up in the mining communities where his father worked, the younger Jones studied at Roanoke College in Salem, Virginia, then received a degree in mining engineering from Columbia University in New York City. After finishing his formal education, Jones returned to southern West Virginia to work with his father in what had become the Pocahontas Fuel Company. The younger Jones was an inventor of labor-saving machinery for the coal mines, including the Jones Coloader, a machine with characteristics that would be incorporated into the modern continuous mining machines. He moved quickly through the management ranks of the Pocahontas Fuel Company, eventually becoming the company's vice president and general manager. While he was focused on business, Jones was equally focused on the education, health, and welfare of his employees and of every child living in McDowell County. He was instrumental in establishing the free dental clinic for all McDowell County children up to age 16, and paid for several hundred young men and women to attend college. He ran unsuccessfully as the Republican Party nominee for the US Senate in 1930, and had been in declining health prior to his death on November 25, 1932. He was playing cards with his friend, Dr. I.T. Peters, when he collapsed and died. He and his wife, Edith (Jenkins) Jones, had two children, Nancy and J.E. "Jimmy" Jones. (Courtesy of the Eastern Regional Coal Archives.)

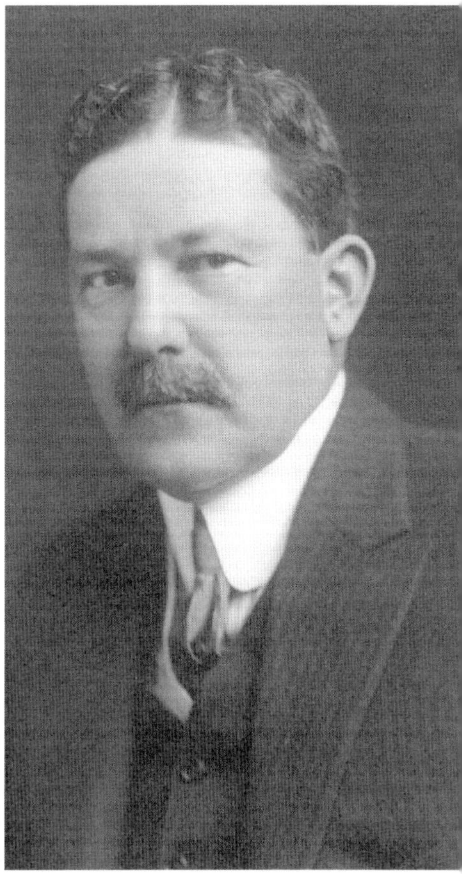

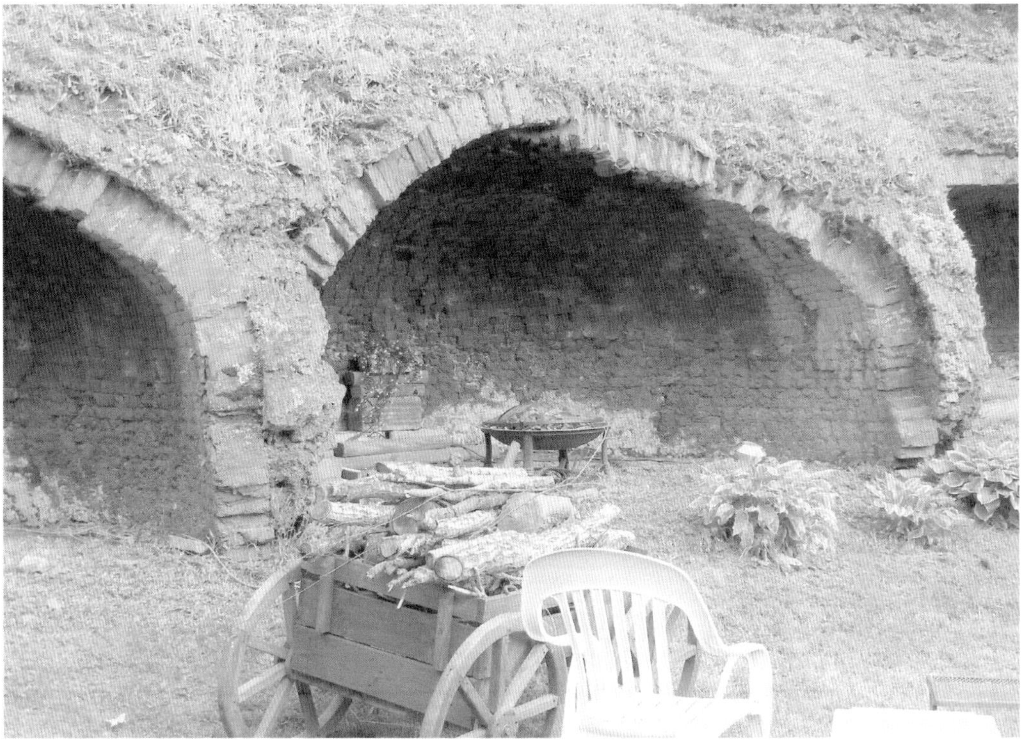

Things Go Better with Coke

The old beehive coke ovens shown here near a residence in Northfork, West Virginia, are remnants of a time when coke was produced near the coal mines. Coke is produced by burning off the impurities of coal at a high temperature (about 2,000 degrees Fahrenheit) in an airtight container. When coke is burned, it produces an intense, smokeless heat that is an essential ingredient of the steel manufacturing process. The southern West Virginia coalfields are important globally because the majority of the regional coal seams produce metallurgical coal, a coal that is already high in carbon content and low in impurities—ideal for producing steel. The beehive ovens were a common sight in McDowell County from the mid-1880s until about 1910, when coke carried a much higher premium sales price. When the coal boom first hit and there weren't enough coal cars for the Norfolk & Western Railway to meet the growing demand, the N&W assigned coal cars to mines based on the number of coke ovens at the mine. When technology improved and steel manufacturers started to use the byproducts of the coke-making process, the old beehive ovens became obsolete. In the 1930s, some were made into homes by families left homeless by the Great Depression. Sam Larry transformed these abandoned coke ovens into an attraction for ATV riders who visit his bed-and-breakfast, Sam's Place. (Photograph by the author.)

Nancy with the Laughing Face (OPPOSITE PAGE)

Nancy Jones, the daughter of Edith and James Ellwood Jones, looks wistfully out of one of the stained-glass windows in the family's mansion in Switchback. Although a native of Pennsylvania, James Jones grew up in the proud coal-mining tradition of his father's native Wales. When the Pocahontas Fuel Company took its first step to capitalize on the growing overseas markets for its coal, the company invested in the world's first super collier ship, the 5,000-ton SS *Jonancy*, named for Jones's infant daughter and launched on November 9, 1914. Much of the metallurgical coal mined in McDowell County continues to fuel a global steelmaking industry. Nancy was studying in Paris when she learned of her father's death in late 1932. (Courtesy of Judy McDaniel.)

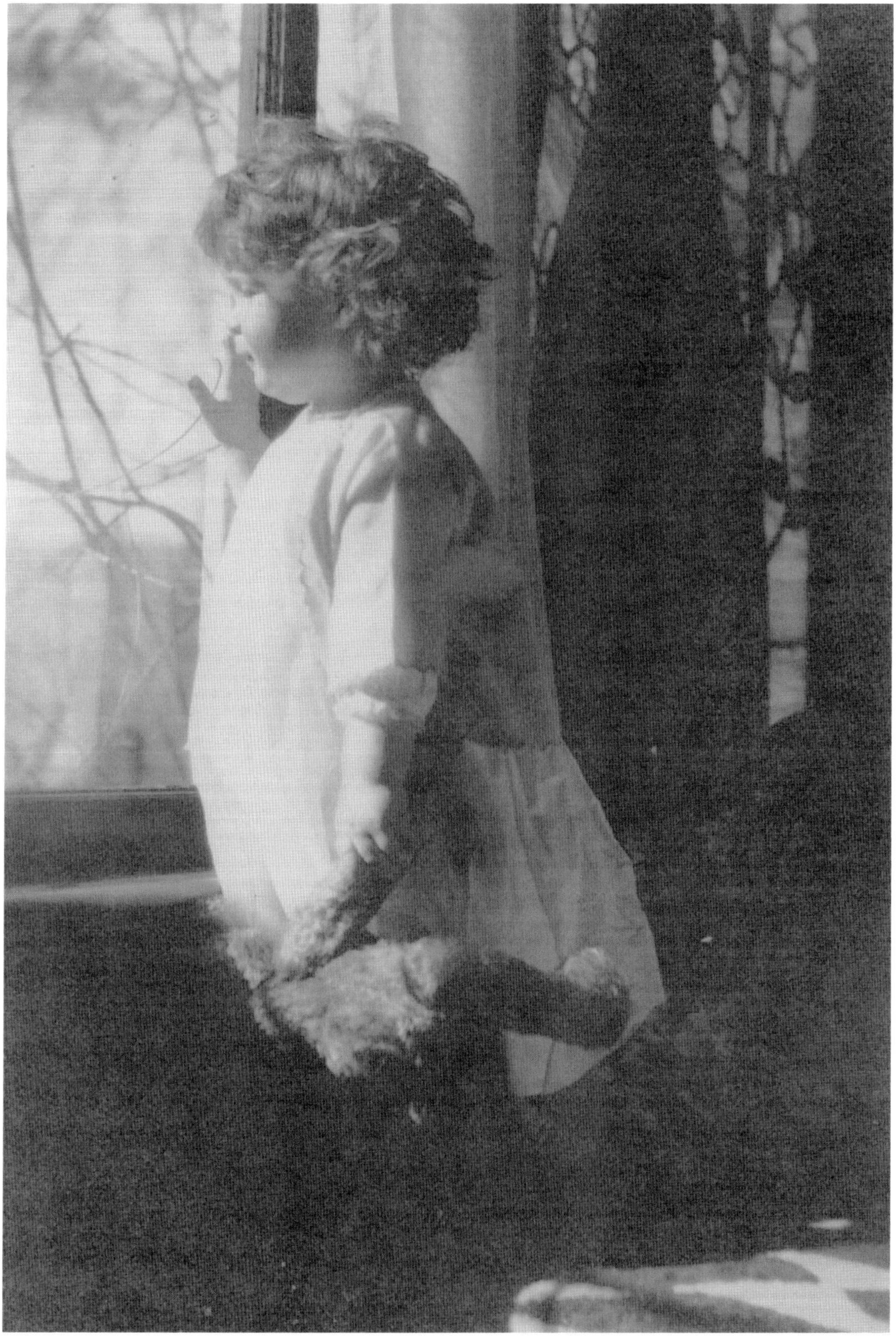

Fuel Satisfaction

The Norfolk & Western Railway transported the first carload of coal mined from the Pocahontas Number 3 seam from Pocahontas to Norfolk, Virginia, on March 13, 1883, and distributed the hand-loaded coal to citizens of that community as a gift. Legend holds that the people who received the coal simply discarded their lumps and went on about their business. In 1883, few households in America used coal for heating or cooking, but all of that was about to change. In 1886, on the eve of the opening of the McDowell County coalfields, E.W. Clark & Company contracted the services of the Philadelphia-based marketing firm Caster and Curran, to promote domestic use of coal—not just any coal, but genuine Pocahontas Coal. Some of the promotional ideas were a little offbeat, like wrapping individual lumps of coal in butcher paper so homemakers wouldn't get their hands dirty. However, the real change came in 1909, when Pocahontas landed the contract to be the exclusive coal source for construction of the Panama Canal, and in 1917, when "smokeless" genuine Pocahontas Coal received the contract to supply all the ships in the US Navy. One of the company's slogans was "fuel satisfaction," and skylines worldwide were about to learn exactly what that meant. (Author's collection.)

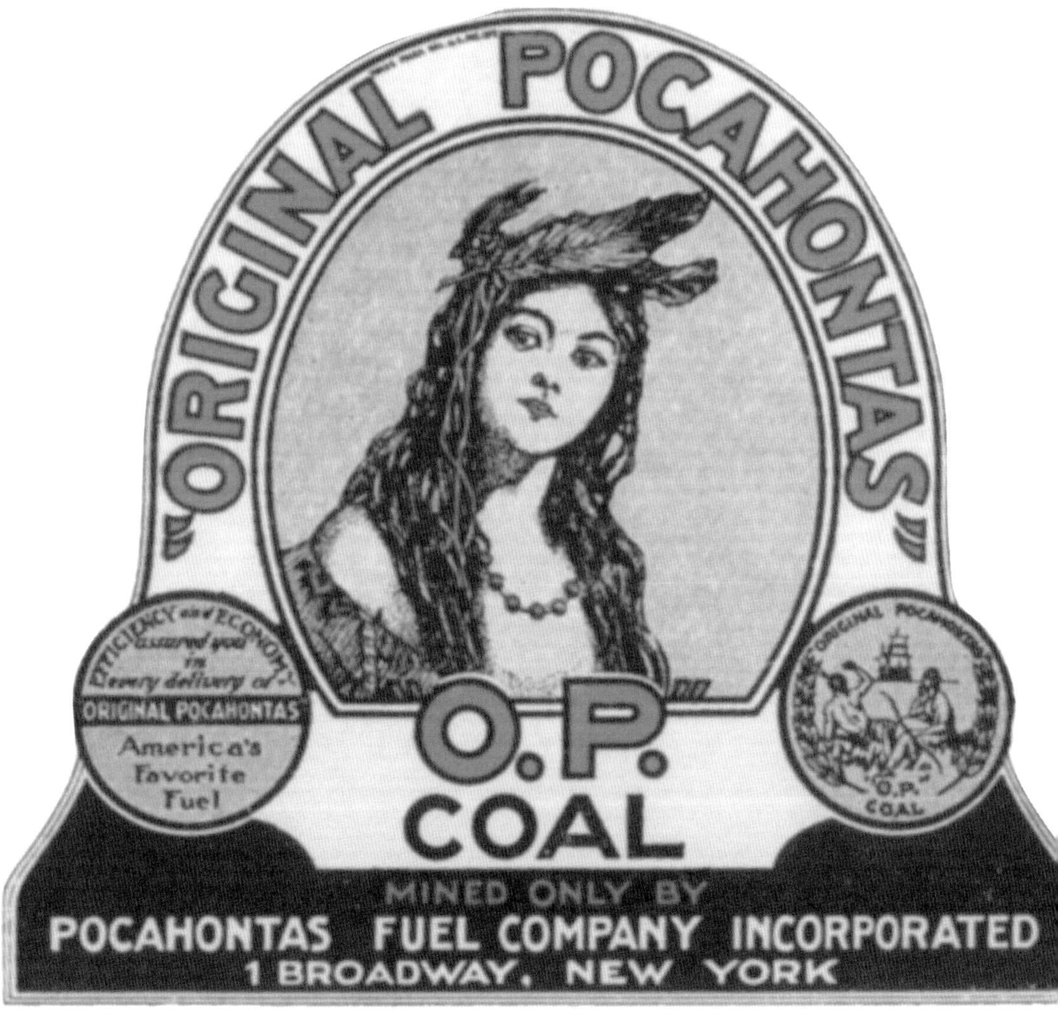

CHAPTER TWO

Natural Gifts

The natural movement of continents, known as plate tectonics, can explain the geological process of how the Appalachian mountain range was formed, but it falls far short of explaining why such a small region would be blessed with such an abundance of natural wealth. Noted geologist Marshall Miller tagged the Pocahontas Number 3 coal seam as the "world standard" for metallurgical coal seams, but the Poca 3 is only one of several premium metallurgical coal seams that underlie the surface of McDowell County. There are a dozen Pocahontas coal seams, along with other named seams like Fire Creek, Red Ash, Sewell, and more that permeate the rock strata beneath McDowell County. That abundance of coal led Danny Smith, vice president of coal development for the Norfolk Southern Corporation, to label the region "the Saudi Arabia of coal." But it's not just any coal. The coal found in McDowell County represents the world's best coking coal, used in the manufacture of steel. Coke, iron ore, and limestone are the primary ingredients in the steelmaking process, and for more than a century, steel has proven to be the most important ingredient in erecting the framework of modern society.

The weather pattern that existed on earth several hundred million years ago, responsible for the almost unbelievable quantity and quality of plant life that flourished and that would ultimately become coal, still exists in the second millennium of the Christian era. On July 8, 2001, when a band of rain showers swept across the mountains of the southern West Virginia coalfields, meteorologists attempting to analyze the storm were puzzled by a singular characteristic that linked the storm to a weather pattern most commonly seen in rain forests: The slow-moving storm appeared to intensify by feeding off the rain that it had brought in the first place. While the modern vegetation, made up of native Appalachian hardwoods, is vastly different from the swamp-basin vegetation that stored solar energy and was transformed into coal over time and under pressure, the moist springs and dry falls form a forest product that has been the envy of the world for more than two centuries. McDowell County's mountains make it difficult to harvest wood products, but the wood that continues to grow is still a source of natural bounty.

However, it was people who came to the region seeking to build successful businesses, or just to make a living from nature's bounty and raise a family, who remain the real strength of nature's gifts to the world. Their story is still being told.

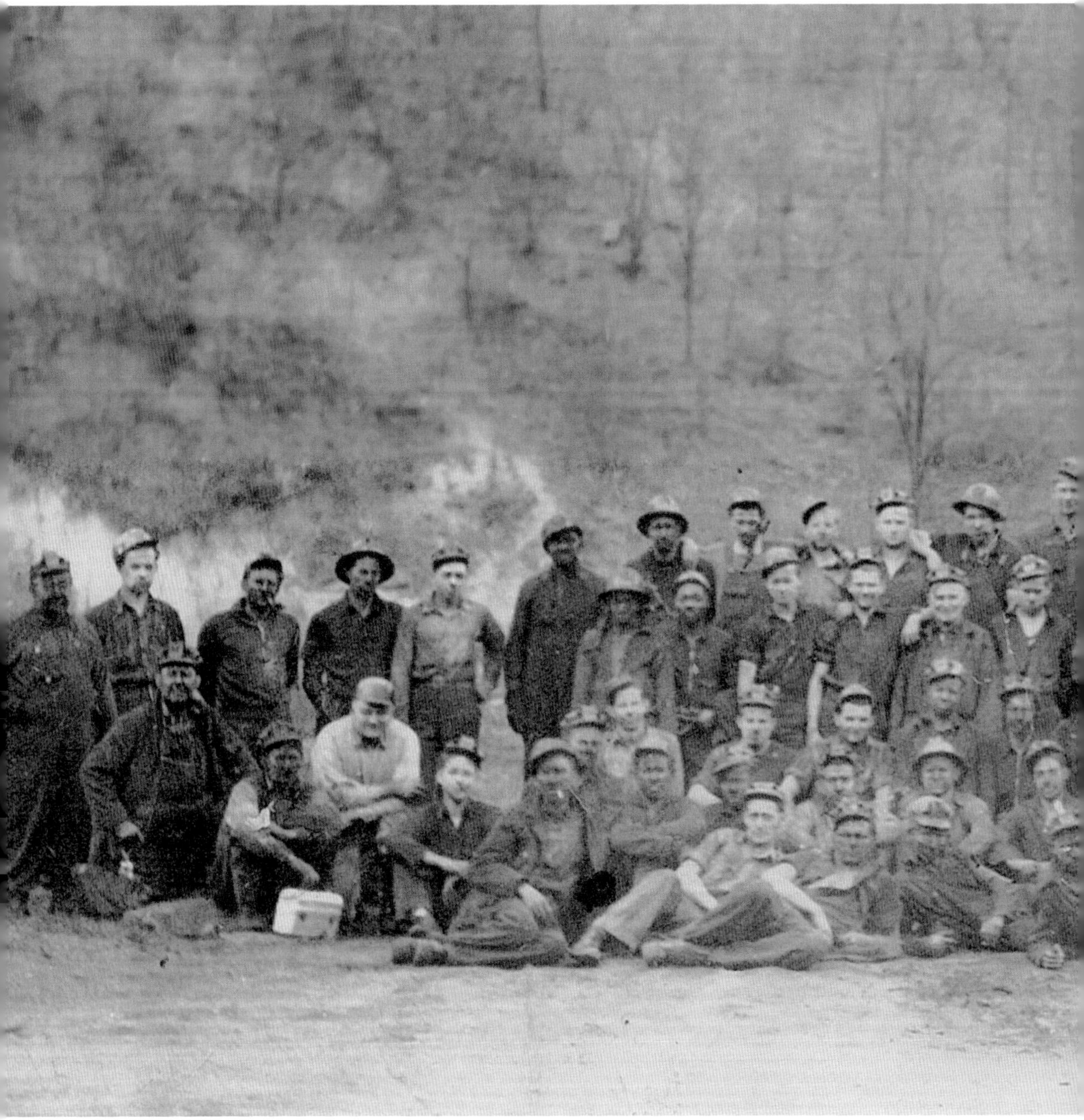

America's Melting Pot

In the late 19th century, the world was undergoing a major economic transformation. European population was rapidly outgrowing the natural resources required to sustain life, and many families who could not find work were willing to sell everything they had and gamble on finding a better life in North America. American industrialists such as J.P. Morgan, Henry Ford, and others were investing money in an industrial revolution that would thrust the United States into global prominence, and the key ingredient for that revolution was the energy that had been trapped in McDowell County's mountains for hundreds of millions of years.The coal miners shown here worked on the day shift of a US Steel surface mine in the Tug Fork fields in Gary Hollow. When Jedediah Hotchkiss started promoting the development of the McDowell County coalfields in the 1880s, he touted the availability of a huge pool of African American laborers who had been born into slavery, but were ready to enter the free enterprise workforce. During

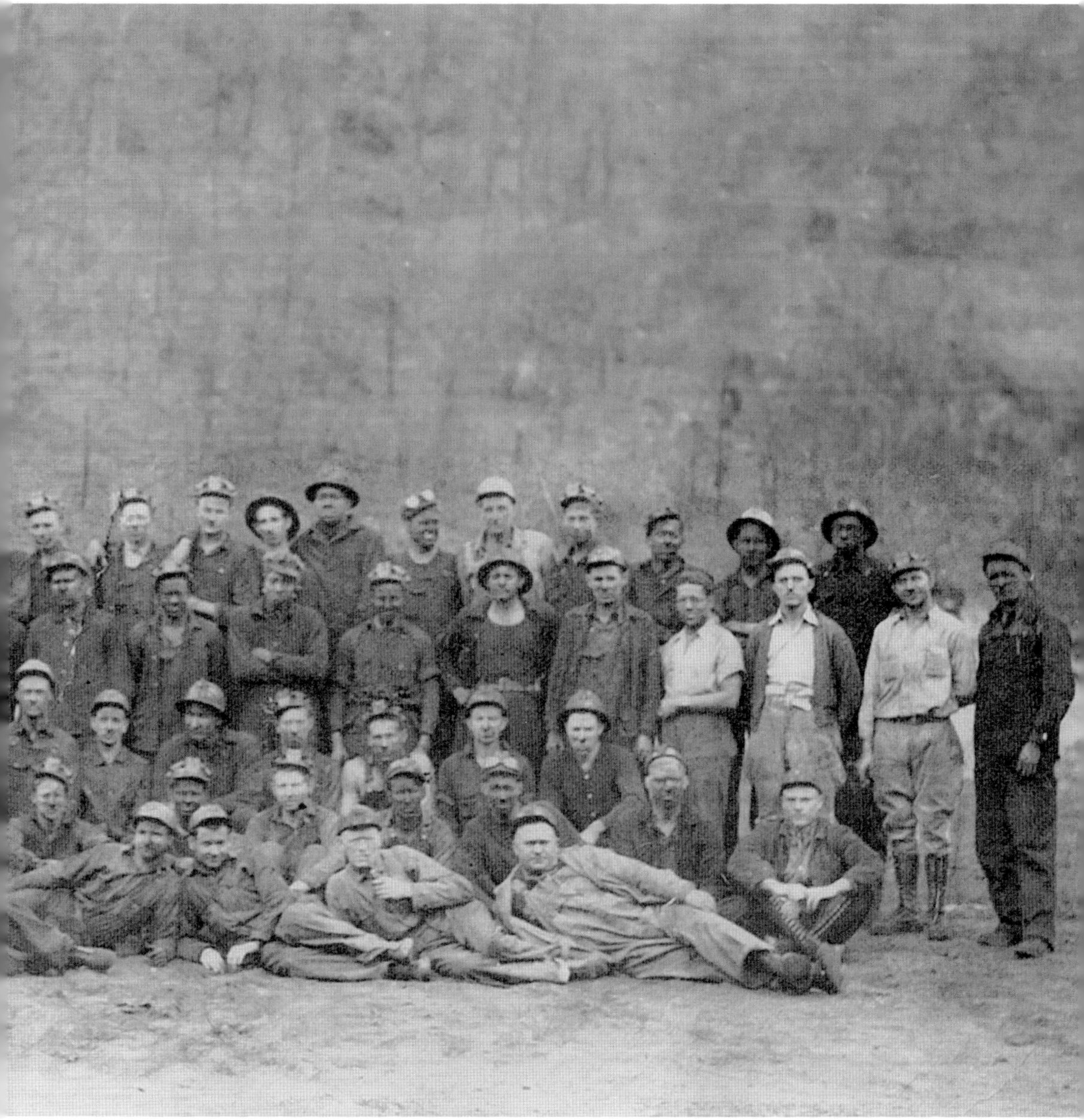

those labor-intensive, hand-loading days, when one coal miner was expected to cut, shoot, and load one ton of coal in one day, the existing workforce could not meet the demand. As a result, representatives of the Southwest Virginia Improvement Corporation started recruiting workers from the thousands of European immigrants who were arriving at Ellis Island in New York almost daily. In time, the coal operators were able to refine their recruitment efforts, selecting specific workers for specific jobs. Mine operators recruited men from northern Italy to build railway bridges, mine entrances, and retaining walls to hold back erosion; men from Hungary and Poland were recruited to work with the native workers—both black and white—as general laborers. The coal mine operators identified good workers and sent them to New York with signs written in the language and dialect of people from their home region. In a short time, the diverse workforce became one of the most productive labor forces the world had ever known. (Author's collection.)

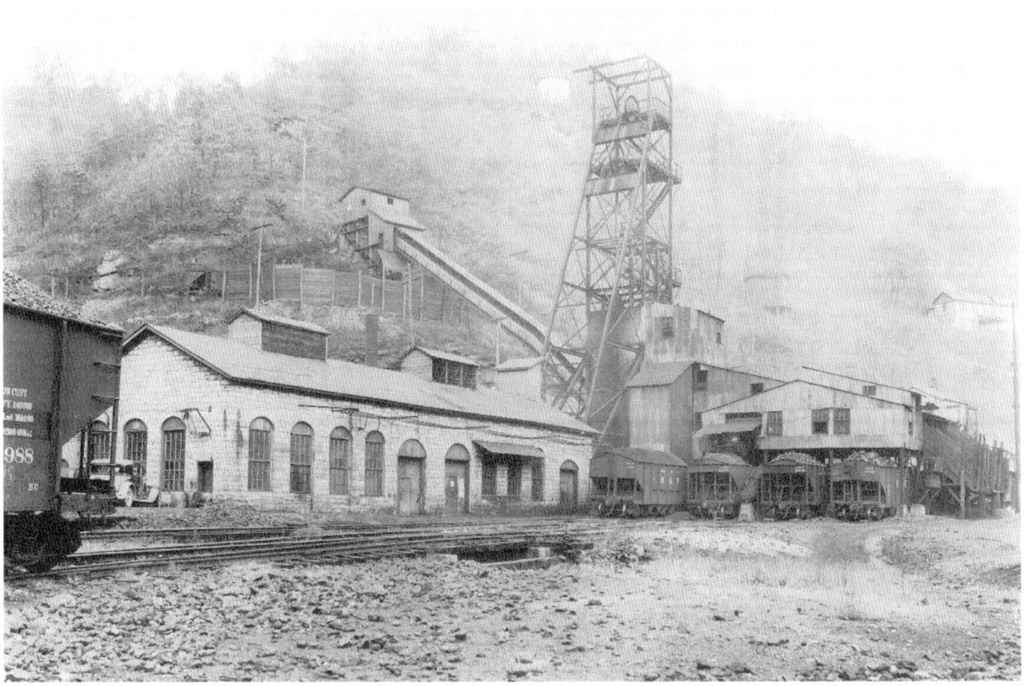

Caples of Good Hope

The new coal tipple at Caples, West Virginia, shown here, was highly successful in terms of coal production. However, after coal mining ceased, developers worked to transform the former mine site into a landfill to process solid wastes from cities of the eastern United States. That project has not yet materialized. (Courtesy of the Eastern Regional Coal Archives.)

Post Office in the Hollow

The building shown here served as the paymaster's quarters for coal miners who worked at Caples, until the mine closed. After a few years, it became the post office for the community. One retired coal miner said that he got his pay at the building when he was working, and drew his pension from the building after he retired. (Photograph by Phil Farmer.)

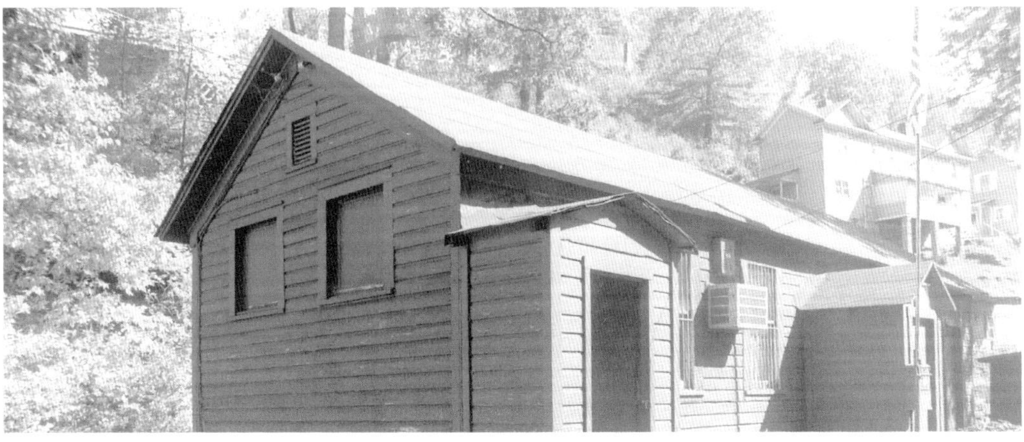

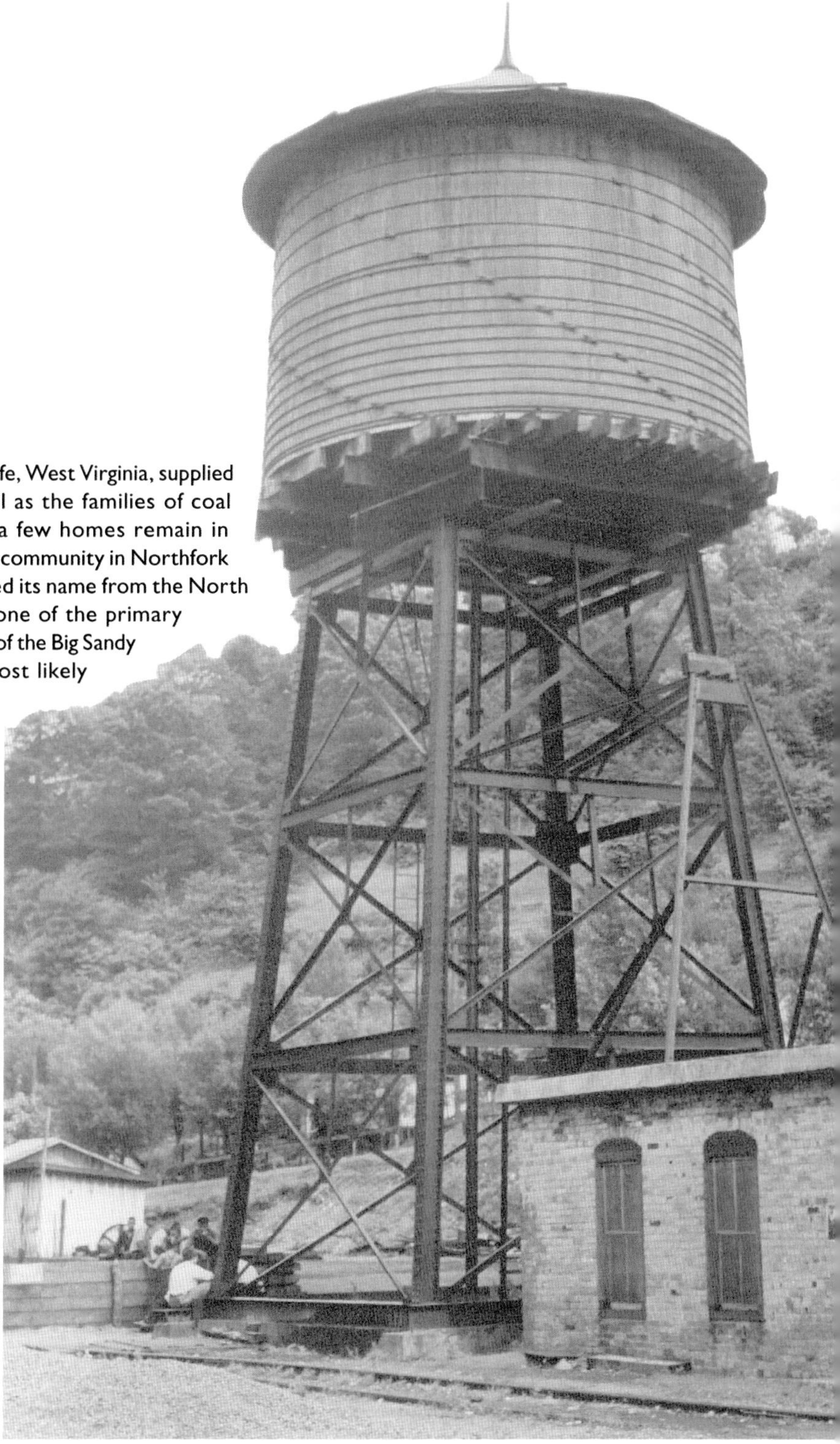

Water Works

The old water tower in Rolfe, West Virginia, supplied the coal company as well as the families of coal miners with water. Just a few homes remain in Rolfe, a McDowell County community in Northfork Hollow. The hollow derived its name from the North Fork of Elkhorn Creek, one of the primary tributaries of the Tug Fork of the Big Sandy River. The name *Rolfe* most likely derived from John Rolfe, the Jamestown, Virginia, settler who married the Indian princess Pocahontas. Several coalfield communities were named to honor people associated with the Pocahontas story. Harriet Lathrop, the wife of William Lathrop, the first superintendent of mining operations in the Flat Top region, is credited with giving the coalfields their name after she saw miners clearing mountain laurel from a mine entrance, and thought the scene was similar to a painting she had seen depicting Princess Pocahontas saving the life of Capt. John Smith. (Courtesy of the Eastern Regional Coal Archives.)

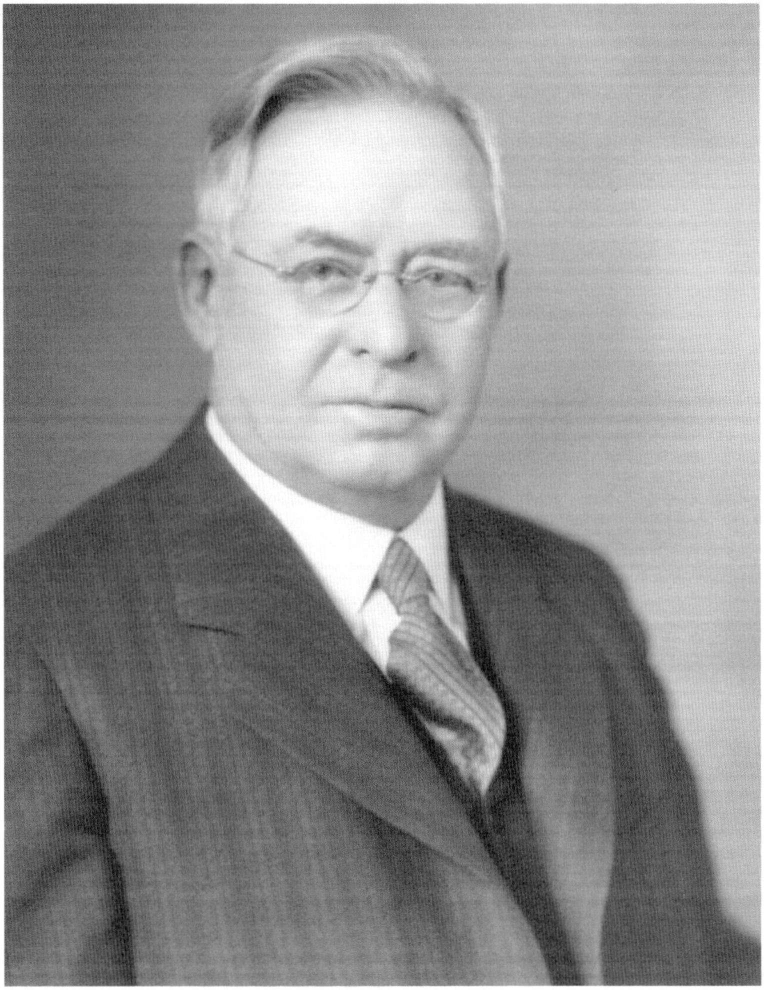

The Genius behind Gary Hollow

While Judge Elbert Gary is often credited with being the architect of J.P. Morgan's United States Steel Corporation, Gary was wise enough to hire a young coal-mining engineer, Edward O'Toole (pictured), to actually make the experiment work. O'Toole was a native of Salineville, Columbiana County, Ohio, in the heart of pottery-making country. He started working in the coal mines of eastern Ohio as a nine-year-old between school terms and, in the process, learned the coal-mining business from the inside out. O'Toole was already an experienced coal-mining engineer when Judge Gary recruited the management team for the new United States Steel Coal & Coke Company based in Gary. O'Toole, a scientist, learned how to blend the different coals of the Gary Hollow region to achieve the optimum steelmaking blend. He invented machinery, including the O'Toole Jeffrey Over-cutting Machine, the O'Toole Cutting and Loading Machine, and the American Coal Cleaning Corporation's Dry Cleaning of Coal Process. He organized the state's first workers' compensation program, and traveled worldwide to examine coal mines in Europe and South America. In addition to his inventions, O'Toole designed the Gary Golf Course, which provided an activity for young US Steel mining engineers who came to the isolated region. His son, William Joseph O'Toole, was born in Fayette County, Pennsylvania, but was raised in McDowell County. William was an officer during World War I, was instrumental in founding McDowell County Post 8 of the American Legion, and served as ambassador to Paraguay during the administration of Pres. Warren G. Harding. (Courtesy of the Eastern Regional Coal Archives.)

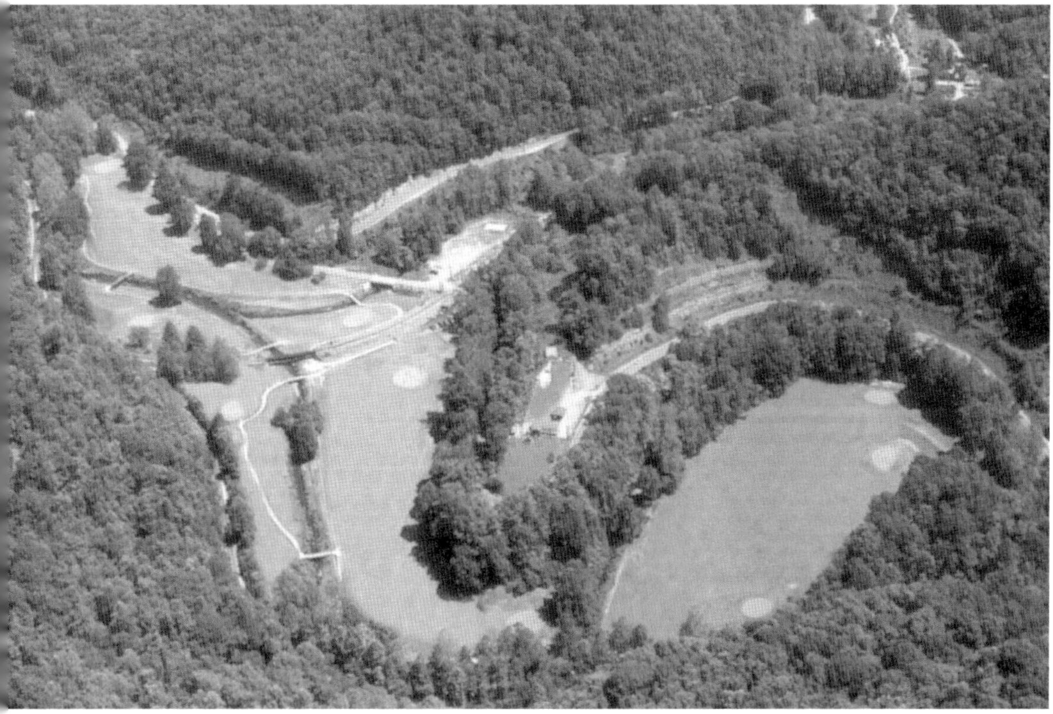

Black Wolf Links

Narrow fairways, the Tug Fork of the Big Sandy River, and a railroad track running through the middle of the course combine to make play on the nine-hole Black Wolf Links challenging. Edward O'Toole employed traction sand, the type used in Norfolk & Western steam locomotives, to make sand traps on the course, which is now operated by the McDowell County Economic Development Authority. (Photograph by Melvin Grubb.)

Alpheus Preparation Plant

The crowning achievement of Edward O'Toole's US Steel Mining operation in Gary, West Virginia, was the erection of the Alpheus Preparation Plant. The plant was named for the Greek god Alpheus and the river in Sicily that flows beneath the surface to the Ionian Sea. In Greek mythology, Alpheus pursued Arethusa, an attendant to the goddess Artemis, who took pity on Arethusa and transformed her into a fountain, and later into an underground stream. Alpheus pursued her underground, where the rivers Alpheus and Arethusa mingle before they enter the sea. The Alpheus Preparation Plant mingled the coal from at least 14 different US Steel coal mines to create the coke that formed the strongest steel the world had ever known. (Photograph by the author.)

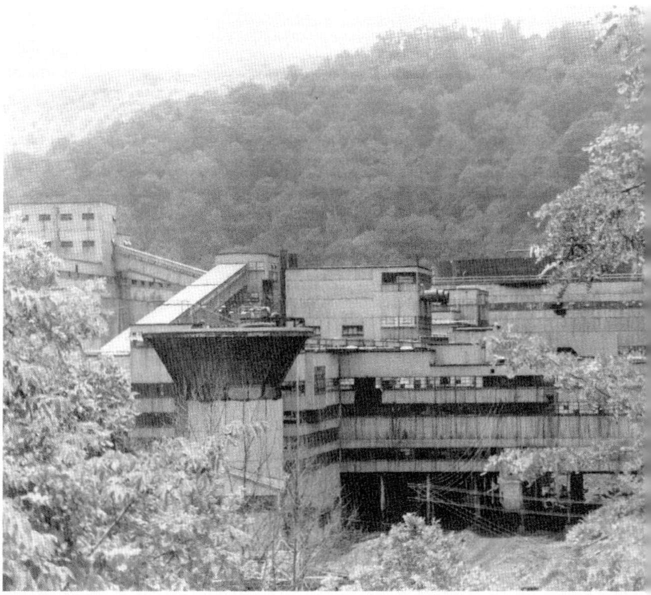

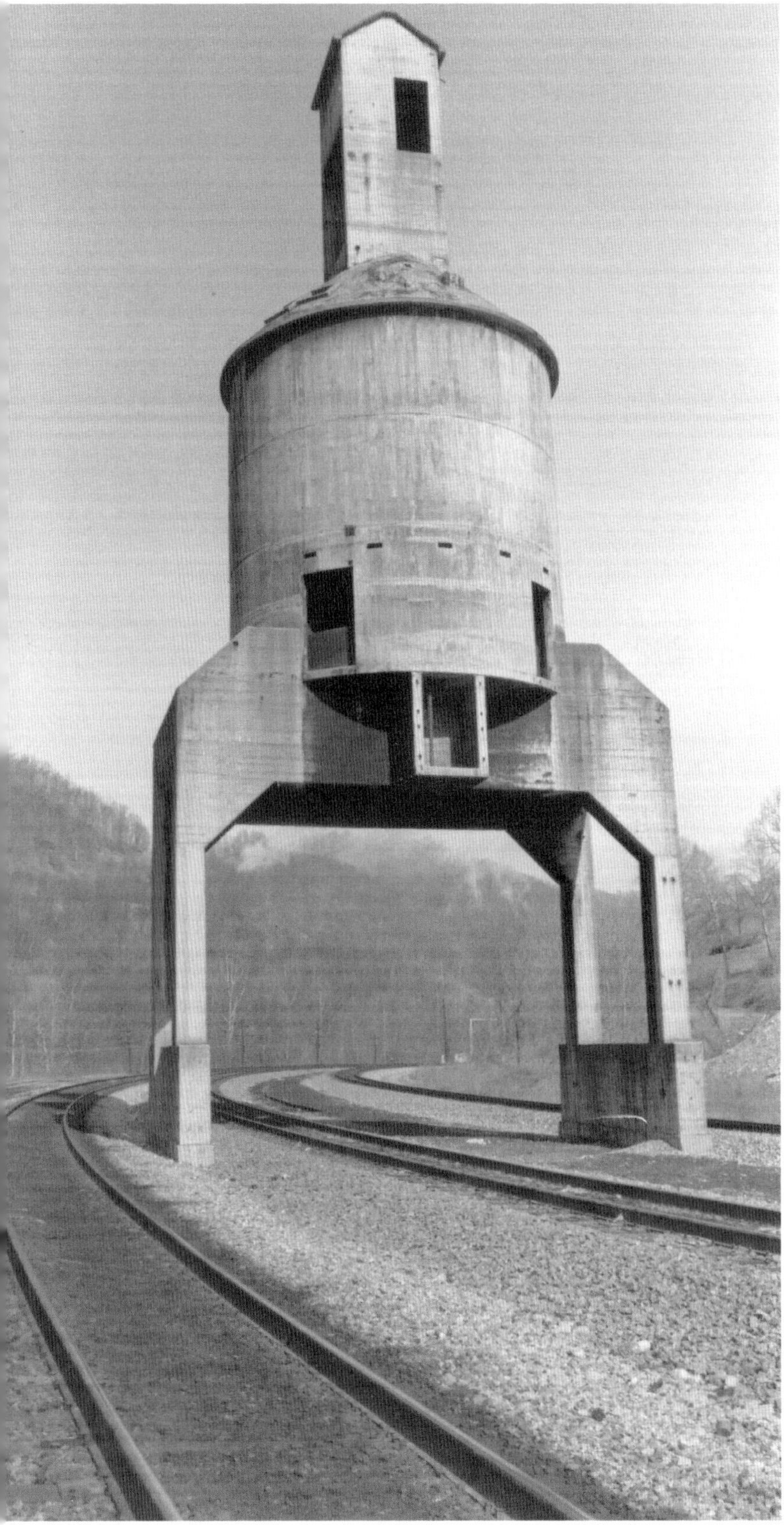

Transformers

Not every iconic remnant of the era when coal was king enjoyed a happy ending. During the early 1940s, the Norfolk & Western Railway decided to enact a plan to improve the efficiency of coal used to power its fleet of steam locomotives, erecting coal-wash stations, like the one shown here in Hemphill, West Virginia, to provide steam locomotives with a pure coal product to fire the boilers. At that time, electric-powered locomotives had already replaced steam for the hardest climbs through the mountains, but steam power was very much in demand for rail passenger service and in locations on the N&W mainline that had not been electrified. The Hemphill wash station was one of three such stations built by the railway, with the others in Williamson, West Virginia, and Bluefield, West Virginia. But the railroad switched from steam to diesel power in the late 1950s, and none of the huge stations was ever put into use. (Photograph by Phil Farmer.)

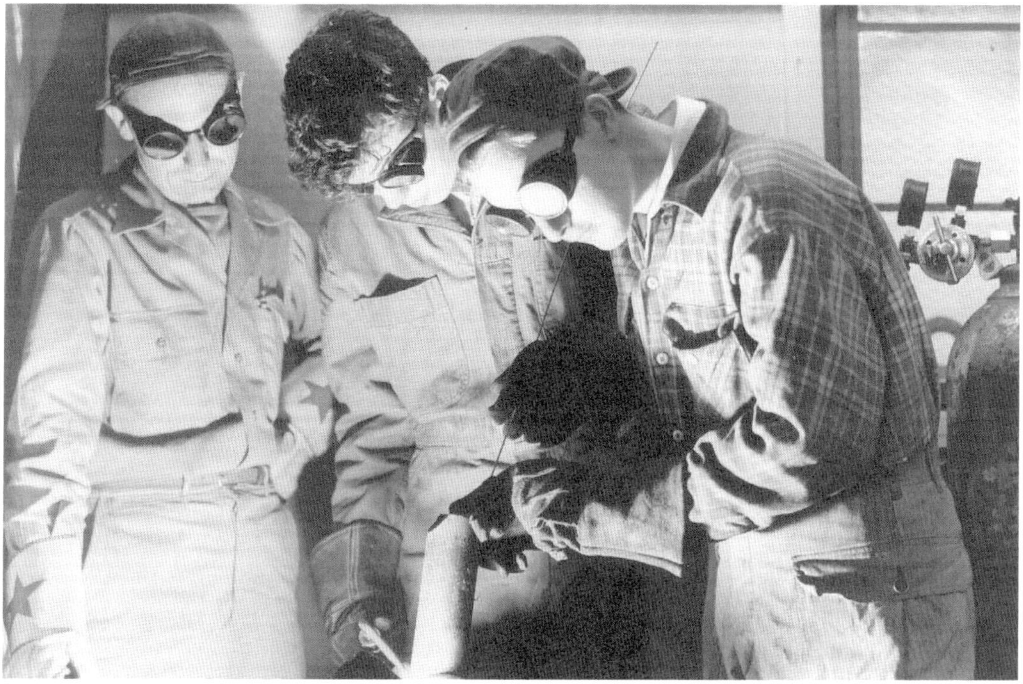

Work Force

Under the eye of welding instructor R.E. Vineyard (left), students James Gross of Elbert, West Virginia, (center) and Billy Kelly of Gary, West Virginia, are shown here working on their welds in the vocational education program of McDowell County Public Schools. In the early 1950s, the county vocational tech program eventually developed a simulated underground coal mine in a large field beside the school in Vivian. (Courtesy of the Eastern Regional Coal Archives.)

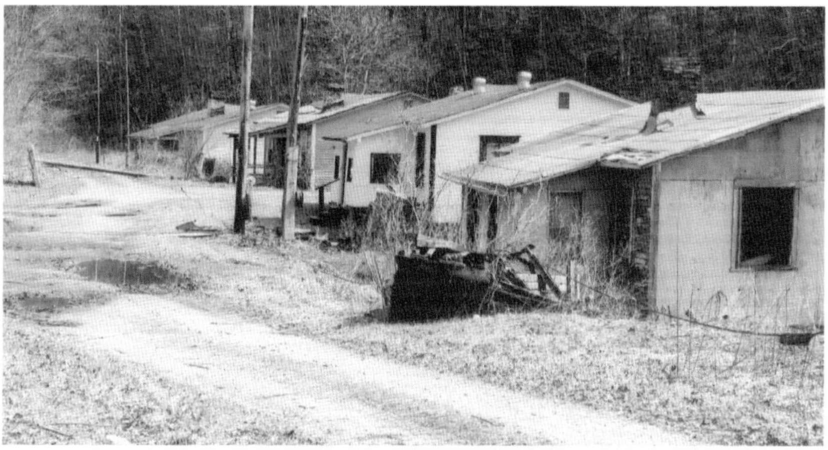

Coal Towns

Company houses were often hastily built and poorly insulated. Those shown here are in the section of Ashland, West Virginia, where the families of African American coal miners lived. One of the residences in this section was the birthplace of Garnett Mimms, the 1960s rhythm and blues singer who was known for the song "Cry Baby." After a brief career in popular music he returned to his gospel roots, where he continues to serve through his ministry and music. (Photograph by the author.)

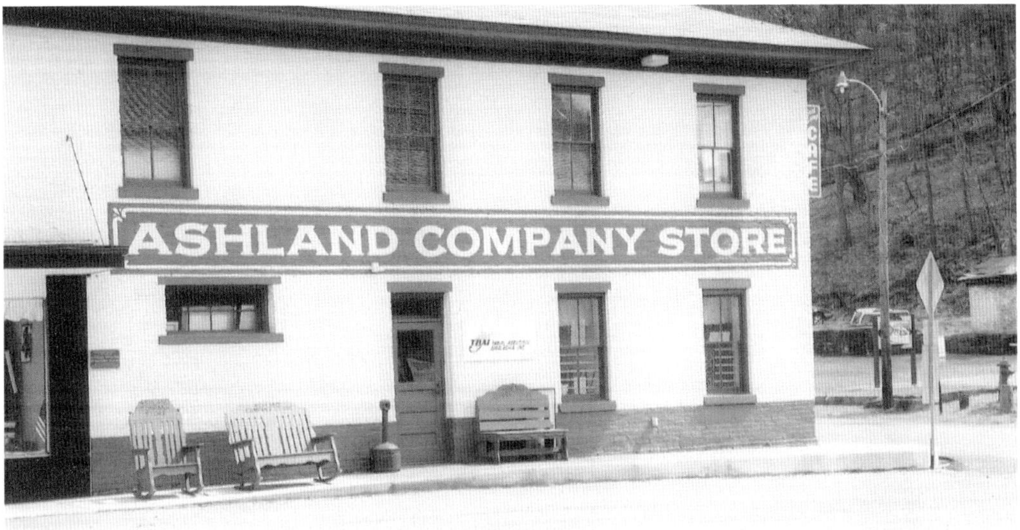

Owe My Soul

The Ashland Company Store, shown here, was resurrected in the first decade of the 21st century to serve as a center for commerce in the developing all-terrain vehicle trail-riding community. The restoration project was done under the guidance of Stop Abusive Family Environments (SAFE). (Photograph by the author.)

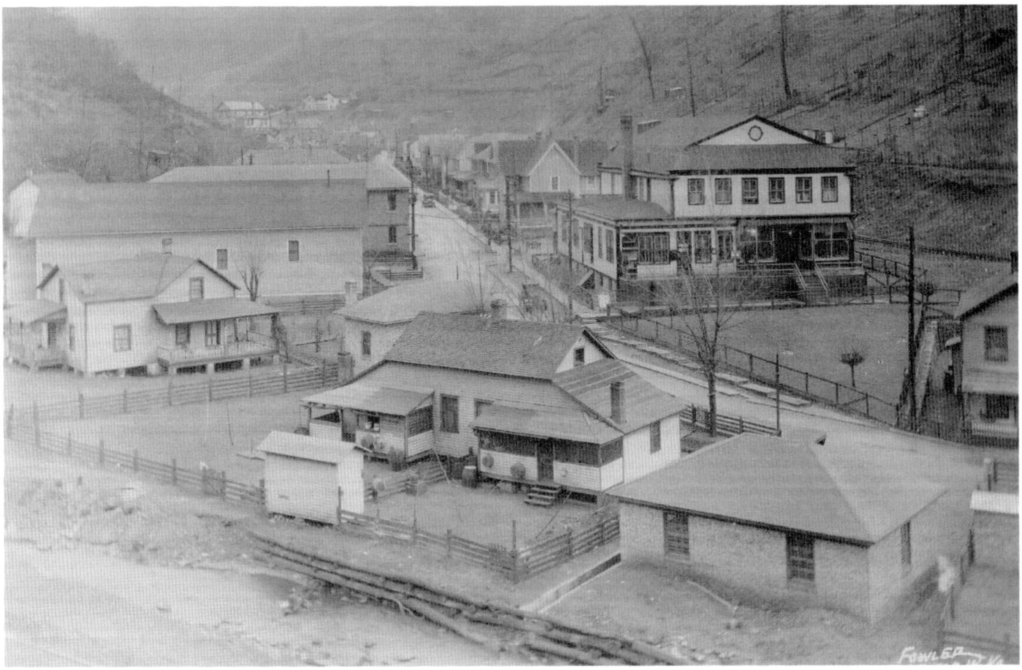

Ashland Heyday

Most of the buildings surrounding the old company store in Ashland are gone now, but the nucleus of the community remains. As part of its efforts to restore the community, SAFE Economic Development helped the town develop a sanitary sewage system that could operate in the steep mountain valley. (Courtesy of the Eastern Regional Coal Archives.)

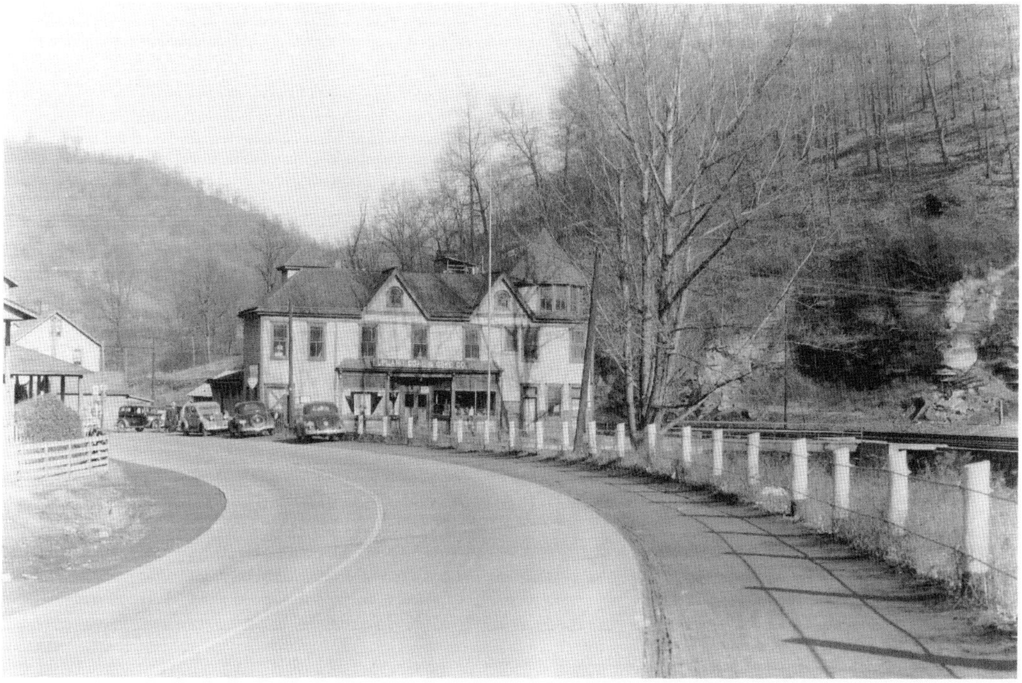

Upland, West Virginia
The Upland Coal Company maintained its offices in the building shown in this photograph. Swedish colonists arrived in what is now Pennsylvania in 1643 and named their first settlement Upland, because it was the first inland location where the ground was firm enough to erect permanent housing. The Swedes held on to their colony for only 12 years before Dutch troops captured New Sweden and ran them off in 1655. The English gained control from the Dutch in 1664. The family of coal pioneer Samuel A. Crozer located a theological seminary in Upland, Pennsylvania, the little-known sister city of Upland, West Virginia. (Courtesy of the Eastern Regional Coal Archives.)

On the Bottom
The community of Bottom Creek, on the Lick Creek tributary of Elkhorn Creek, near Kimball, West Virginia, was the site of a November 18, 1911, mine explosion that killed 14 coal miners and 4 engineers with the Crozer Land Company. The engineers were in the mine to determine if the coal operators were using proper mining techniques to safely extract all the coal that could be mined. (Courtesy of the Eastern Regional Coal Archives.)

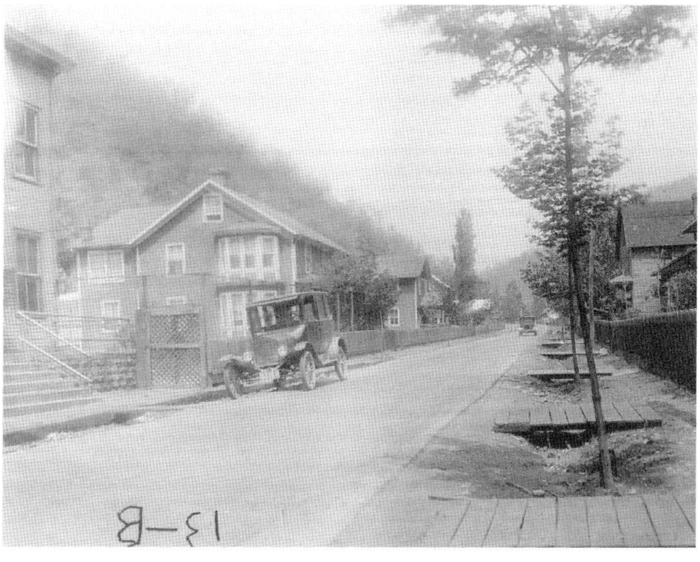

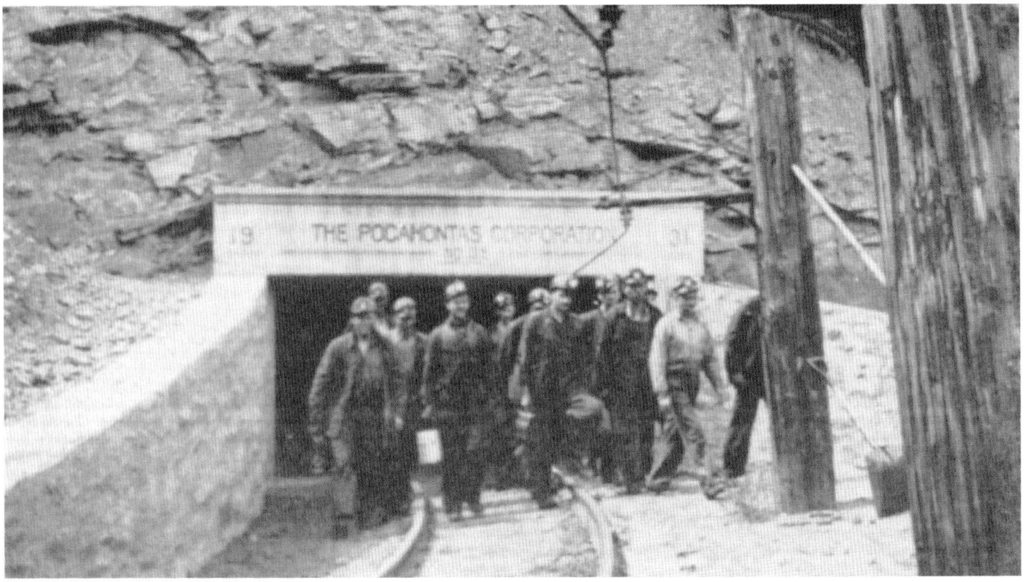

Underground River

Coal miners are shown here leaving the Bishop Mine in 1932 after completing their portion of the massive 18.6-mile underground drainage tunnel in McDowell County, West Virginia, and Tazewell County, Virginia. The tunnel drained 12,000 acres of coal. Each of the workers involved in the massive project received a medallion from the Pocahontas Fuel Company. (Author's collection.)

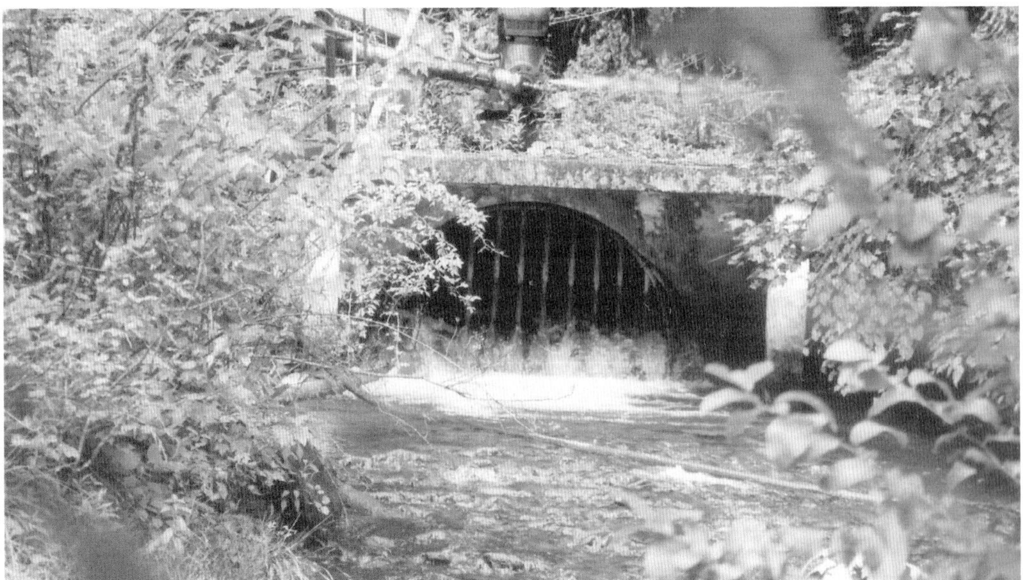

Dry Fork No More

The Pocahontas Fuel Company's incredible tunnel system drained 12,000 acres of Pocahontas Number 3 seam coal into the headwaters of the Dry Fork of the Big Sandy River. The modest exit for that huge area is located in McDowell County near the town of Amonate. The project was started in the fall of 1931 and completed in 1936, opening up unmined coal reserves of 400 million tons. (Photograph by the author.)

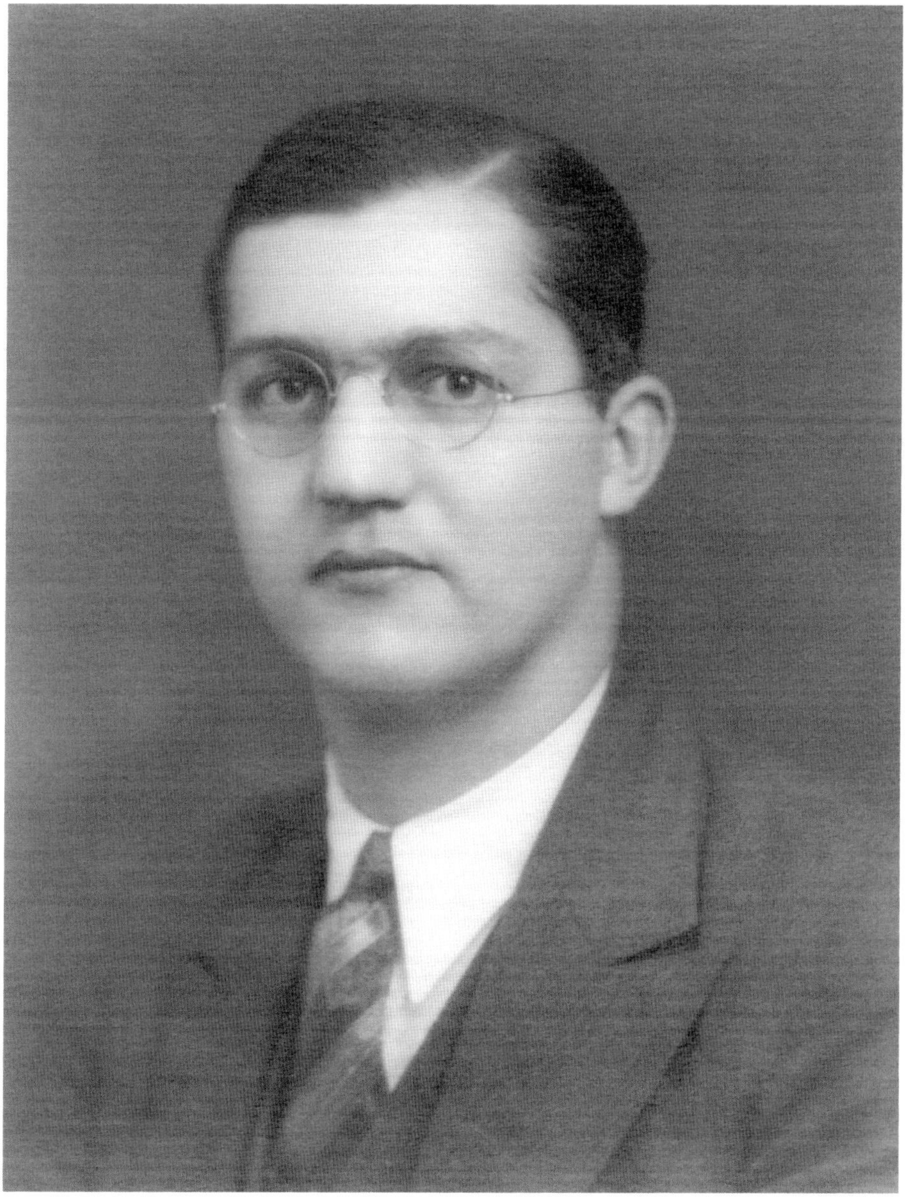

Algoma
William Beury, owner of the Algoma Coal Company, near the junction of Elkhorn Creek and its North Fork tributary, named his company by forming a contraction of the Indian name *Algonquin* with the Indian name for waters, *goma*. Beury was the brother of Joseph Lawton Beury, also a pioneer coal man, who opened the first mine in the New River smokeless coalfields at Quinnimont, Fayette County, West Virginia. *Quinnimont* is Latin for "five mountains." The Beury family was from Schuylkill County, Pennsylvania, where Joseph and William Beury's father was in the anthracite coal-mining business. Joseph and William became partners with John Cooper in the first mine in the Flat Top coalfields, the Mill Creek Mine, which opened in 1884 near Bramwell. William Beury then moved into the McDowell County coalfields and opened Algoma. Interestingly, Beury's name (and that of Col. A.J. May) is used to form part of another McDowell County town, Maybeury. (Courtesy of the Eastern Regional Coal Archives.)

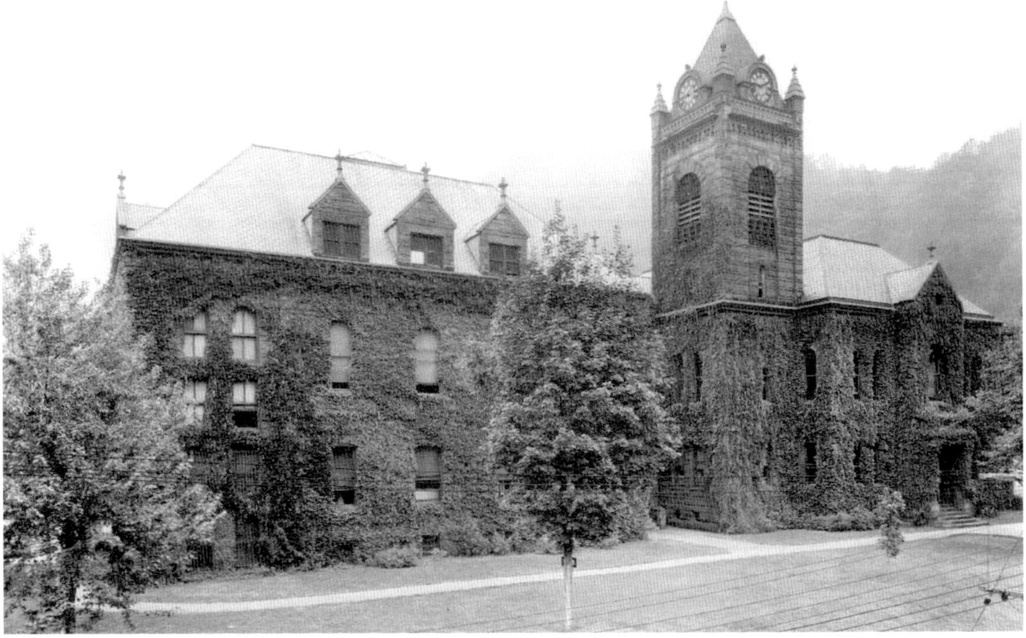

County Court

The McDowell County Courthouse in Welch is one of the state's most storied, yet apparently unappreciated, courthouses. It was erected in the early 20th century, and retains much of its architectural design. The building is filled with history, but possesses little of the trappings of modern living. The county lacks the revenue to bring it up to modern standards. (Courtesy of the Eastern Regional Coal Archives.)

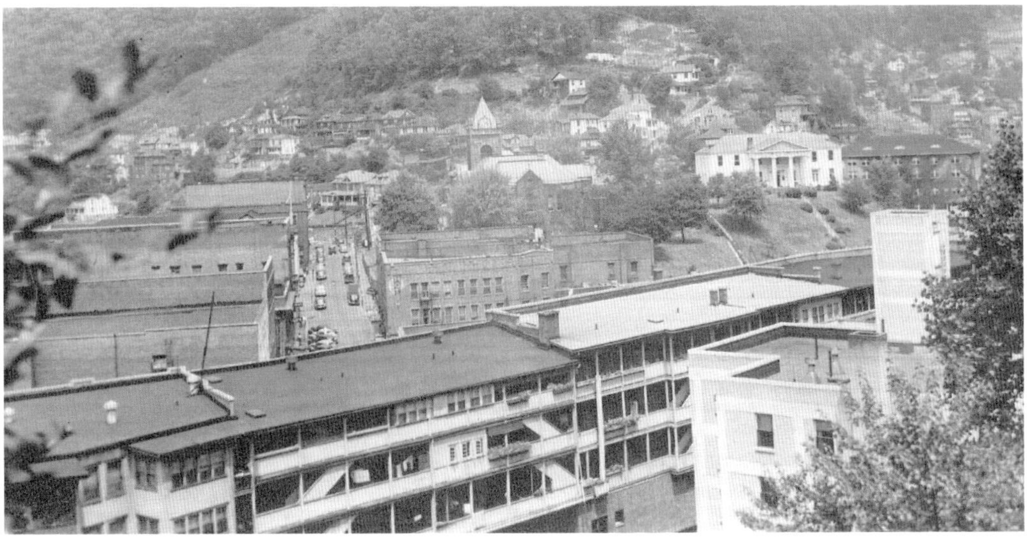

Wyoming Street in the Summer

This view of Welch, West Virginia, shows Wyoming Street at a time when the community was bustling with activity. Mine mechanization, mine consolidation, and the closing of some county mines caused a dramatic reduction in McDowell County's population. But the county continues to reinvent itself to take advantage of its fascinating history and beautiful scenery. (Courtesy of the Eastern Regional Coal Archives.)

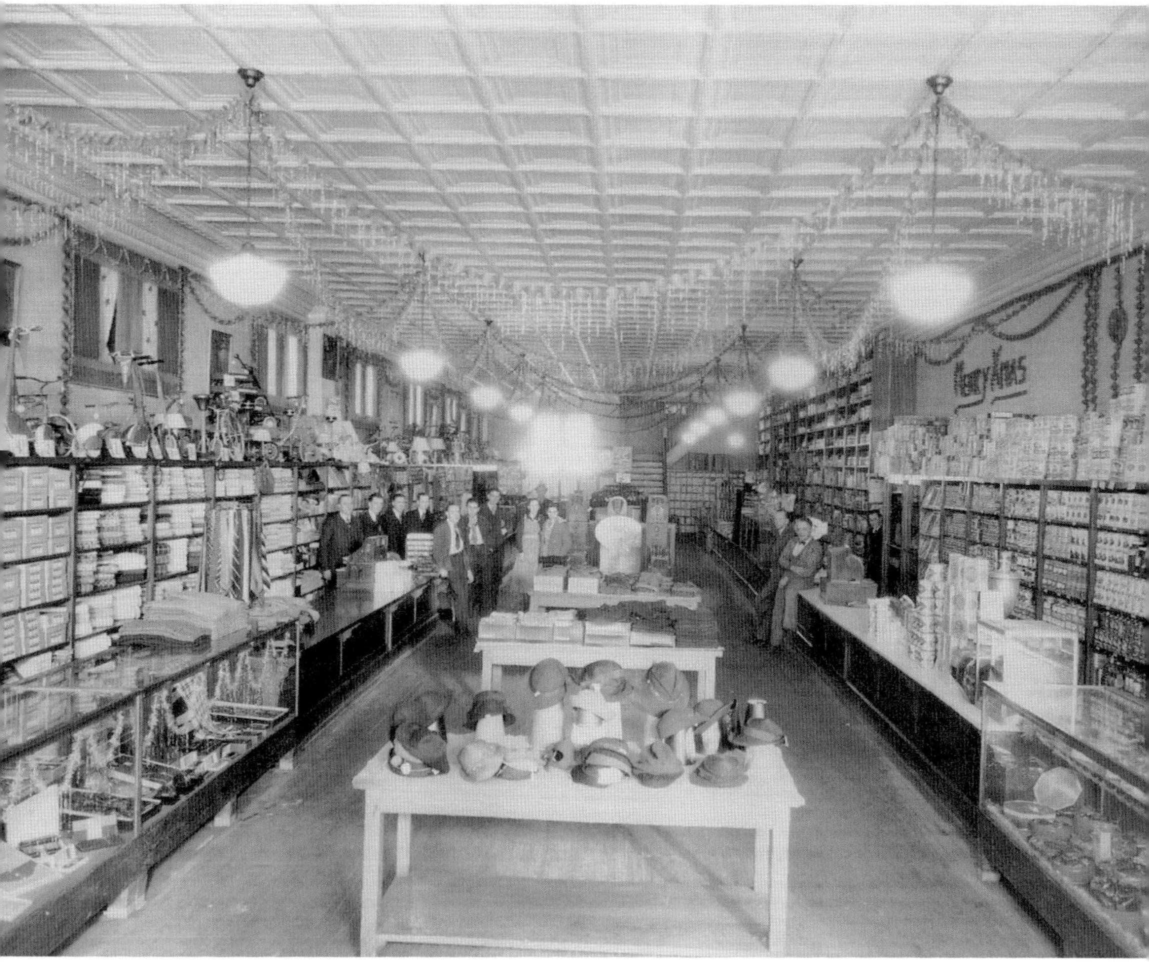

You Can Get Anything You Want

The staff of the company store in the town of Berwind is shown here ready to serve customers. Edward J. Berwind was among the most powerful coal operators in the United States during the late 1800s until his death in 1936. He was born into a family of great wealth in the Philadelphia area, and acquired 30,000 acres of "smokeless" coal in central Pennsylvania. The Berwind White Coal Company provided most of the coal for the Pennsylvania Railway and handled most of the coal for steamship bunkering in New York, Cuba, and the Caribbean Islands. Berwind acquired coal property in Thurmond, West Virginia, and invested in a large tract of coal property on Dry Fork in McDowell County at roughly the same time. Berwind was one of the major players in the coal industry during the early 20th century. (Courtesy of the Eastern Regional Coal Archives.)

Two for the Show

W.E.E. "Kep" Koepler (left) and William A. Bishop are shown here at an unidentified location. Keopler was the executive director of Bluefield, West Virginia–based Pocahontas Operators Association, and Bishop developed the Bishop Mine on the McDowell County border with Tazewell County, Virginia. Bishop would later sell his mine operations to Inland Steel Company and the Consolidation Coal Company, now known as Consol. Koepler, born in 1884 in St. Charles, Missouri, was a trade paper journalist. He joined the staff of *The Black Diamond* in 1907, and in 1913, came aboard the *Colliery Engineer*, a trade publication that eventually became *Coal Age Magazine*. After a short stint with the *Philadelphia Public Ledger*, he came to Bluefield in 1918 to assume the post with the Pocahontas Operators Association. (Courtesy of the Eastern Regional Coal Archives.)

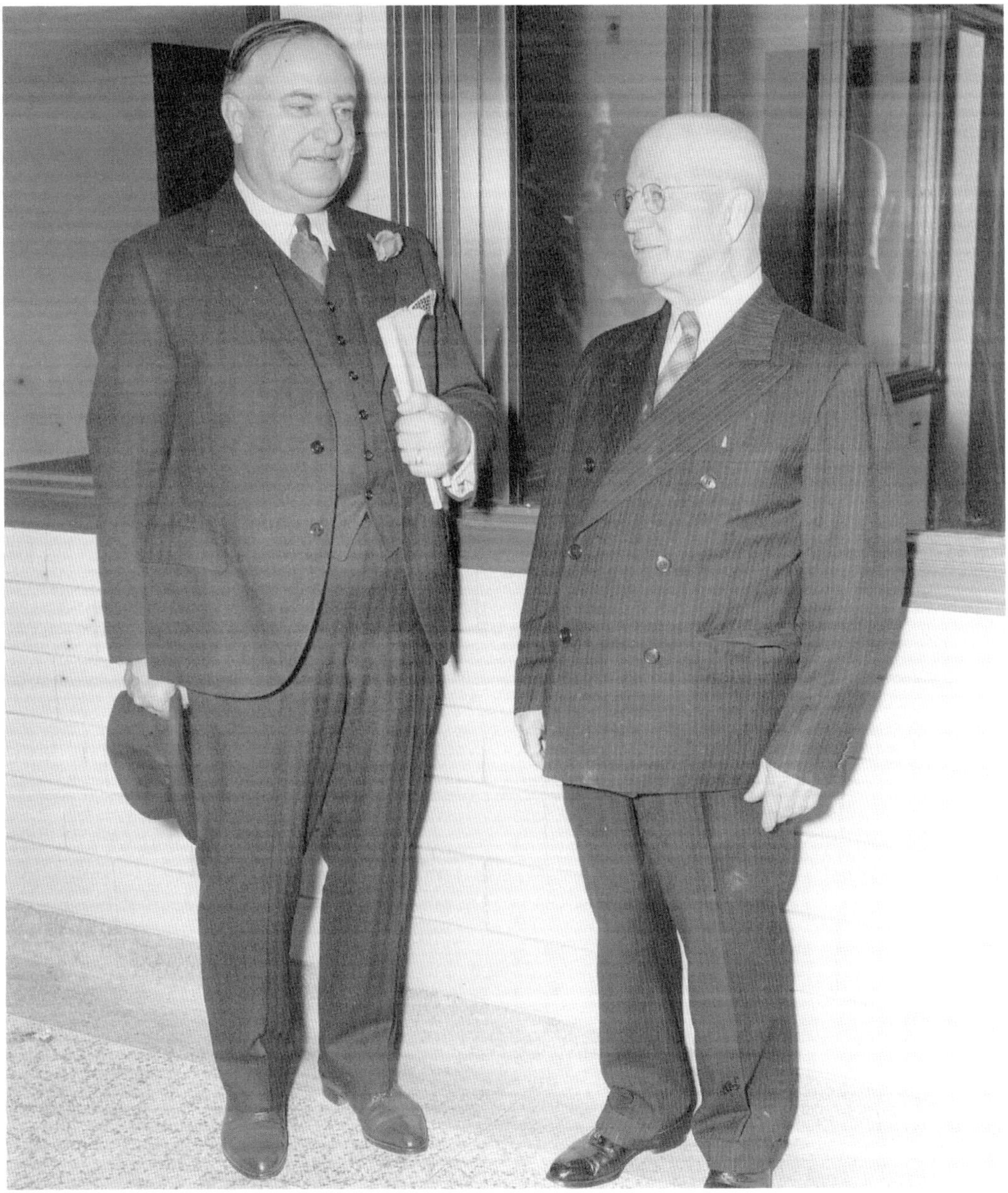

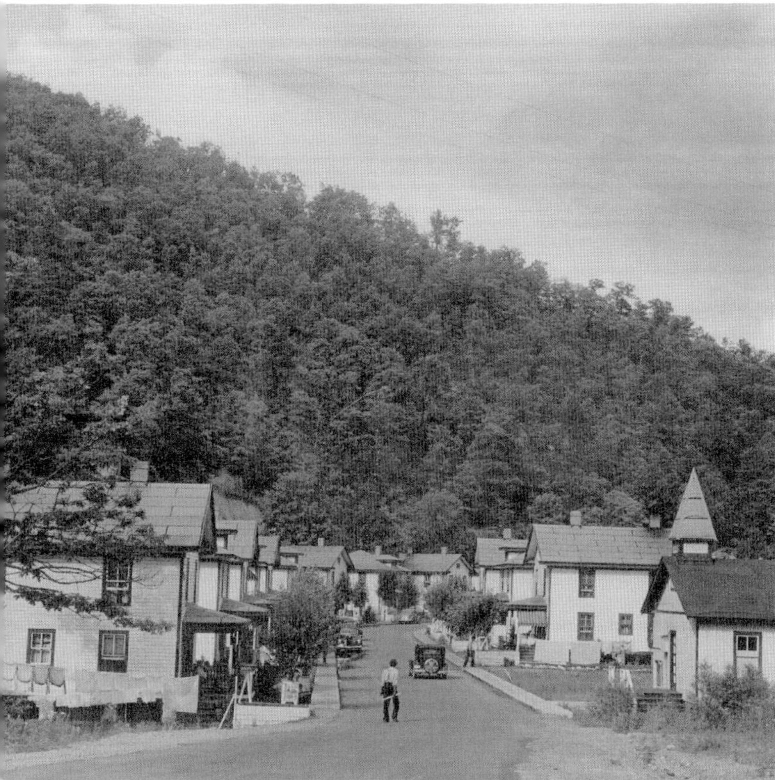

Segregation
While most of the town of Bishop was located in Tazewell County, Virginia, the African American section was in McDowell County, West Virginia. Segregation was prominent throughout McDowell County, but coal miners and their families, of all races, creeds, and countries of origin, learned to work and play together. (Courtesy of the Eastern Regional Coal Archives.)

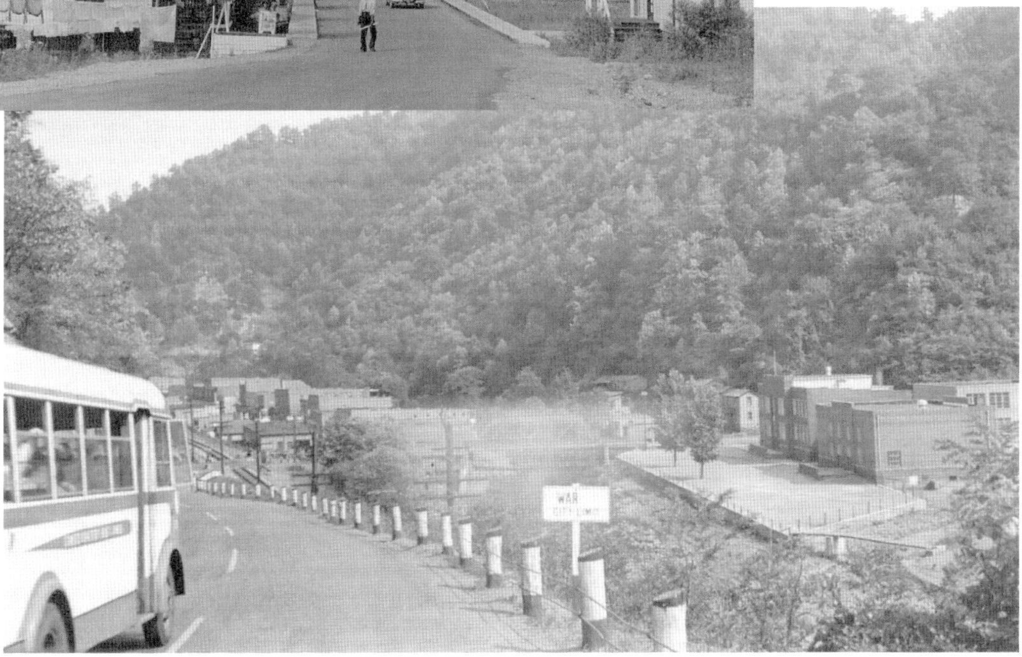

West Virginia's Southernmost City
The town of War, shown in this photograph, was a place where people of all races achieved their dreams. Coaches like Merrill Gainer, Glyn Carlock, and Jim Hickam achieved success, and athletes including Oscar Patrick and Bob Gresham excelled. Photographer Jim Clark, general Robert Stephens, and author Homer Hickam all have ties to War and its two high schools, Big Creek and Excelsior. (Courtesy of the Eastern Regional Coal Archives.)

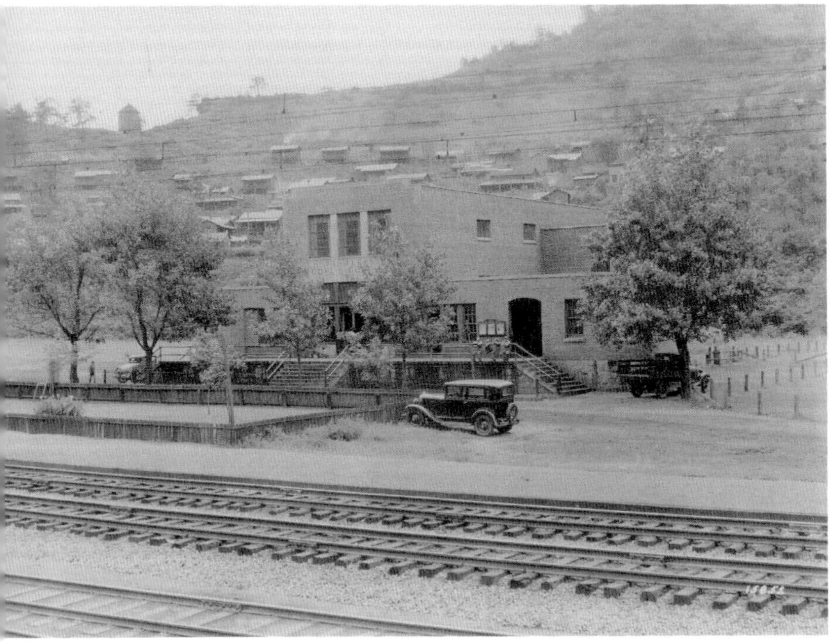

On the Right Track
The Peerless Coal Company in McDowell County was one of several coal-mining operations that provided "fuel satisfaction" to customers worldwide. (Courtesy of the Eastern Regional Coal Archives.)

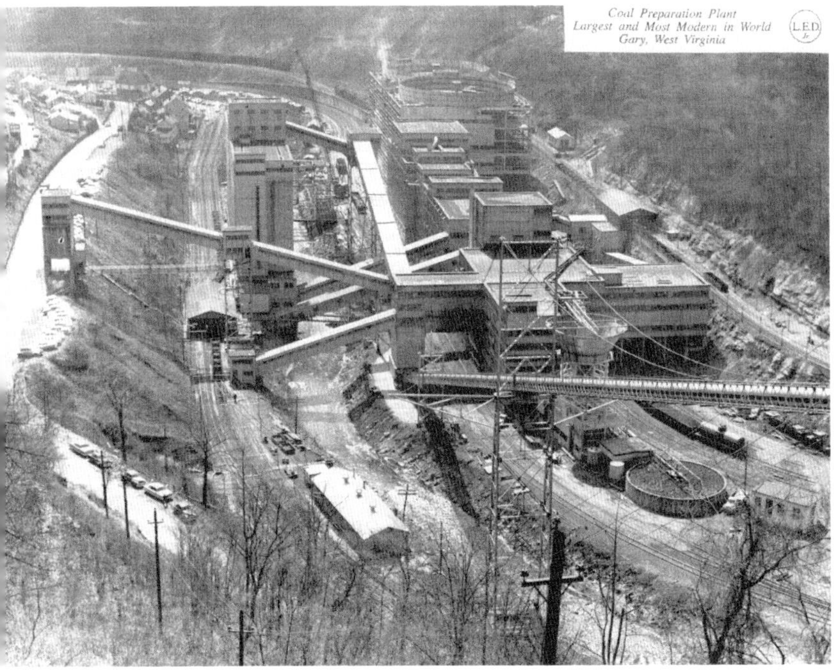

Coalfield of Dreams
At its height, the mighty US Steel Coal & Coke Alpheus Preparation Plant was capable of sending the right blend of coking coal to US Steel plants throughout the United States. The steel produced at plants in Chicago, Pittsburgh, and elsewhere established a strong infrastructure for the nation to build upon. (Courtesy of the McDowell County Library, Welch Branch.)

CHAPTER THREE

Answering the Call

McDowell County, Virginia, was established just three years before the start of the American Civil War, and joined the counties of western Virginia that refused to secede from the Union in 1861. The county became part of the 35th state of West Virginia on June 20, 1863. Since that time, West Virginians have played a role in every major war involving the United States, starting with the Spanish-American War, when Genuine Pocahontas Coal powered the ships of Adm. George Dewey when he entered Manila Bay, and the *Iowa* under Capt. Robley "Fighting Bob" Evans, who steamed around Cape Horn to assist US Navy ships in Santiago Bay.

While McDowell County coal was used to make the steel for tanks, ships, and weapons of war, able-bodied men and women from the county served with distinction in the branches of every military service. The ranks of World War I doughboys were made up of both white and black soldiers, and their service was honored through the construction of war memorials for both races. Men and women answered the call to fight in World War II. Lt. Sara Blanche Vance of Vance Hollow, near Iaeger, West Virginia, was the first woman from the state killed in action during World War II. She was killed in Italy on October 22, 1944. Another Vance with roots in the Iaeger area, Sgt. Gene Arden Vance Jr., of Morgantown, serving with the 19th Special Forces Group (Airborne), was killed in action in Afghanistan on May 19, 2002. He was the first soldier with the West Virginia National Guard killed in action since World War II.

Through the years, the people of McDowell County have always honored those who have served in the military by making the annual observance of Veterans Day something very special. The people of McDowell County have always taken very seriously their duty to serve the nation in the armed services.

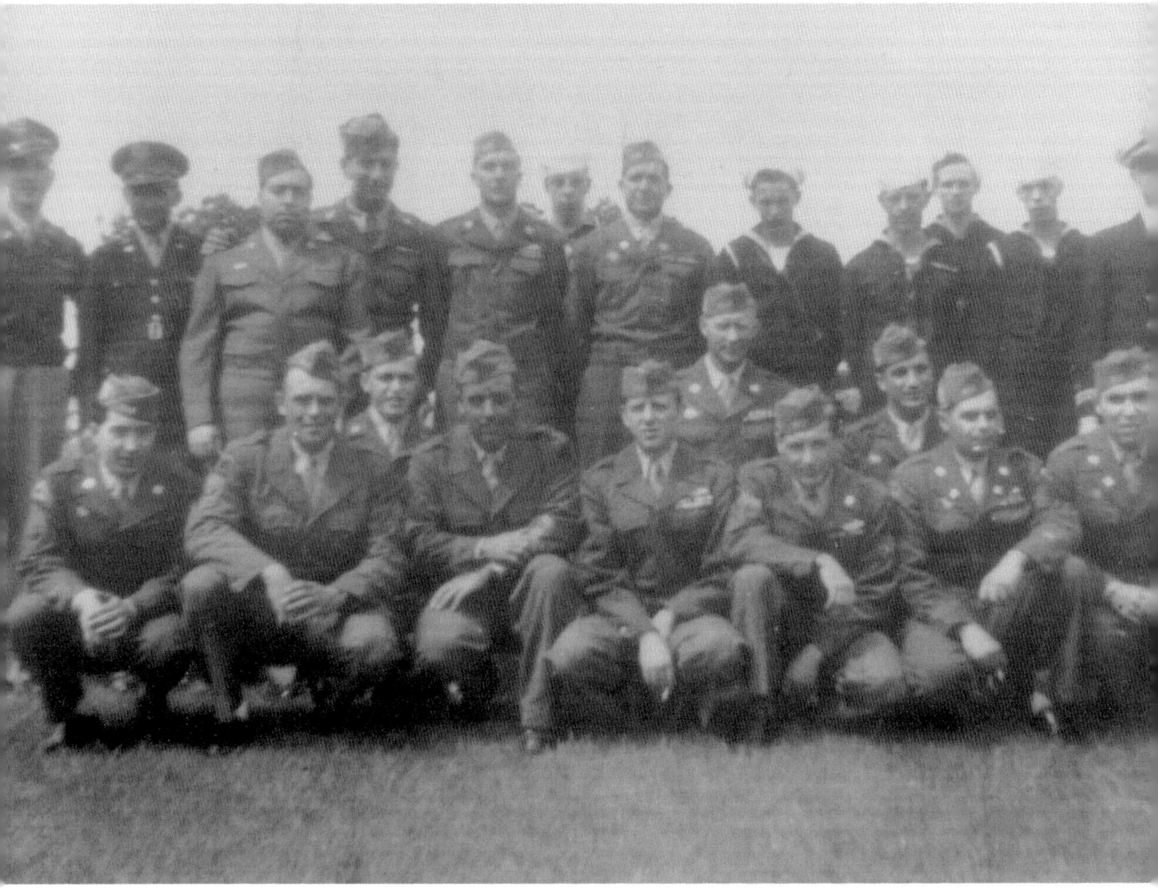

Kimball Served

At the end of World War II, several soldiers, sailors, airmen, and marines—all from the town of Kimball, West Virginia—posed for this photograph. Shown are, from left to right, (first row) Jimmy Gianato, Von Rector, unidentified, Jess Hardy, Lloyd Woolwine, J.W. Scott, Lew Lumpkins, Frank Sorrell, Luke Gianato and ? Leckiel; (second row) unidentified, Kelly Marrs, Johnny Gianato, Sammy Catuso, two unidentified, Kelly Napier, unidentified, Edgar Sawyers, Stafford George, and three unidentified. (Courtesy of Jimmy Gianato.)

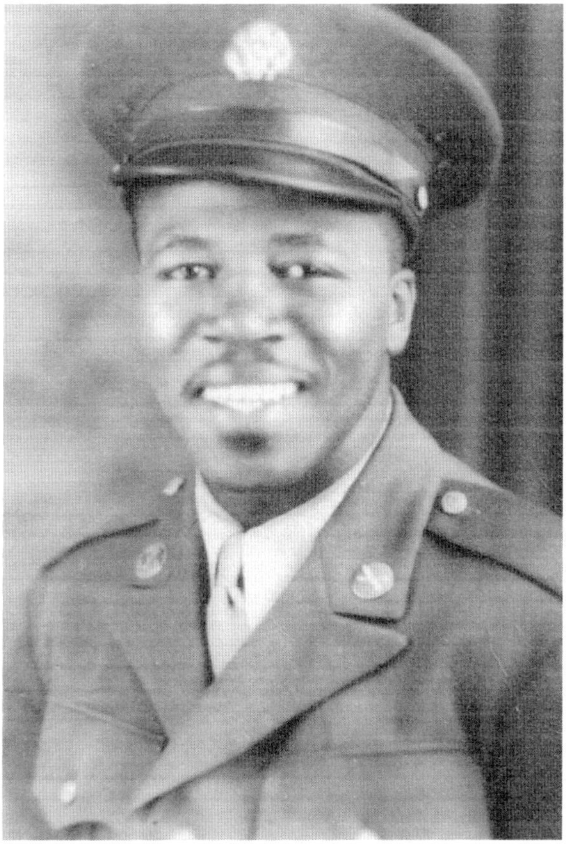

Combat Veteran
Ellis Ray Williams served in the US Army during World War II, but unlike most blacks who served, Williams was a combat veteran, fighting in the Battle of the Bulge. After the war, Williams returned home to continue working for veterans and was instrumental in the restoration effort of the World War I Memorial Building in Kimball, which honors African American veterans of that war. (Courtesy of Ellis Ray Williams.)

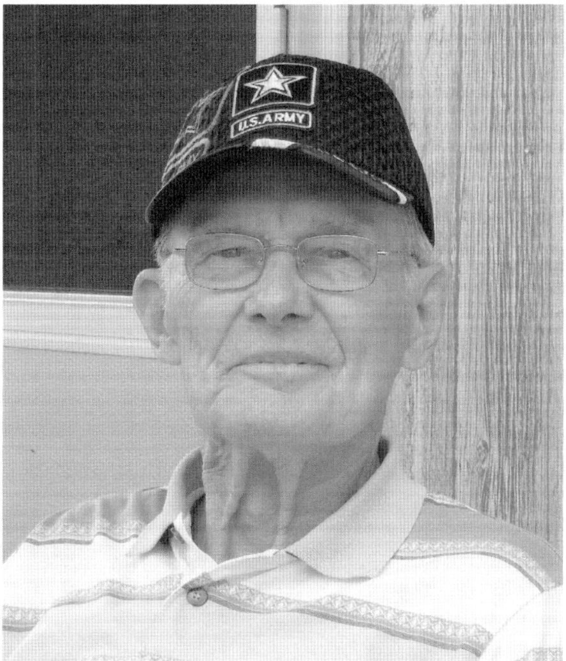

D-Day
Walter W. Kowaleski, a 1943 graduate of Elkhorn High School in Switchback, West Virginia, was among the thousands of US Army soldiers who landed on Omaha Beach in Normandy, France, on June 6, 1944. He served with the 29th Infantry Division, 115th Infantry Regiment, a unit that was intended to land on the second day of the invasion. Due to heavy losses suffered by the first wave, however, Kowaleski and his comrades landed at 10:30 a.m. on D-Day. (Photograph by the author.)

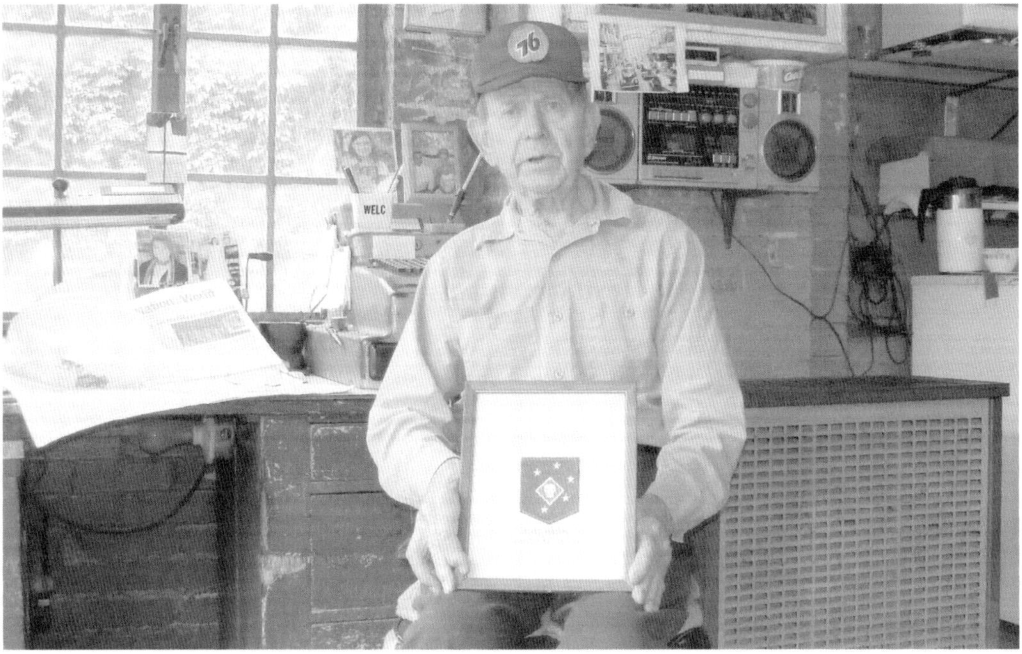

One of Edson's Raiders
Ed Shepard displays his Edson's Raiders emblem in the office of his service station in Welch. Shepard joined the US Marine Corps on January 7, 1942, exactly one month after the Japanese attack on Pearl Harbor. He was assigned to the 1st Marine Raider Battalion, Edson's Raiders, and served as a sniper in the battles of Guadalcanal, Tulagi, New Britain, Peleliu, and Okinawa. (Photograph by the author.)

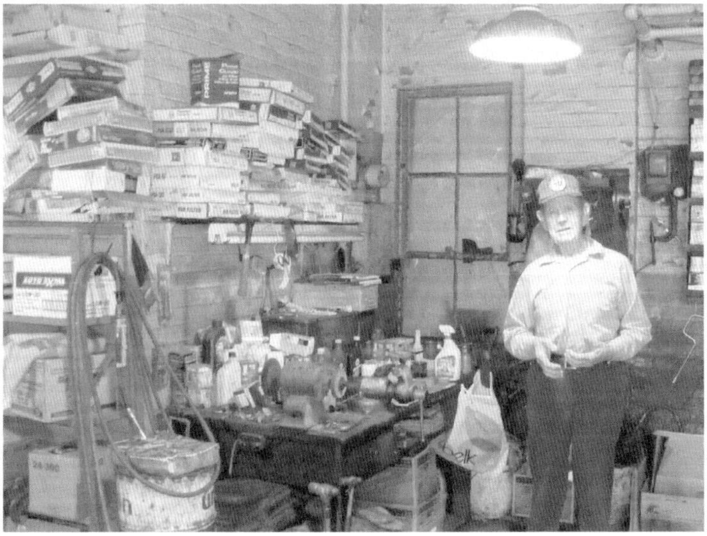

Service with Pride
Although he hasn't sold gasoline in recent years, Ed Shepard still does oil changes and minor repairs at his former Pure Oil, and later Union 76, station in Welch. He was born in Garland, a small community up Dry Fork, near Iaeger. After World War II, Shepard returned home to Welch, took a job at the station, and became its owner a few years later. (Photograph by the author.)

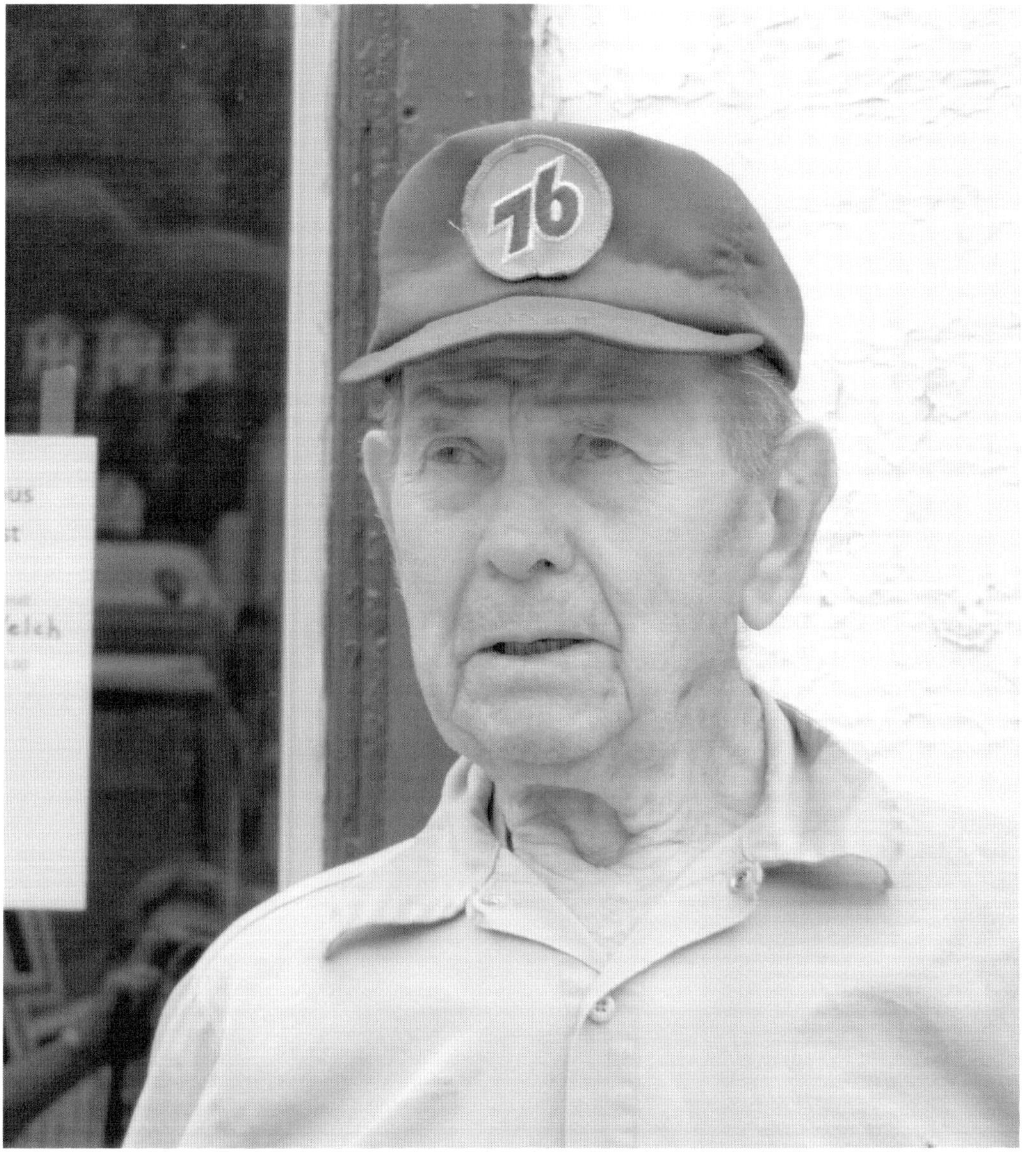

American Hero

As a sniper in the 1st Marine Raider Battalion, Ed Shepard knew what his fate would be if he was ever captured by the enemy. He knew the enemy would torture him without hoping to get any information from him at all, and that they would keep him alive as long as they could. Although he didn't talk much about his service after the war, he is mentioned prominently in the two most respected books about Edson's Raiders, *The 1st Marine Raider Battalion at Guadalcanal*, by George W. Smith, and *The 1st Marine Raider Battalion in World War II*, by Joseph H. Alexander. Both books discuss an incident when he and a fellow Marine were wounded and trapped behind enemy lines at Guadalcanal, and provide details of Shepard's miraculous escape. Although he was born in McDowell County, his family moved to 30 different homes. When he was just 14 years old, he wound up living with an aunt in Idaho. He returned to McDowell County after he completed his tour of duty. "By the time I was 21 years old, I had done and seen more than most men see in a lifetime," he says in a quote for this book. (Photograph by the author.)

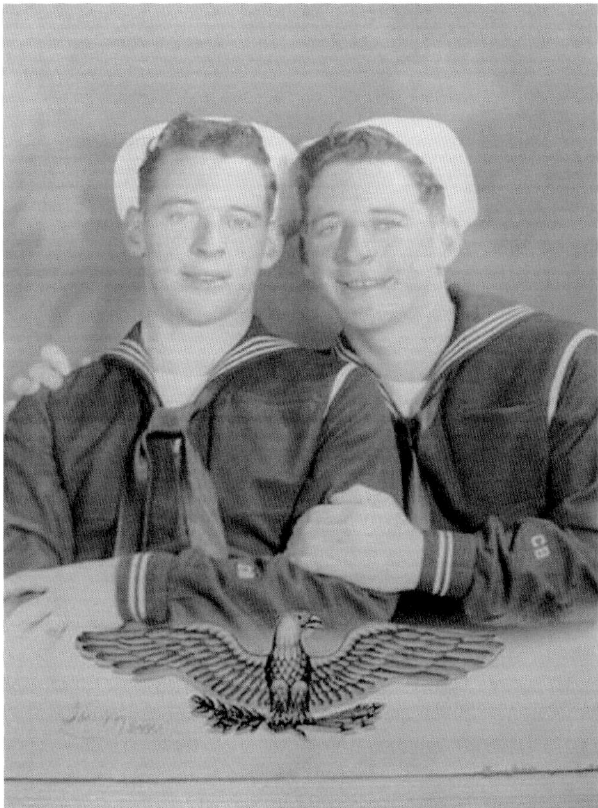

Double Trouble
Twins Rush (left) and Riley Justice of War, West Virginia, served in the US Navy Seabees during World War II. The Justice family had a long history of military service. The twins' great-grandfather John Justice served in the Revolutionary War, and their grandfather, Solomon Justice, fought for the Confederacy and served in the 34th Mounted Cavalry during the American Civil War. (Courtesy of Anita Moody.)

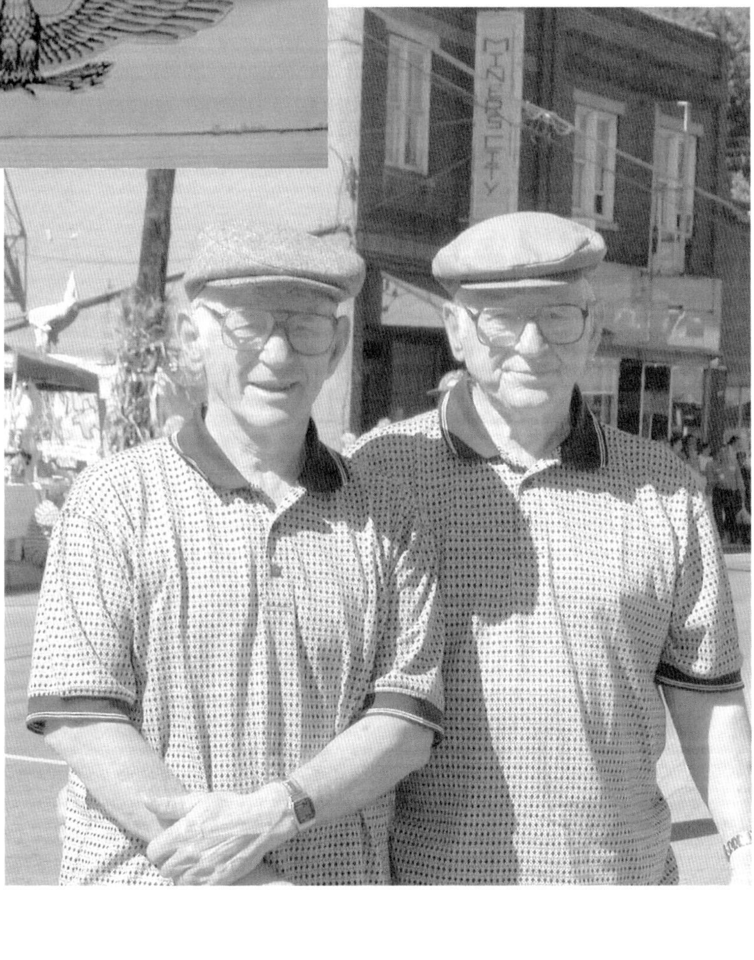

Twin Blades
After World War II, the Justice twins, Rush (left) and Riley, attended Wheeling Barber School and operated the Justice Twins Barber Shop in War for 55 years. The Justice twins were extremely popular and were featured in many publications through the years. The city of War honored them with a celebration in 2001. (Courtesy of Rush Justice's daughter, Anita Moody.)

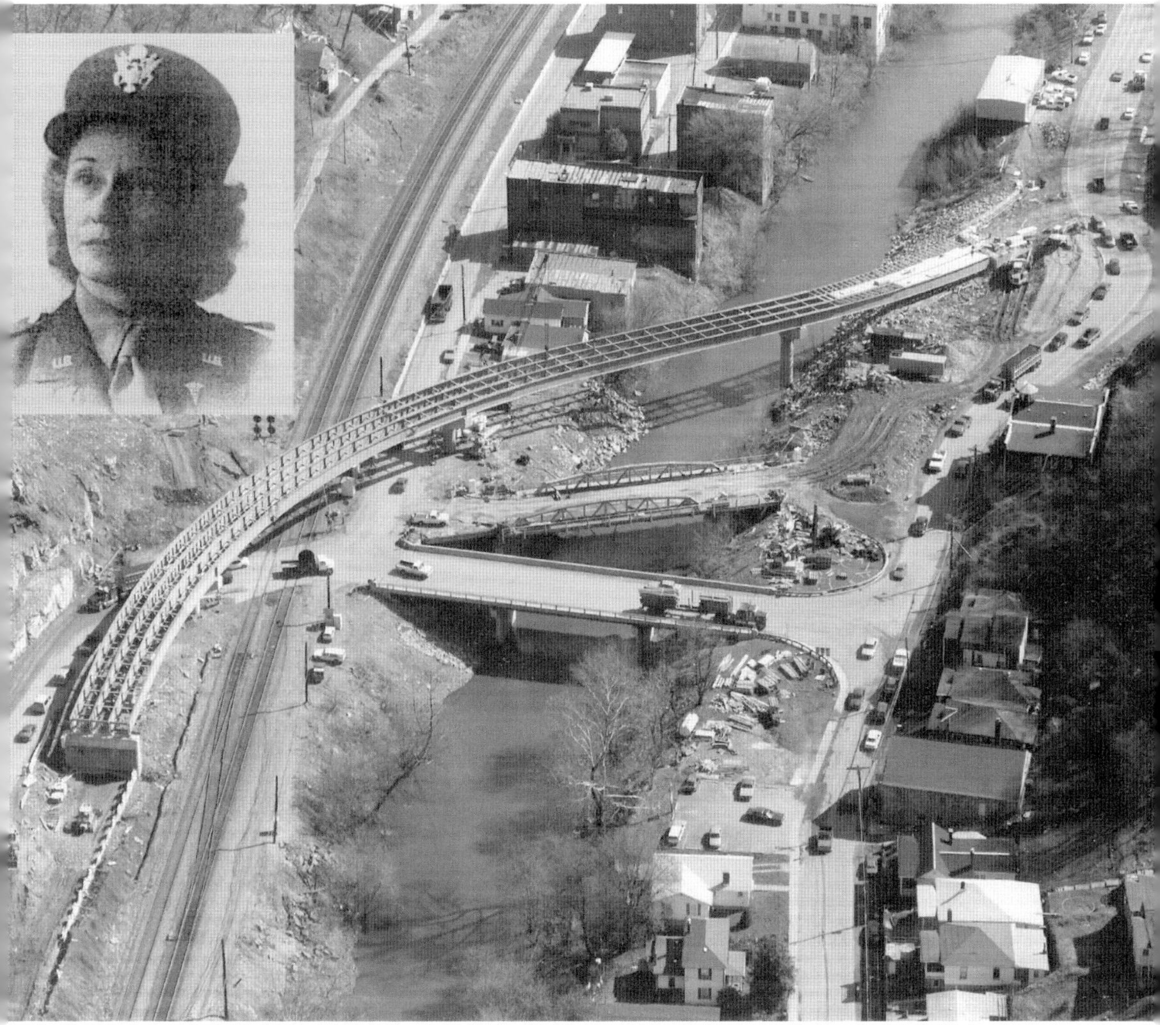

Bridging Troubled Waters

Lt. Sara Blanch Vance grew up in Vance Hollow, outside Iaeger, McDowell County, and graduated from the Raleigh General Hospital School of Nursing in Beckley, West Virginia. After finishing school, she worked for a time at Cincinnati General Hospital in Cincinnati, Ohio, and Pinecrest Sanitarium in Beckley. She joined the US Army Nursing Corps in November 1942, received her basic training at Camp Campbell, Kentucky, and was sent to North Africa in 1943. Lieutenant Vance was among a group of Army nurses who were later called the "Anzio Nurses," because of their landing at Anzio. In a letter home, she wrote that the nurses wore fatigues for the landing and that enlisted men carried them ashore. According to her nephew, Joe Stafford, a long-serving mayor of Iaeger who had spoken to a soldier from McDowell County who had served with Lieutenant Vance, she had been inside a hospital as it was being shelled by the enemy, and stepped outside and was killed on October 22, 1944. She was the first woman from West Virginia killed in action during World War II. There are now 18 women on the state's honor roll of those killed in action. Vance is buried in the Sicily-Rome American Cemetery in Nettuno, Italy. The bridge over the Tug Fork and Norfolk Southern Railway tracks at Iaeger, shown under construction during the late 1990s, was dedicated in her honor in 1999. (Photograph by Melvin Grubb. Insert image courtesy of Joe Stafford.)

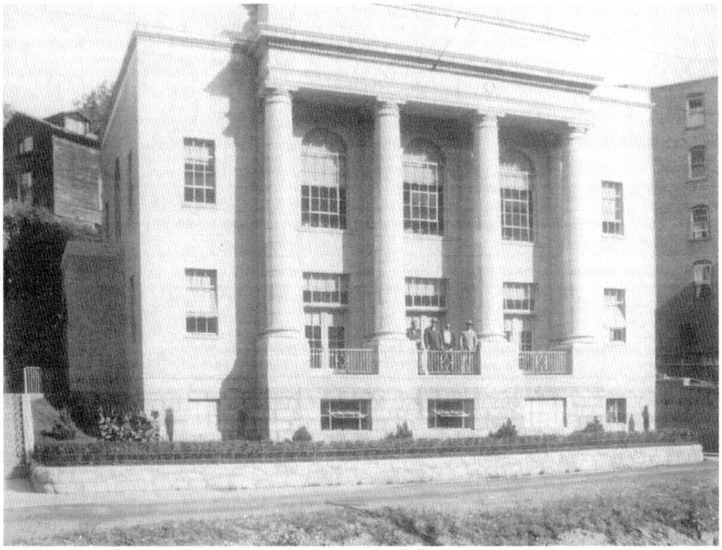

War Memorial

After World War I, the McDowell County Commission authorized the construction of a war memorial building in Welch. In that era of segregation, the many African American soldiers from McDowell County demanded a war memorial as well. The War Memorial in Kimball, West Virginia, believed to be the only memorial of its kind dedicated to black doughboys, was dedicated on February 11, 1928. (Author's collection.)

Inside the Kimball War Memorial

More than 1,500 blacks from McDowell County served in the US Army during World War I. The War Memorial, designed by Welch architect Hassel T. Hicks, became home to the Luther Paterson Post Number 36 of the American Legion, the first black American Legion post in the United States. The building was gutted by fire in 1991, and restored in 2009, thanks to the support of the late US senator Robert C. Byrd. (Courtesy of Hassel T. Hicks family.)

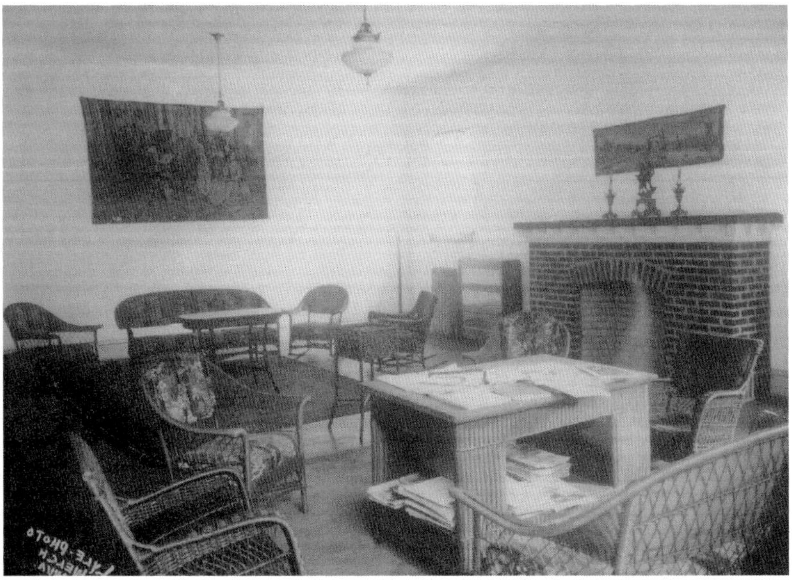

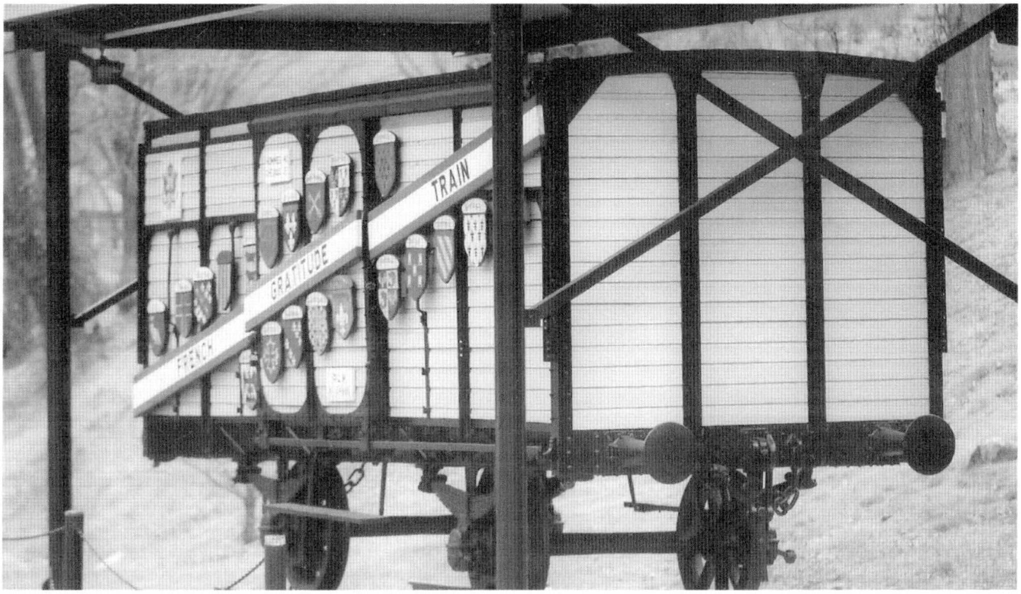

War to End All Wars
After World War I, the people of France presented all 48 states and the District of Columbia with a railroad boxcar filled with gifts for the American people, in appreciation for freeing France from German occupation. Many of the boxcars, including the one given to West Virginia, were displayed for a time and discarded. Members of the Welch-based W.E. Eubank Voiture 1171, Societe Des 40 Hommes Et 8, found the state's boxcar in a field in St. Albans, West Virginia, restored it, and displayed it at Coney Island in Welch. The "40 & 8" is associated with the American Legion and is so named because a typical French boxcar could transport 40 doughboys and 8 mules to the trenches during World War I. (Photograph by the author.)

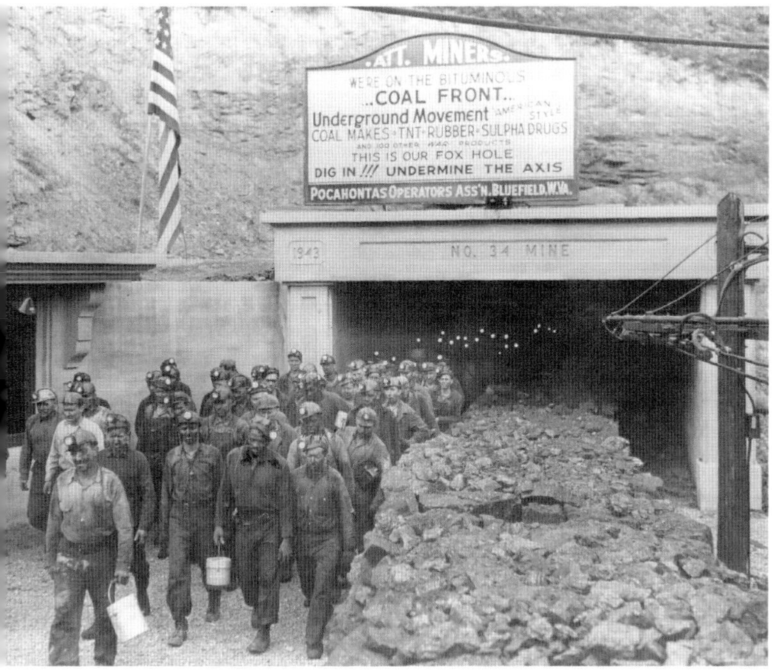

A Different War
Coal miners are shown here exiting the Pocahontas Fuel Company's mine at Jacob's Fork, West Virginia, near Bishop, Virginia, during World War II. Coal mining was considered essential to the war effort and, as a result, many coal miners were deferred from the draft. (Courtesy of Grubb Photo Service.)

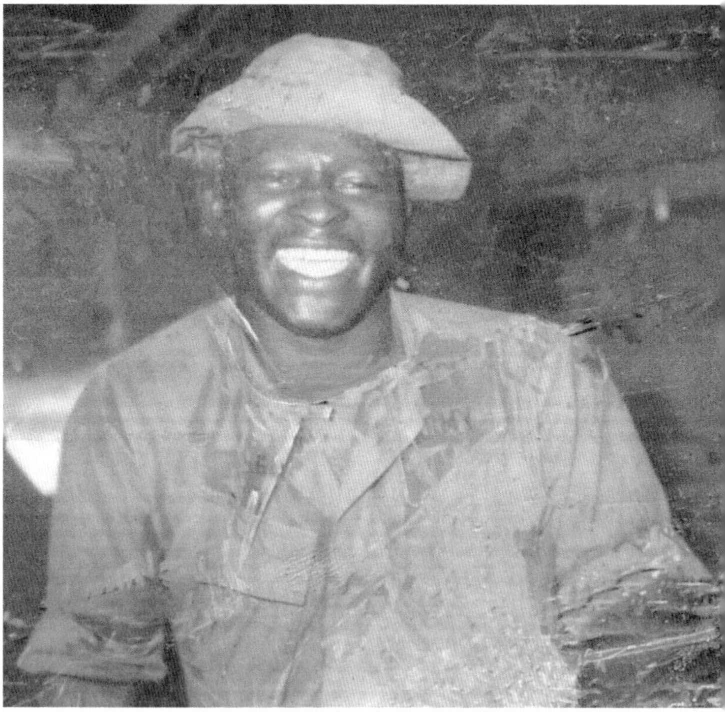

Doc

After finishing high school, SP5 Phillip "Doc" Rogers left his home in Davy, West Virginia, to stay with his sister in North Babylon, New York, where he could earn money to go to medical school. He was drafted into the US Army and assigned as a medic with the 2nd Battalion, 47th Infantry, 9th Infantry Division, and sent to Vietnam. On June 25, 1968, his unit came under heavy fire. Rogers went into the firefight to aid wounded soldiers, and was shot and killed by a sniper as he worked to bandage the wounds of one of the soldiers. (Courtesy of the Reverend Dr. Earl Rogers.)

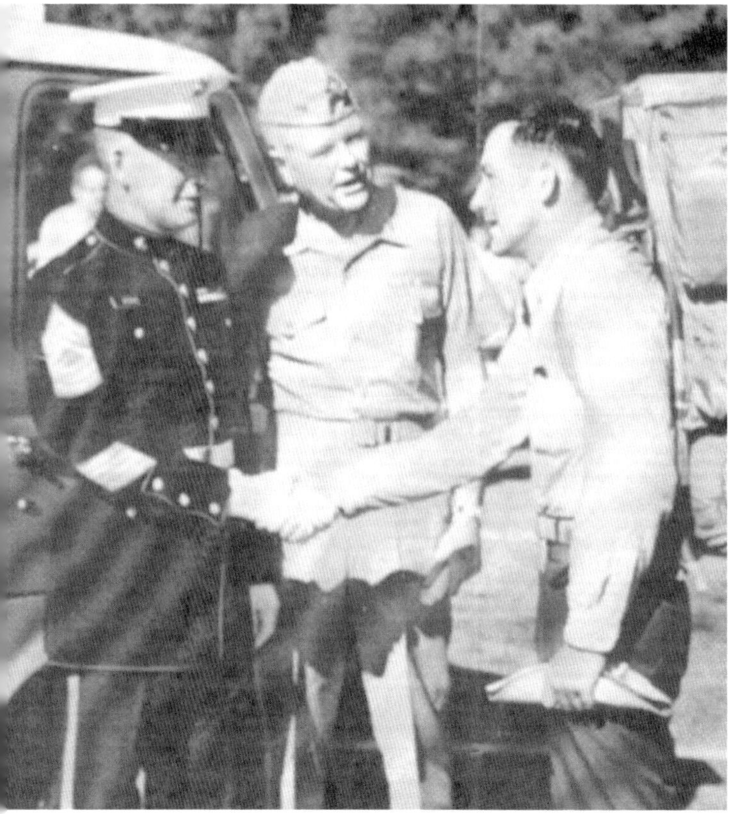

Intent to Win the War

L.Cpl. Julius C. "Corky" Foster (right) is shown here in a 1967 *Leatherneck* magazine photograph being greeted at Camp Lejeune by M.Sgt. F. King and Maj. Gen. J.O. Butcher after walking 404 miles from Welch, West Virginia, to enlist for active duty to demonstrate his "intent to win" the war in Vietnam. Foster was in the Marine Reserves when he made the walk in August–September 1967, and had been a student at West Virginia University. He was killed in action at Khe Sanh, Vietnam, on February 25, 1968. (Courtesy of *Leatherneck* magazine.)

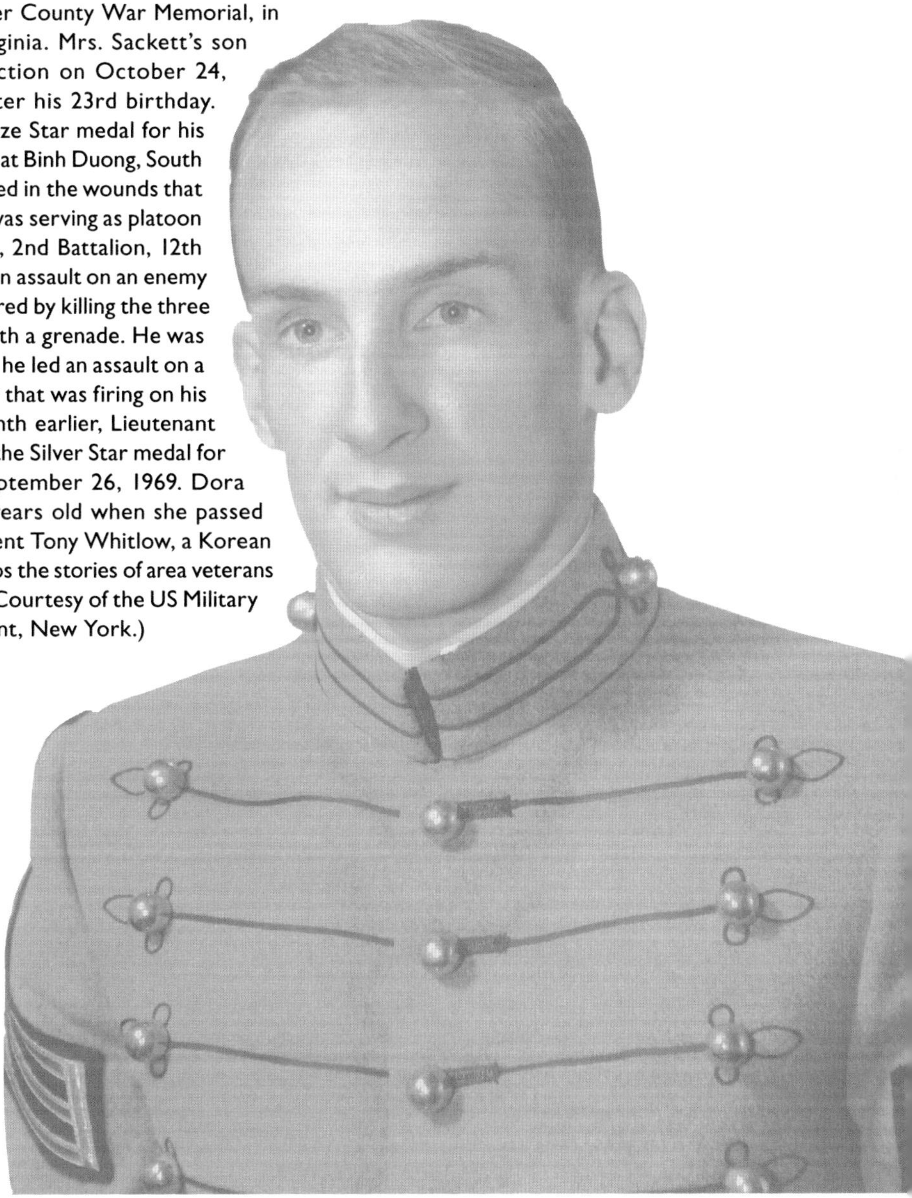

Service Remembered

After Dora Lee Sackett of Twin Branch, West Virginia, died on February 12, 2008, her caregiver, Priscilla Cecil, fulfilled Sackett's final request by delivering the dress uniform her son, 1st Lt. David Lee Sackett, had worn while he was a cadet at the US Military Academy, to the For Those Who Served Museum in the Mercer County War Memorial, in Princeton, West Virginia. Mrs. Sackett's son had been killed in action on October 24, 1969, just 16 days after his 23rd birthday. He received the Bronze Star medal for his actions during combat at Binh Duong, South Vietnam, which resulted in the wounds that caused his death. He was serving as platoon leader in Company A, 2nd Battalion, 12th Infantry, when he led an assault on an enemy bunker, which he secured by killing the three enemy combatants with a grenade. He was fatally wounded when he led an assault on a second enemy bunker that was firing on his platoon. Just one month earlier, Lieutenant Sackett was awarded the Silver Star medal for heroic actions on September 26, 1969. Dora Lee Sackett was 90 years old when she passed away. Museum president Tony Whitlow, a Korean War–era veteran, keeps the stories of area veterans alive at the museum. (Courtesy of the US Military Academy at West Point, New York.)

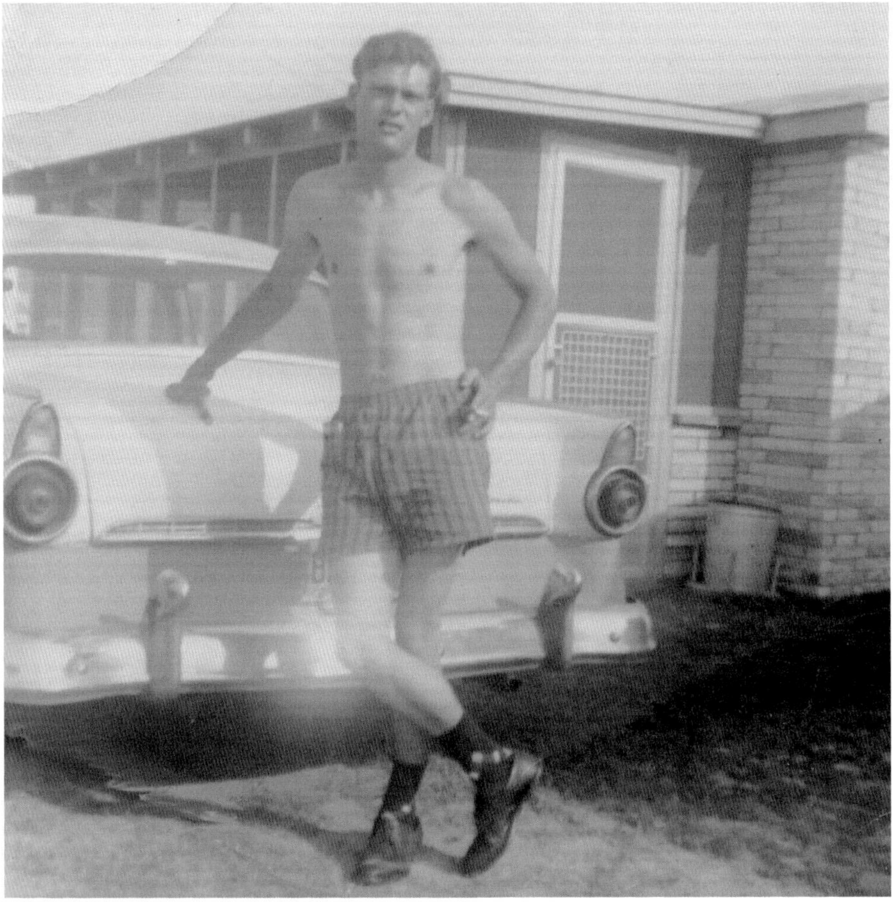

Calm before the Storm

Phill Gene McDonald was born in Ritter Hollow, near Avondale, McDowell County, West Virginia, and attended grade school at Blevins School, before going to Iaeger High School for grades 7–11. McDonald dropped out of school in his senior year and did odd jobs in the Iaeger area before relocating to Greensboro, North Carolina, where he landed a full-time job and lived with a sister. He was one of 14 children in the family of Oscar and Vandora (Roberts) McDonald. Pfc. Phill Gene McDonald was just a few days shy of his 26th birthday when he received his draft notice in the late summer of 1967. After receiving his basic and specialized training, McDonald was assigned to the 14th Infantry Regiment, 4th Infantry Division, and sent to the Republic of Vietnam. During a battle near Kontum City on June 7, 1968, as Pfc. McDonald was serving as team leader of 1st platoon, Company A, his unit came under heavy fire. Pfc. McDonald volunteered to escort two wounded soldiers back to an evacuation point. Along the way, he used grenades to silence an enemy position that was threatening the evacuation. After he returned to his unit, McDonald provided covering fire to enable his unit to reposition itself into a non-exposed position. Enemy gunners concentrated fire on McDonald's position, wounding him. Despite being wounded, he manned the machine gun of a wounded comrade and provided covering fire so the wounded gunner could be evacuated. When the enemy pinned down his fellow soldiers, McDonald crawled toward the enemy position to destroy it with grenades. During that action, he was mortally wounded. On June 7, 1988, Guilford County, North Carolina, dedicated the Phill G. McDonald Plaza at the Guilford County Governmental Center in his honor. In addition, the state of West Virginia named an extremely high mountain bridge on I-64 crossing Glade Creek in Raleigh County, West Virginia, the Phill G. McDonald Bridge. (Courtesy of Dean Burroughs.)

One Humble Soldier

Three of Pfc. Phill Gene McDonald's sisters traveled to the White House on April 7, 1970, to receive the Medal of Honor awarded to their brother posthumously. Pfc. McDonald's twin sister, Phyllis (McDonald) Waldron, is shown here receiving the medal from Pres. Richard M. Nixon as Dean (McDonald) Burroughs (left) and Bernice (McDonald) Jablonowski (right) look on behind her. "It was one of the worst heartaches I've ever had," Dean Burroughs said. There was only 14 months separating her from the twins, Phyllis and Phill, and they were very close. At the time Phill was drafted, the Vietnam War was receiving a lot of criticism from a growing number of people. While some of the dissent was coming from people who had sincere concerns about the nation's military policy in Southeast Asia and absolute support for American military personnel, a more radical faction of the anti-war movement directed scorn toward active and/or returning military veterans, going so far as to assault the soldiers on their return to US soil. "Phill was a very devout Christian," Dean Burroughs said of her brother. "He told us before he left that if he could save one life before he died, it would be worth it. Phill would not want to be called a hero. He just wanted to protect and save others." (Courtesy of Dean Burroughs.)

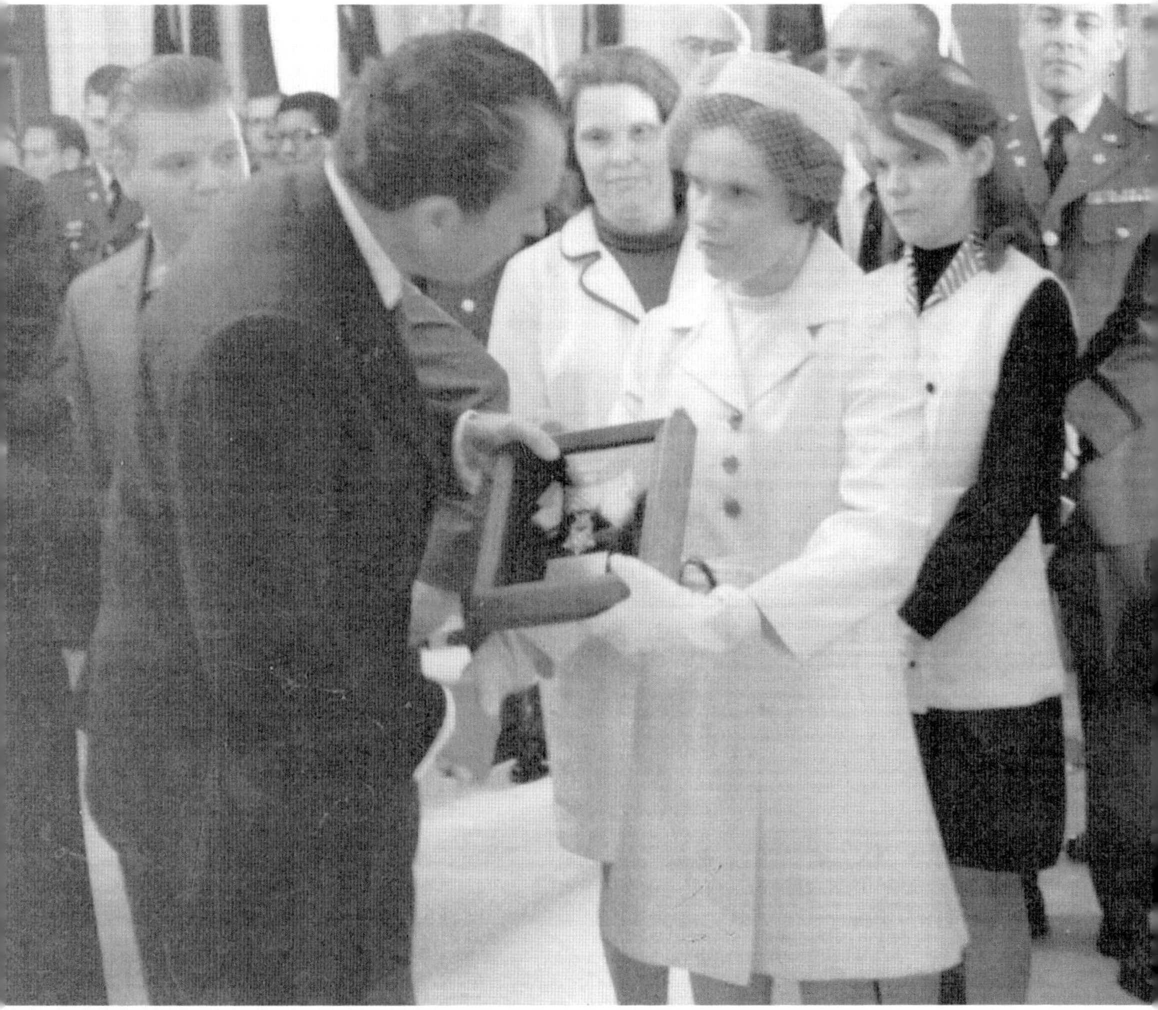

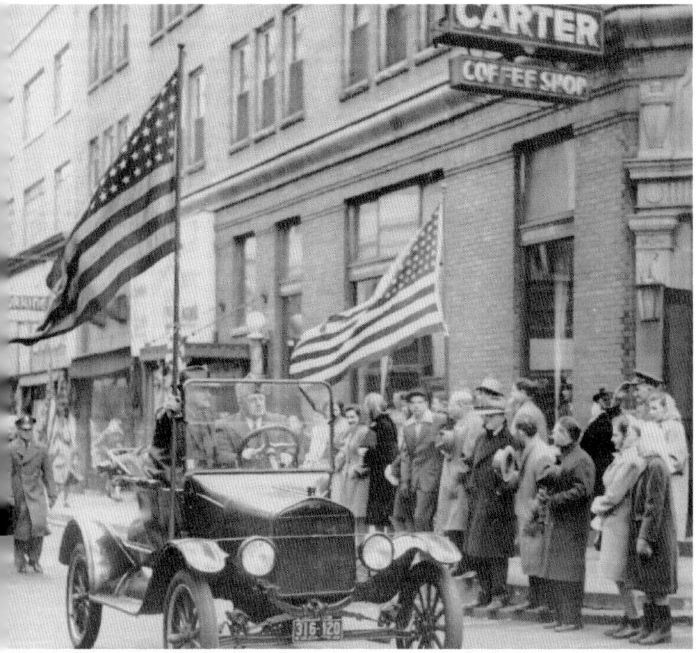

McDowell County Veterans Day Parade

Sam Solins, a World War I veteran who served in the same unit with future president Harry S. Truman, was the longtime organizer of the annual McDowell County Veterans Day Parade. In this photograph, Solins is behind the wheel transporting a speaker to the podium, past the old Carter Hotel on McDowell Street in Welch. (Courtesy of the McDowell County Library, Welch Branch.)

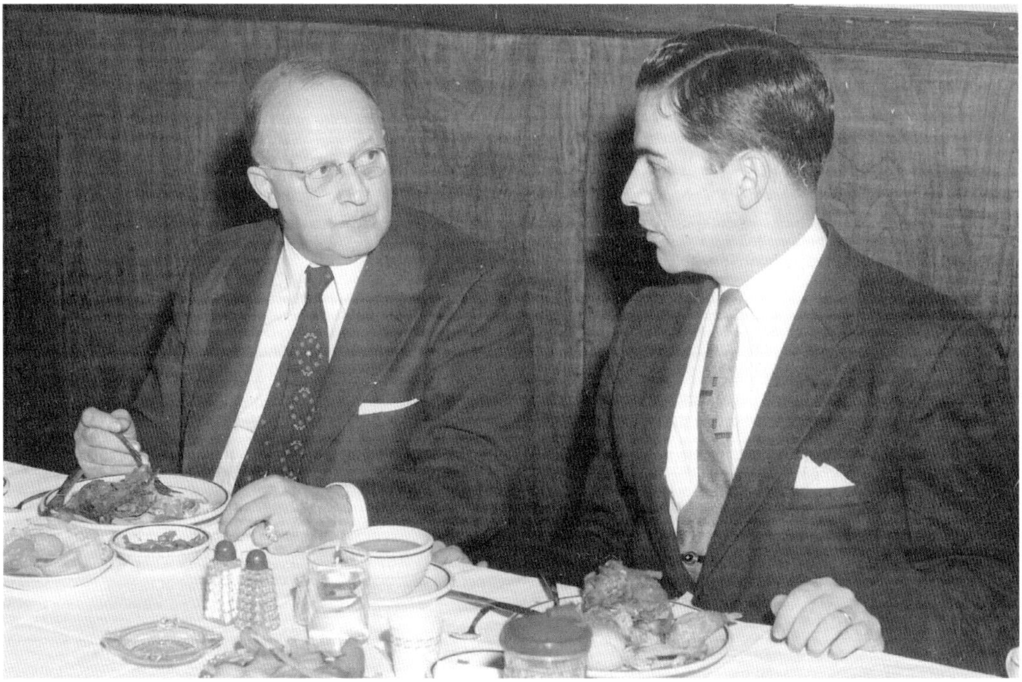

Dinner for Two

Sam Solins (left) is shown here dining with Gov. Cecil Underwood prior to the Veterans Day Parade on November 11, 1958. The 1958 parade was special, because McDowell County was celebrating its centennial that year. All of the parades have special significance, of course. Two US presidents, Harry Truman and Lyndon B. Johnson, have served as speakers, as have countless other military and political leaders. (Courtesy of the McDowell County Library, Welch Branch.)

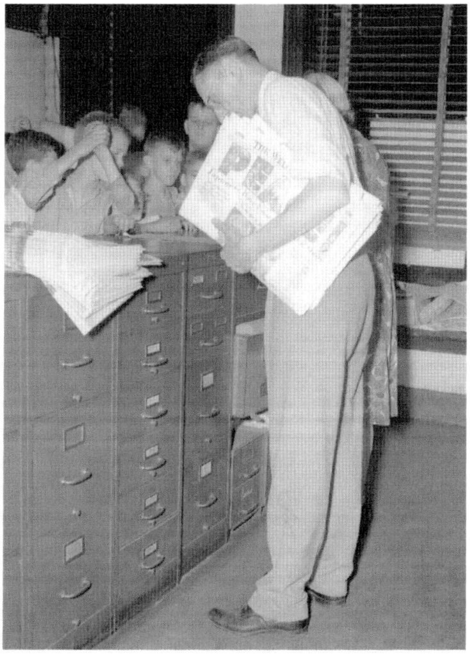

Peace in Our Time
W.R. "Will" Kiser, general manager of the *Welch Daily News*, is shown distributing copies of the special V-J edition of the paper to city newsies following Japan's surrender on August 14, 1945. (Courtesy of Jay Chapman.).

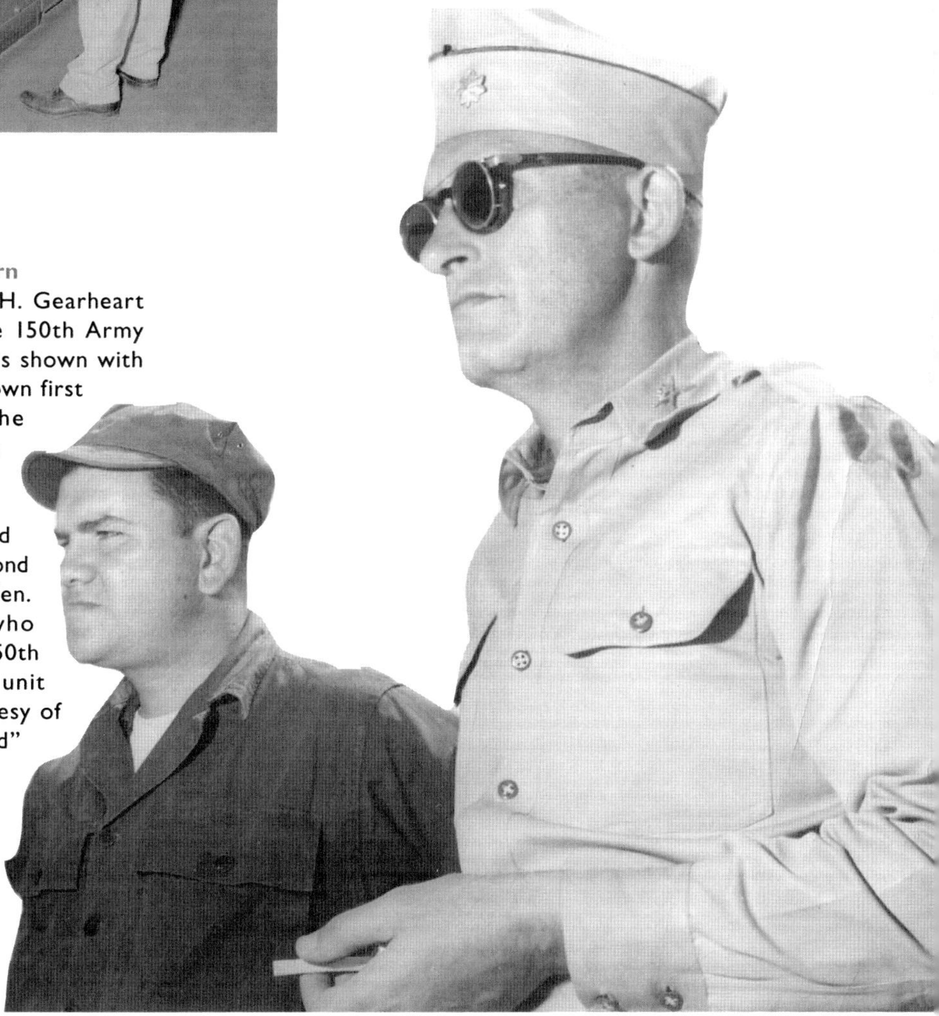

They Shall Return
Lt. Col. Charles H. Gearheart Sr. (right), of the 150th Army National Guard, is shown with Hammond (unknown first name) during the 150th's deployment to Panama during World War II. Gearheart served many years as second in command to Gen. W.E. Eubank, who established the 150th National Guard unit in Welch. (Courtesy of Charles H. "Bud" Gearheart Jr.)

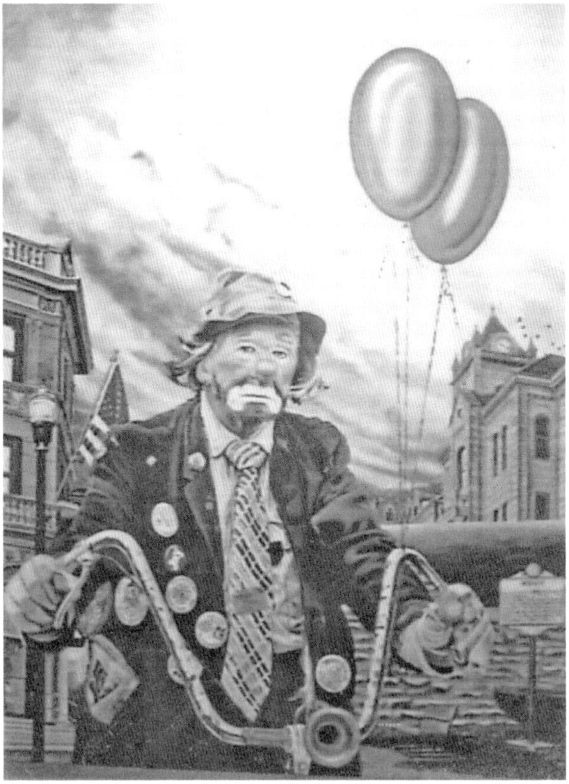

Red Baron

Jimmy Hampton, also known as "The Red Baron," is depicted in this painting by McDowell County artist Tom Acosta in his traditional pose, riding a wobble-wheeled bicycle down McDowell Street to the thrill of onlookers. Hampton has been a fixture in parades for several years. (Courtesy of Jimmy Hampton.)

Clowning Around

The Red Baron is shown here aiming his bent-wheeled bicycle at the author as he attempts to take video for the *Bluefield Daily Telegraph* at the November 11, 2011, Veterans Day Parade in Welch, West Virginia. (Photograph by Michael Quick.)

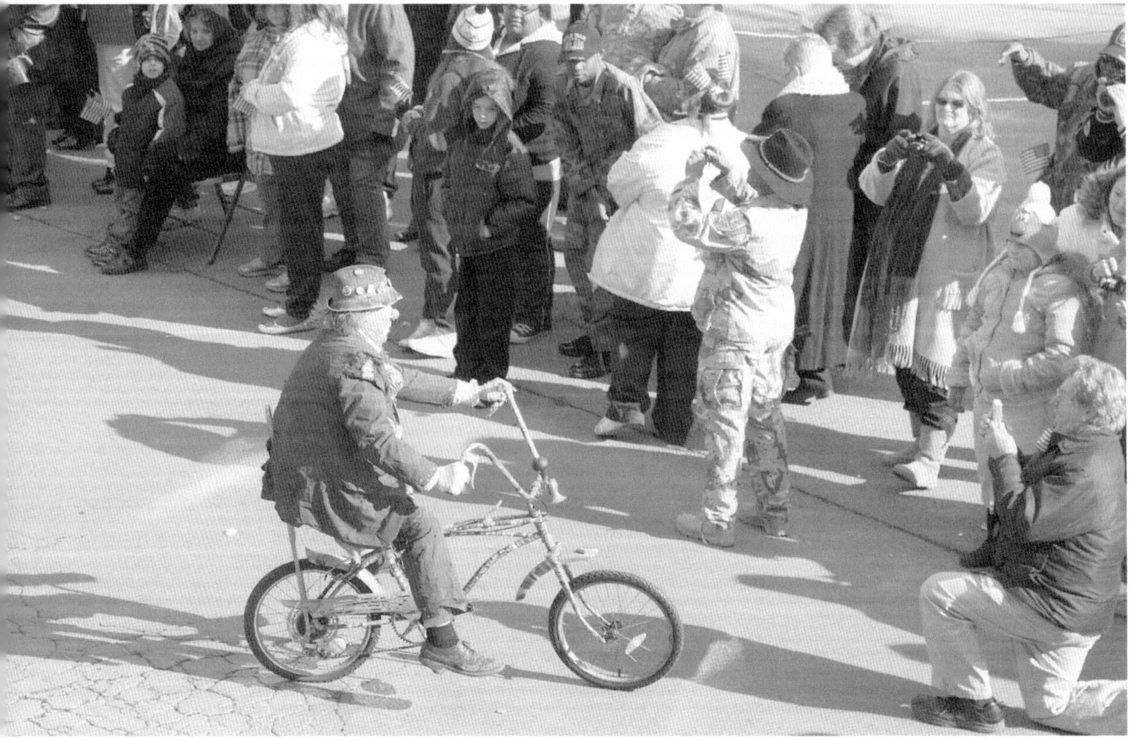

Postwar Collateral Damage

Steelmaking coal was in great demand during World War II, pushing the pool of available labor to its limits and causing strained relations between organized coal miners represented by the United Mine Workers of America and the various companies that were mining coal. But nothing stopped the nation's thirst for coking coal. Companies that had spent four years building one of the greatest war machines the world had ever seen, retooled to make cars, appliances, and other trappings of the newly defined family unit. At noon on January 15, 1946, an explosion at the Havaco Mine destroyed most of the tipple workings, shattered windows in the community, and was heard and felt by people 25 miles away. There were 200 coal miners working at the mine that day, and most families feared the worst. After all, 83 coal miners had died when the same mine (known then as the Jed Mine) exploded on March 26, 1912. Coal operators had changed the name to reduce the fear factor for a new generation of miners. While families feared, the surviving coal miners knew what to do. After the 1912 blast, the coal mine operator was required to sink a new shaft, and the old entry, featuring a spiral staircase, was intended for use as an escape hatch. New federal and state laws concerning the application of rock dust since the January 10, 1940, explosion at the Bartley Mine that claimed the lives of 91 coal miners made a difference for most of the coal miners at Havaco, and skilled mine rescue teams were at the site within two hours to assist the living, transport the injured, and remove the dead. There were 15 deaths in the explosion, which was isolated to a poorly rock-dusted area near the base of the mineshaft. Unlike 1912, when the mostly foreign-born coal miners with no family to claim them were buried in an unmarked graveyard that remains unmarked today, the families of the 15 victims could identify the remains and carry them to their final resting place. The identity of the rescuers shown here are unknown. (Courtesy of the Eastern Regional Coal Archives.)

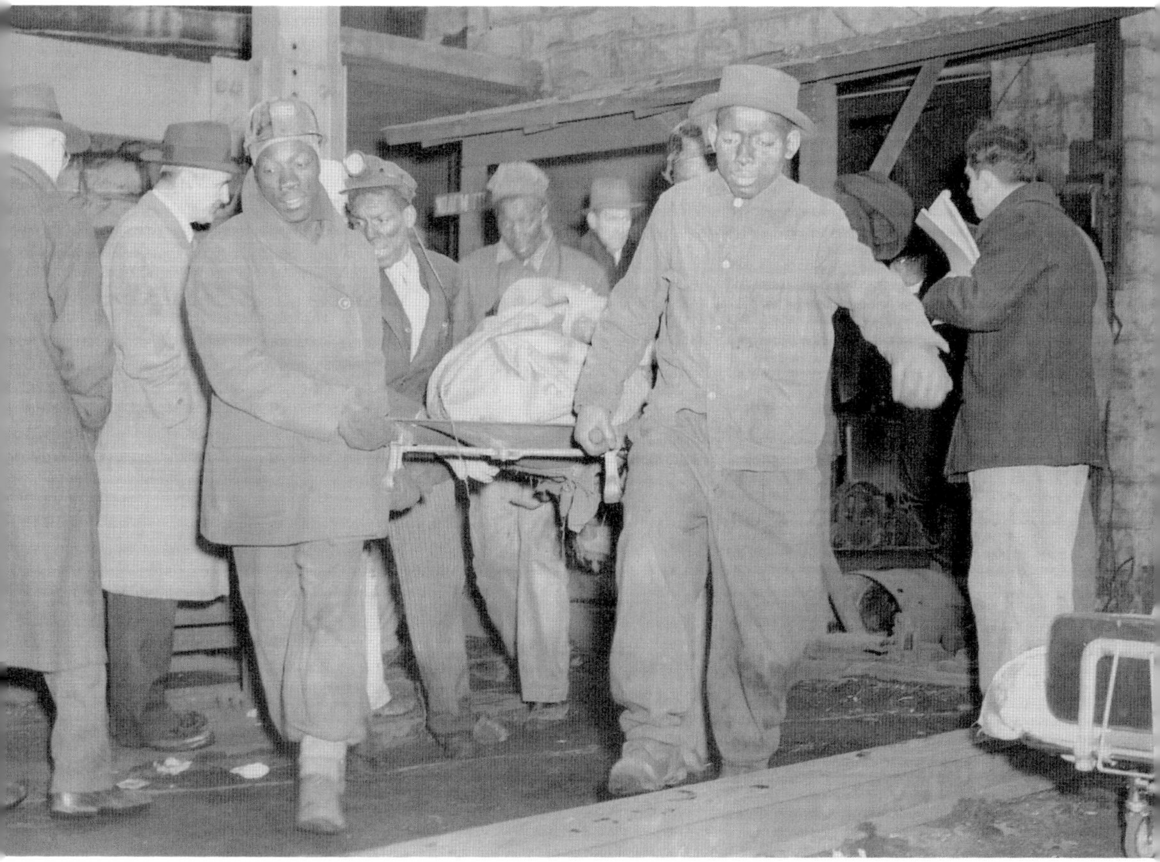

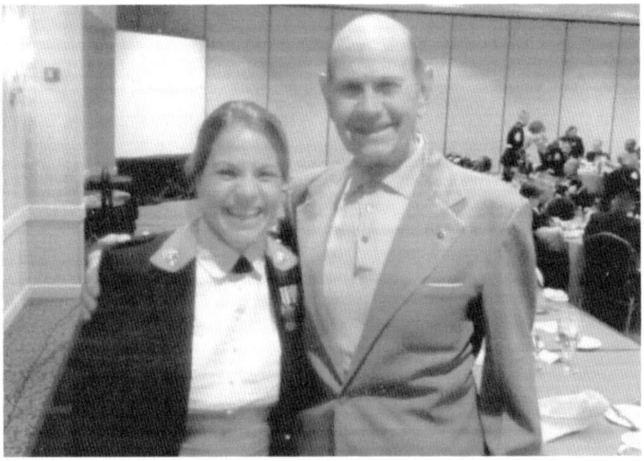

Honored Guest
Maj. Lauren S. Edwards (left) is shown here prior to introducing Ed Shepard as the honored guest at the US Marine Corps celebration of the 236th anniversary of its origin, held on November 10, 2011, in Lexington, Kentucky. Major Edwards introduced Shepard as "a true Marine warrior. Mr. Shepard has passed into the halls of legends. He is exactly what storybooks of American heroes are made of." (Courtesy of Ed Shepard.)

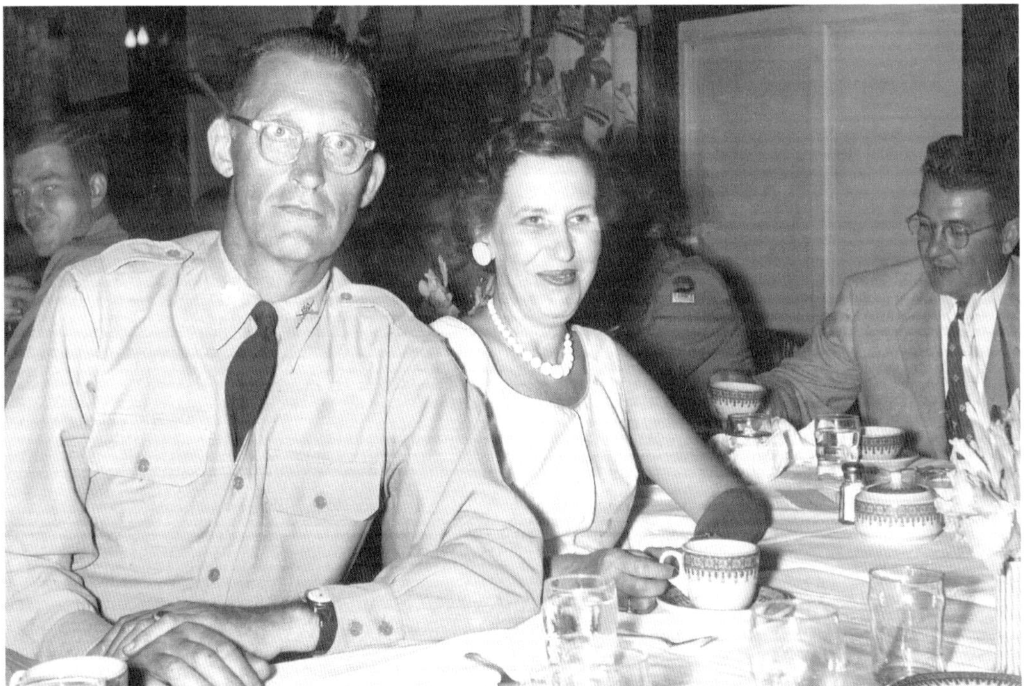

Formal Dinner
Col. Charles H. Gearheart Sr. and his wife, Virginia, are shown here enjoying a formal dinner for West Virginia governor William C. Marland at the West Virginia National Guard's summer camp, A.P. Hill. The National Guard continues to play a vital role in the safety of America's interests at home and abroad. (Courtesy of Charles H. "Bud" Gearheart Jr.)

CHAPTER FOUR

Newsmakers

Not every legendary story of McDowell County made headlines. In southern West Virginia, stories like the Hatfield and McCoy family feud made international headlines while the feud was taking place, and even draws attention in 2012. But the stories about extraordinary people who triumphed over oppression, battled discrimination, faced isolation and disappointment with a smile, and followed a path that most would have turned away from, shine through time after time in the McDowell County story, although they often are little less than historical footnotes.

The people of McDowell County are the first to applaud the success of the county's native sons and daughters, and remain supportive when times are hard. No matter how difficult things get, they traditionally see the proverbial glass as being half full. In the world of news, sports, entertainment, the arts, and so much more, the people of McDowell County never stop applauding all of those who have tried and made it, as well as those who have tried and failed. It makes no difference, for after you've heard the siren song of the wind whipping through the forest-covered mountains of McDowell County at night, you never forget.

Comedian Steve Harvey left McDowell County when he was five years old, but he still recalls his upbringing in Gary as he warms up his audiences in Atlanta, Georgia, who have come to watch *The Family Feud*. Philadelphia Phillies' manager Charlie Manuel was born in Northfork, West Virginia, and although he learned the game of baseball in Southwest Virginia, the seeds of his passion for the sport were planted in McDowell's mountain soil. And although Jeannette Walls only spent a few years of her nomadic life in Welch, her McDowell County stay helped her discover an individual approach to life that strips away excessive and unnecessary trappings and leaves only the marrow to explore.

Rich and famous, poor and infamous—McDowell County has had them all. Their stories continue to form one of the fibers that combine to make communities strong no matter where their faith and the fates lead them.

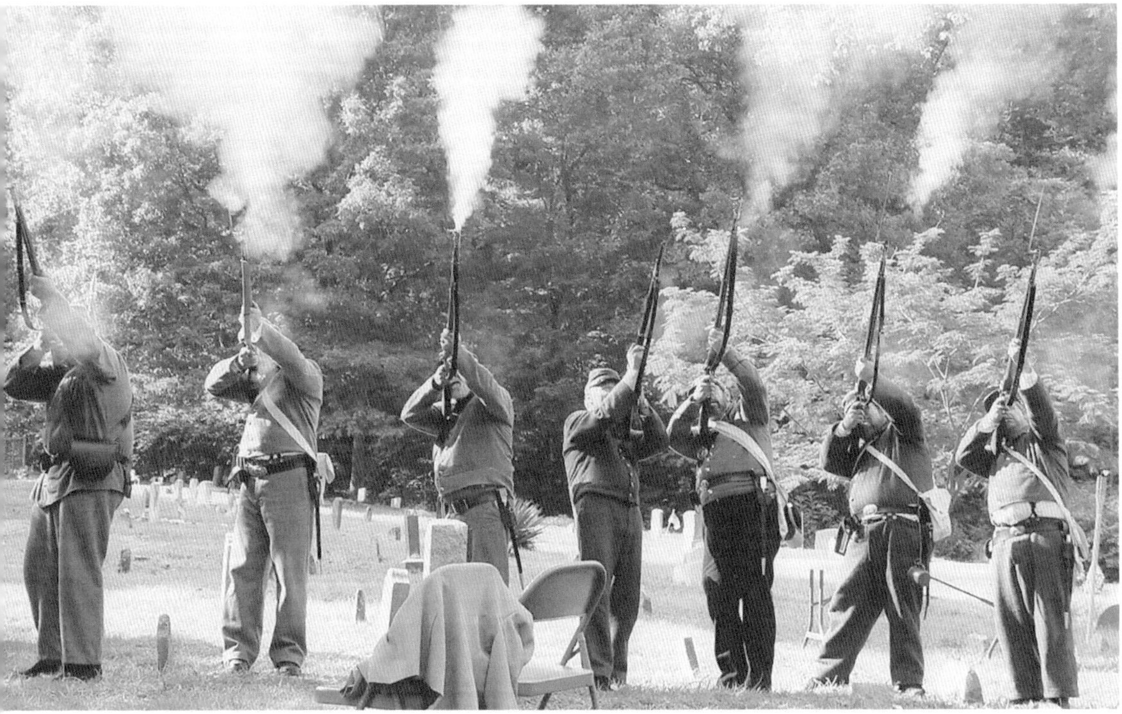

Unforgotten Cause

A rifle team with the Sons of the Confederacy is shown firing a seven-musket salute to honor the reburial of Solomon Justice at the Justice Family Cemetery in Asco. In August 1862, Solomon Justice joined the Confederate Army's 34th Mounted Calvary, fought in several key battles, including the Battle of Gettysburg, and returned home to find his farm on Huff Creek, West Virginia, ravished and his wife, Jane (Cook) Justice, abused and hanging in the corn crib. Solomon was reburied beside his wife in the family cemetery on August 9, 2004. (Courtesy of Anita (Justice) Moody.)

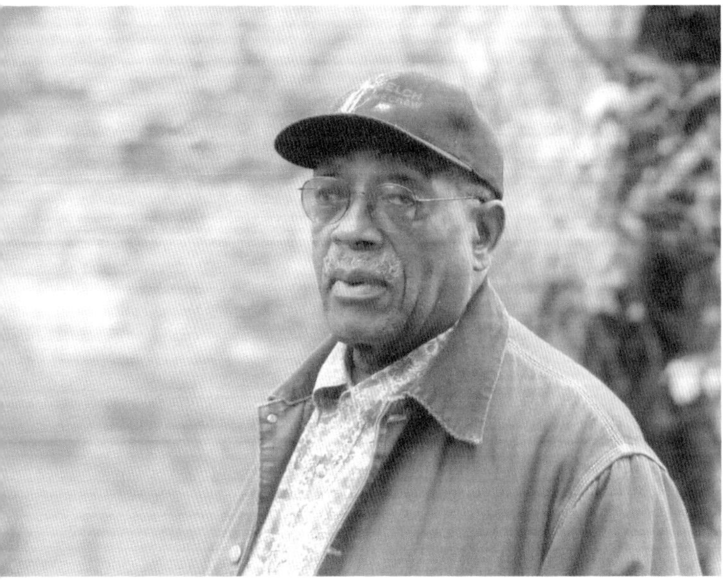

The Buck Stops Here

William "Buck" Wade has been a leader in the McDowell County coalfields throughout most of his life. He started working in the coal mines as a teenager, and after about a decade underground, accepted a position as a safety man with District 17 of the United Mine Workers of America, remaining in that position until his retirement. During his tenure, he fought to improve working conditions for all coal miners. After his retirement, he was elected and served several years as mayor of the city of Keystone, West Virginia. (Photograph by the author.)

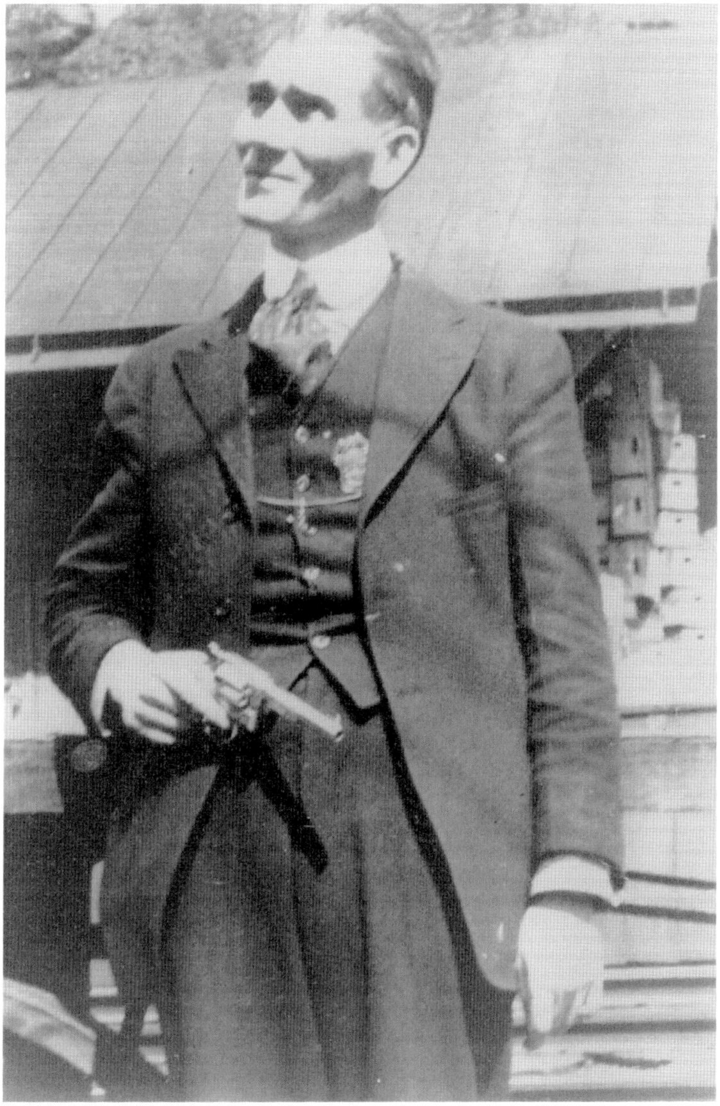

Smiling Sid

One of the most volatile moments in the history of organized labor in the United States occurred on August 1, 1921, when Sid Hatfield (shown here), the former sheriff of Matewan, West Virginia, was gunned down on the steps of the McDowell County Courthouse in Welch. Hatfield was propelled into national prominence following the May 20, 1920, shoot-out between striking coal miners and agents of the Baldwin-Felts Detective Agency in what has come to be called "The Matewan Massacre." Hatfield, and fellow United Mine Workers of America organizer Ed Chambers, had been summoned to the courthouse to testify concerning a shooting in the spring of 1921 at a coal mine in Mohawk, West Virginia. McDowell County officials believed the UMWA was behind the shooting. As Hatfield and Chambers, along with their wives, Jessie Hatfield and Sallie Chambers, reached the top of the courthouse steps, they were met by Baldwin-Felts detectives, and a gunfight ensued. Three detectives—C.E. Lively, George Pence, and William Salters—were tried on the charge of killing Chambers, and the jury acquitted them of the crime on December 17, 1921. The McDowell County court has no record of any trial on charges related to the death of Sid Hatfield. (Courtesy of the Eastern Regional Coal Archives.)

Les Modernes

The Les Modernes, a civic organization of the McDowell County area, pose for an undated photograph while attending the Black & White Ball. Shown are, from left to right, (first row) Bernice Reeves Summers, Elizabeth Richardson Morrison, Queenie Belle Turaman, Mary Leftwich Brammer, Elizabeth Johnson, Viola Johnson, Letitia Johnson Byrd, and Imogene Neal Trapp; (second row) Lois Leftwich Miller, Jane Satterfield Shelton, Equilla Satterfield Mack, Juliette Gregory Brown, Dorothy Jordan Thomas, Grace Mack Toler, Marion Jones Capehart, Glady Damridge Odlam, Claudia Stafford Wilks, Christine Neal Williams, Shirley Painter Lilly, Florence Leftwich Edwards, and Ruby Hutchinson Smalls. (Courtesy of McDowell County Public Library, Welch Branch.)

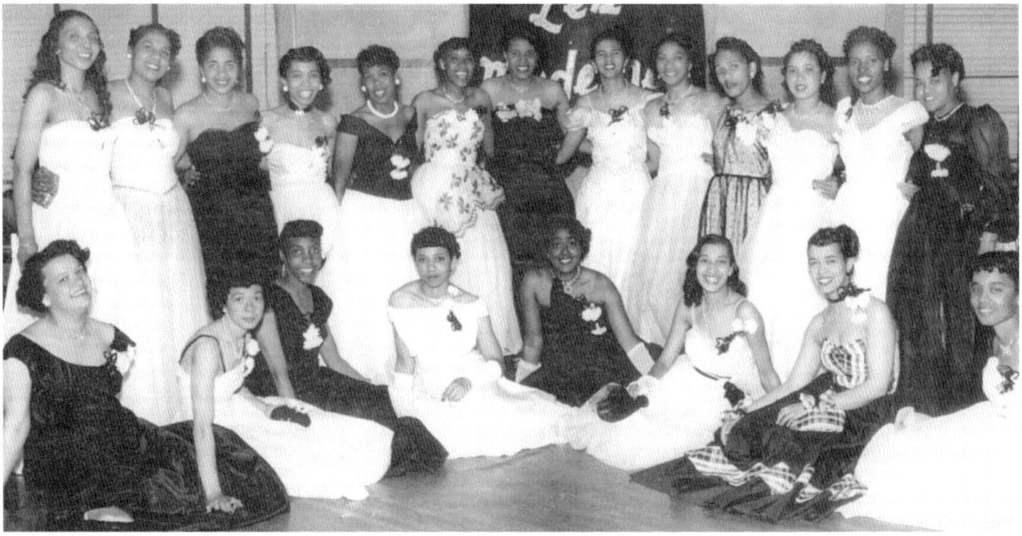

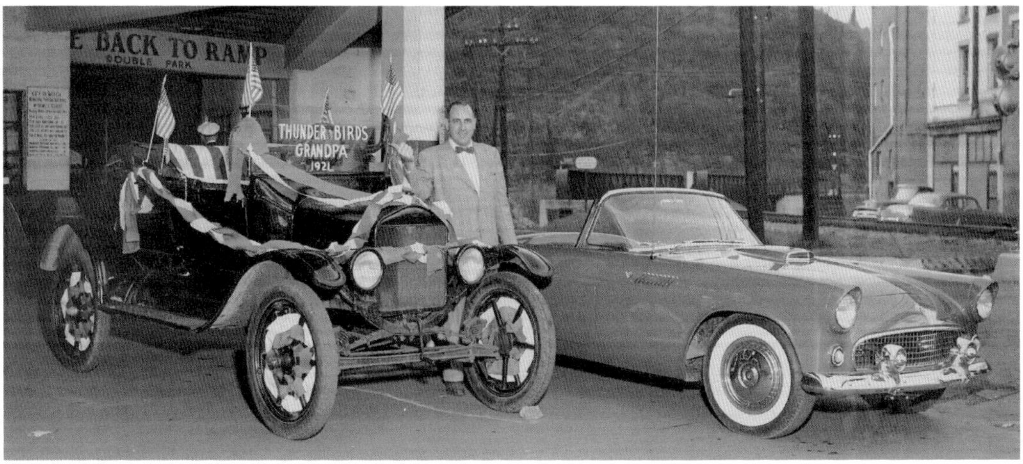

Cars Tuned

Jack Moses is shown here in front of the Welch Municipal Parking Garage, flanked by a Model T Ford on one side and a late-1950s model Thunderbird on the other as he prepares for the start of the big Veterans Day Parade. The McDowell County Veterans Day Parade on November 11, 1955, was a well-attended event, but that turnout was eclipsed in 1963 when 10,000 to 12,000 people came out for the Veterans Day Parade and to hear Vice Pres. Lyndon B. Johnson. (Courtesy of McDowell County Library, Welch Branch.)

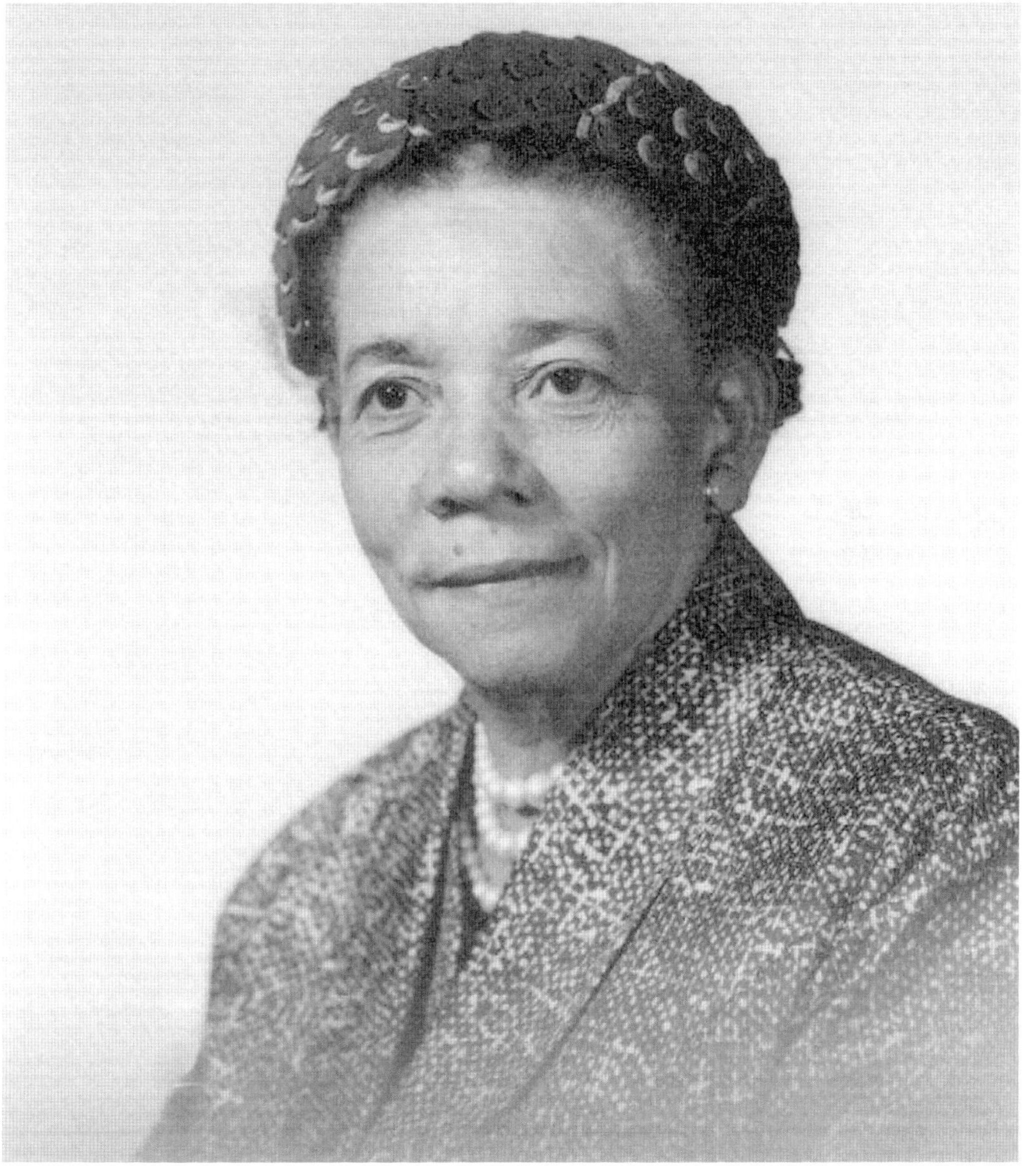

Civic Leader

During the height of the Jim Crow segregation laws throughout the South, Elizabeth Simpson Drewry, of Northfork, West Virginia, worked her way up through the McDowell County Democratic Party's ranks to earn the position as chair of the county's Democratic Executive Committee, and eventually, in 1950, became the first African American woman elected to the West Virginia House of Delegates. She was, in fact, the first black female to be elected to any state legislature in the nation. The national black press, including the *Chicago Defender* and the *Pittsburgh Courier*, provided the country with insights into how the schoolteacher from McDowell County was holding her own in a legislative body made up mostly of white males. In 1956, she was honored by *Ebony* magazine as one of the 10 most outstanding black women in government. Throughout her 13-year career in the state legislature, Drewry stood as an advocate for education and labor. She died in Welch on September 24, 1979, at age 85. (Courtesy of the Eastern Regional Coal Archives.)

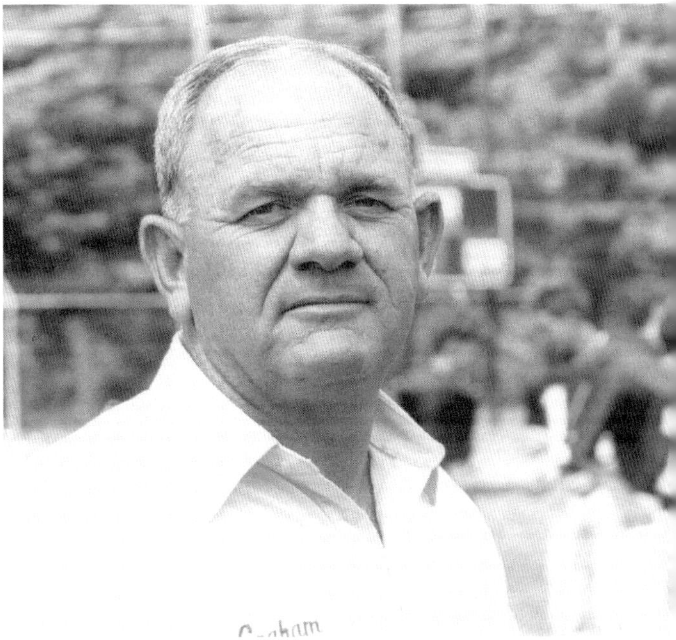

Coach

Glynn Carlock was born in Yukon, West Virginia. He played football for the Big Creek Owls under Coach Merrill Gainer, served in the US Marine Corps from 1957 to 1960, and, after earning degrees at Concord and Radford Universities, went into coaching. Carlock was an assistant at Bluefield High School in Bluefield, West Virginia, for 10 years, then became head coach of the Graham High School G-Men from 1973 until his death on August 8, 2005. During his coaching tenure at GHS, his teams won state championships in 1989 and 1995. He was inducted into the Virginia High School Hall of Fame in 1998. (Photograph by the author.)

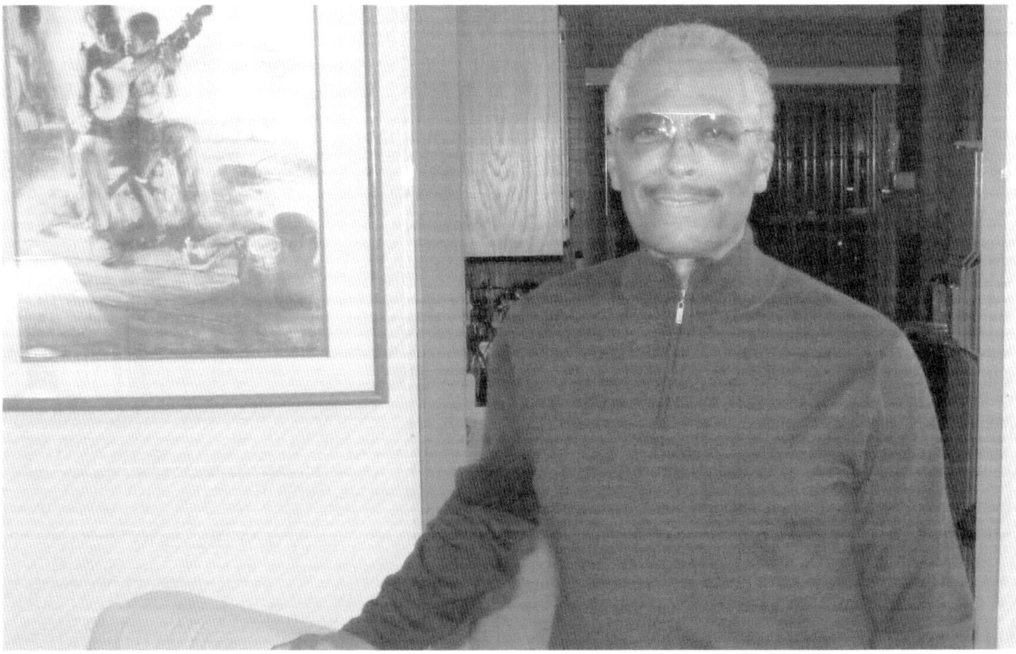

Sportsmanship

Ergie Smith was born in Keystone, West Virginia. He went to Bluefield State College, where he achieved All-America recognition as the star tailback with the BSC Big Blues, and returned to his native McDowell County in 1953 to teach and coach at the segregated Gary District High School. In 1965—the last year of segregated schools in McDowell County—Smith took his Gary District basketball team to perform in the All Black Schools state tournament, and won. That fall, the McDowell County Board of Education did not offer him a job as a teacher or a coach in the integrated school system. (Photograph by the author.)

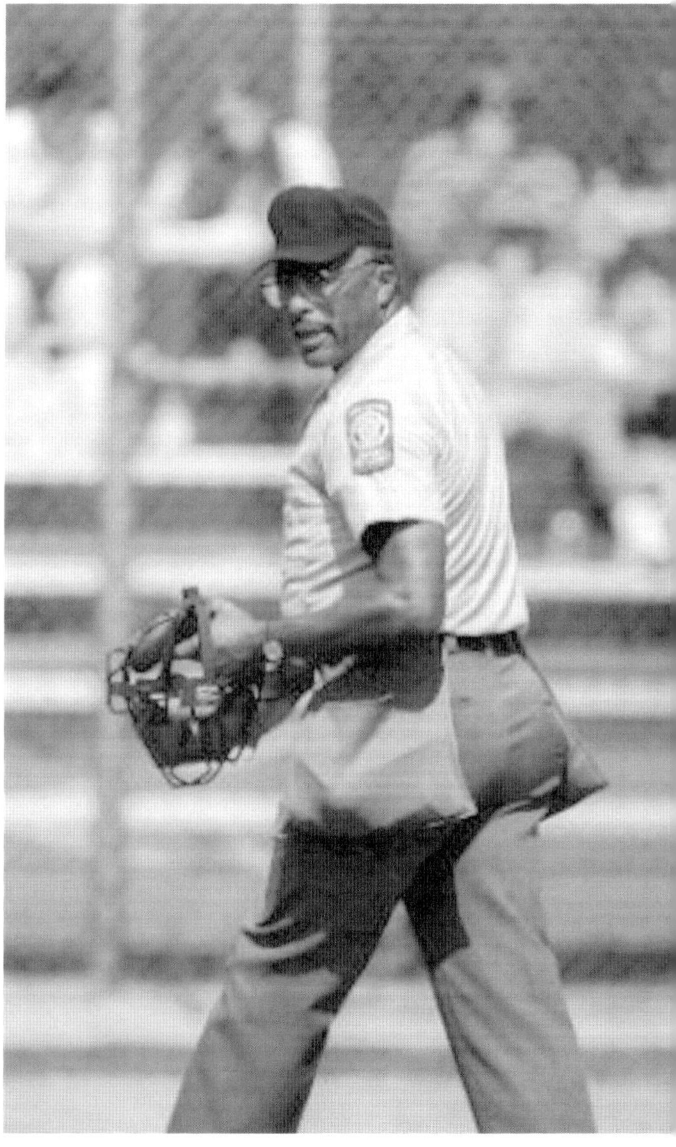

Dedication
Although his dreams of teaching and coaching had been shattered by his lack of opportunities in public education in McDowell County, Ergie Smith, shown here working as an umpire in a Little League World Series game, accepted a position as the director of the Council of Southern Mountains, helping McDowell County families deal with the onset of poverty that struck the region. He also helped young people of all races achieve their goal of getting a higher education. Among them was future US district judge Irene C. Berger of the Southern District of West Virginia, the first black woman appointed to the federal bench in the state. In the fall of 1972, the job of coaching basketball at the integrated Gary High School came open, and Smith applied and got the job. Smith led the integrated Gary Coal Diggers to the West Virginia Class AA state basketball championship, and in the process, became the only coach in state history to lead a team to both the All Black Schools state championship and a state championship in the integrated school system. (Courtesy of Ergie Smith.)

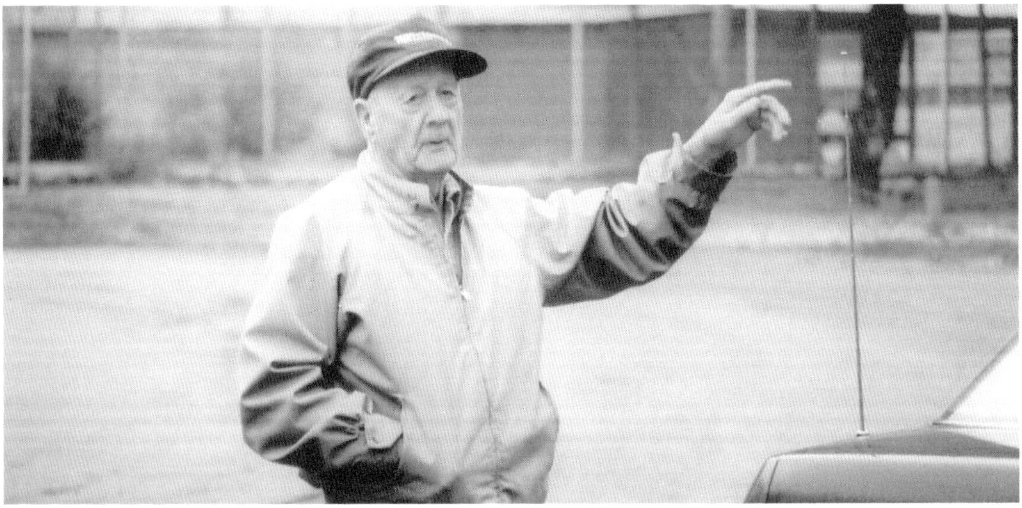

Coalwood Ambassador

Ernest O'Dell "Red" Carroll was always the kind of person who would drop everything and help a friend or stranger in whatever way he could. After the publication of the book *Rocket Boys*, by Homer Hickam Jr., and the interest generated by the 1999 movie *October Sky*, Red Carroll became the unofficial tour guide for Coalwood until his death on January 8, 2011. He helped people understand the community in the late 1950s, when Big Creek High School students believed they could reach for the sky. (Photograph by the author.)

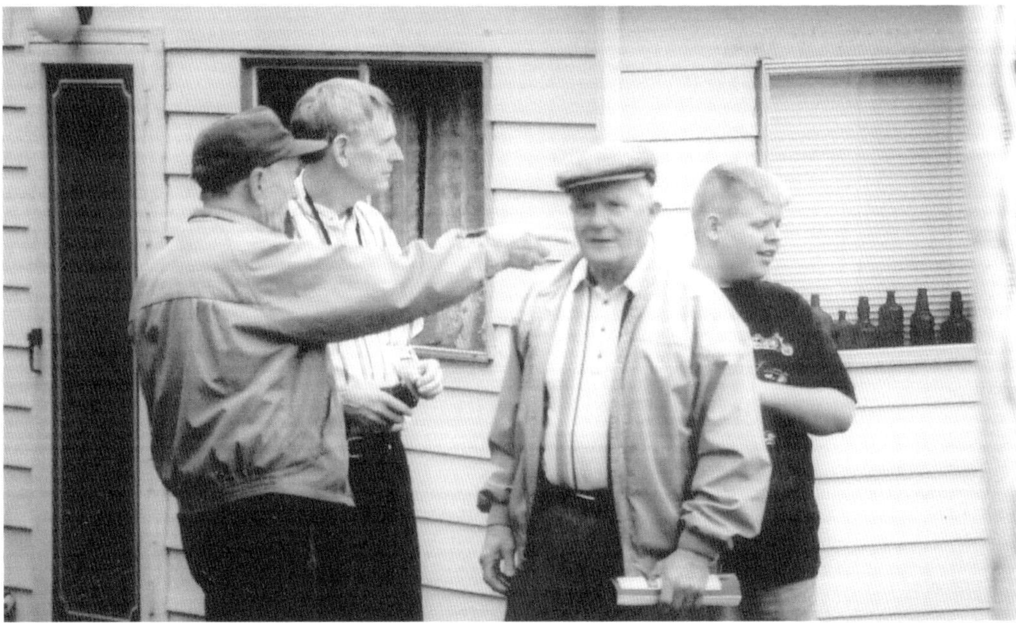

Photograph of the Past

Ernest "Red" Carroll (left) is shown here pointing out a Coalwood scene to famed West Virginia photographer Arnout "Sonny" Hyde (second from left) as Early Smith (third from left) and Red's son, Josh Carroll, look on. Arnout Hyde became captivated by the rocket boys' story, and was a frequent visitor to Coalwood until his death on August 9, 2005. (Photograph by the author.)

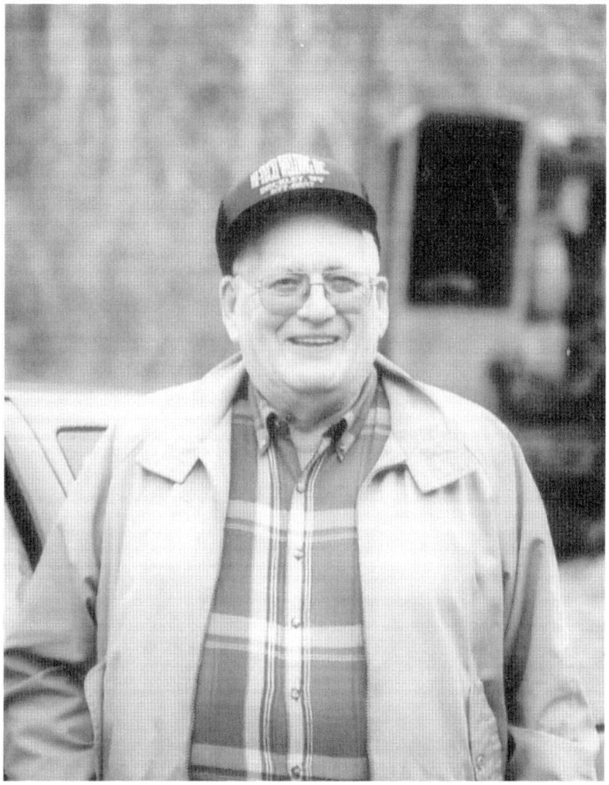

A Bolt to Hold Them Together
Bill Bolt, retired supervisor of the Olga Coal Company machine shop, actually fabricated several of the parts used in the rockets that the Big Creek High School students who called themselves the "rocket boys" would launch. Bolt continues to be a great supporter of McDowell County, and still calls Coalwood, West Virginia, home. (Photograph by the author.)

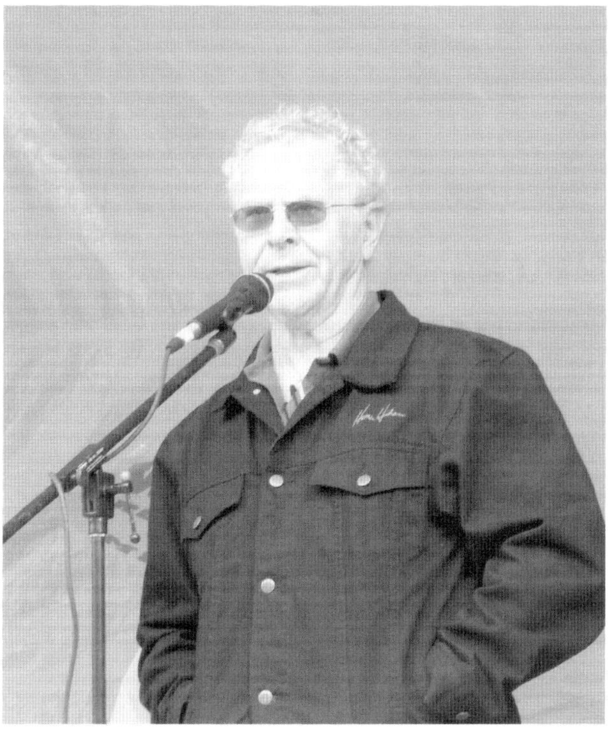

Rocket Man
Noted West Virginia author Homer H. Hickam Jr. is shown here addressing the audience at one of the October Sky Festivals, held in Coalwood from 1999 through 2011. In his memoir, *The Rocket Boys*, Hickam told the story of how he, Jimmy (O'Dell) Carroll, Quentin Wilson, Roy Lee Cooke, Sherman Siers, and Billy Rose received a National Science Award for their work in launching rockets from 1957 to 1960. (Photograph by the author.)

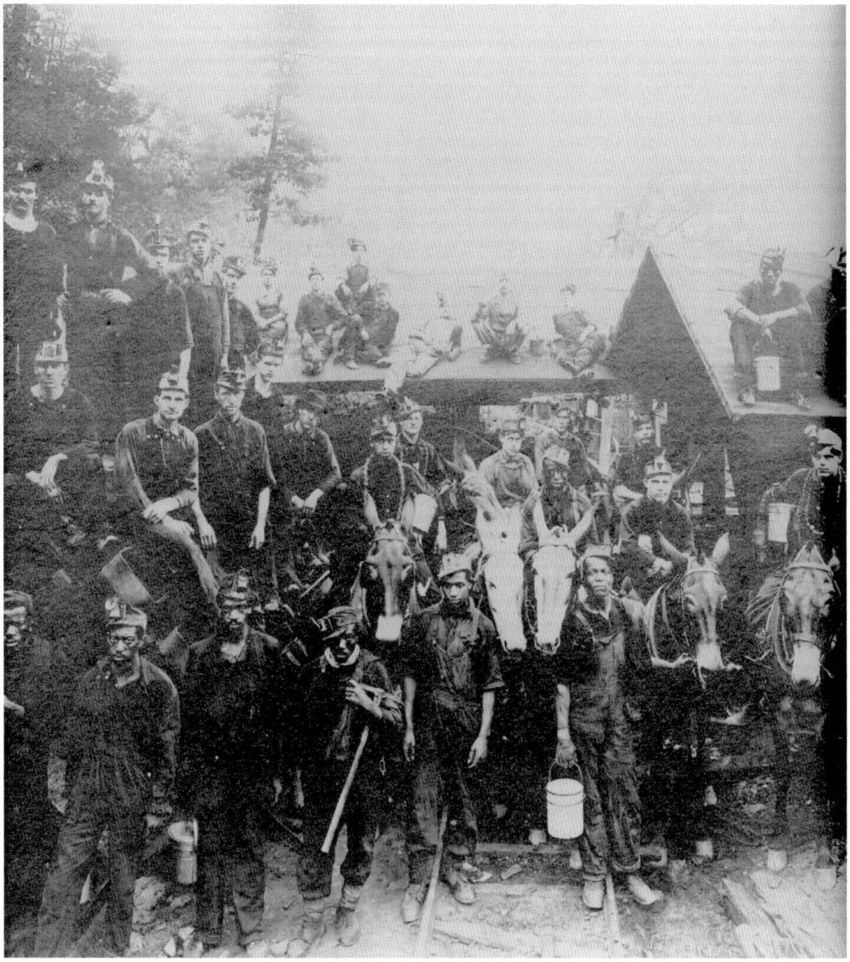

Leckie Coal Miners and Mules
Carol Jacks of Gallipolis, Ohio, noticed that the Welch Branch of the McDowell County Public Library had developed a West Virginia Collection, and, to help the library with its collection, she donated this photograph (shown only in part) on August 8, 2001, just one month after the main floor of the library had been flooded. At the time, there were several stories in the press concerning the many losses in the county and about efforts to rebuild. The photograph had hung in the Leckie Coal Company Offices in the Hartman Theater Building in Columbus, Ohio, during the 1960s and had come into the possession of Jim Blum, who had worked as a dispatcher for Leckie Coal for 35 years. (Courtesy of the McDowell County Public Library, Welch Branch.)

Study in Glass (OPPOSITE PAGE)
Jeannette Walls is a well-known American writer whose memoir, *The Glass Castle*, remained on the *New York Times* bestseller list for 100 weeks after its publication in 2006. The book recounts her nomadic family life. She spent some of her formative years in Welch, where her public school teachers encouraged her to explore her creative gifts. Following the national attention she received after the publication of her memoir, Walls returned to southern West Virginia and southwestern Virginia to lend her celebrity to the cause of helping at-risk families and in support of education. She is shown here autographing books during a recent visit to Bluefield College in Bluefield, Virginia. (Courtesy of Bluefield College.)

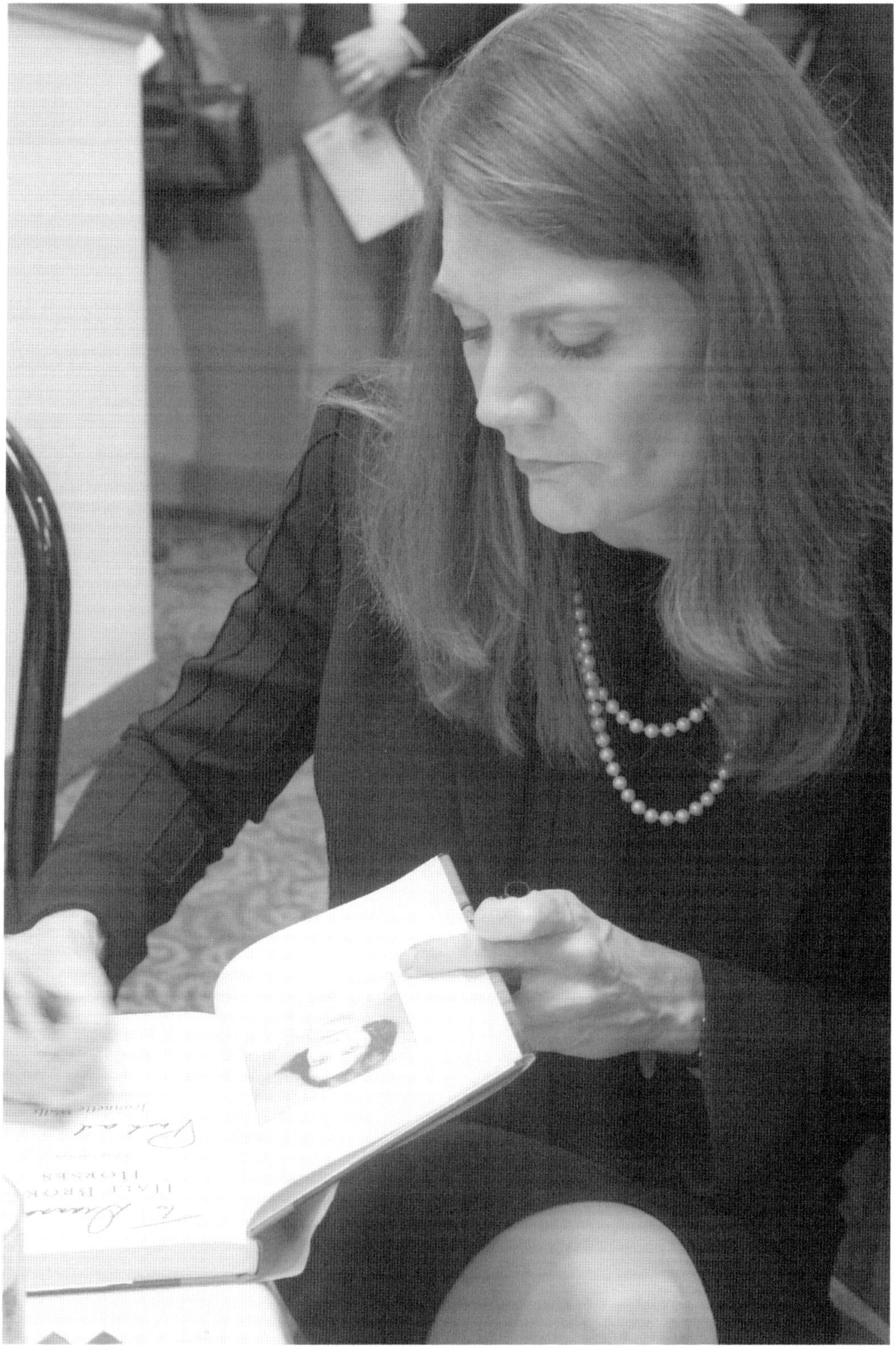

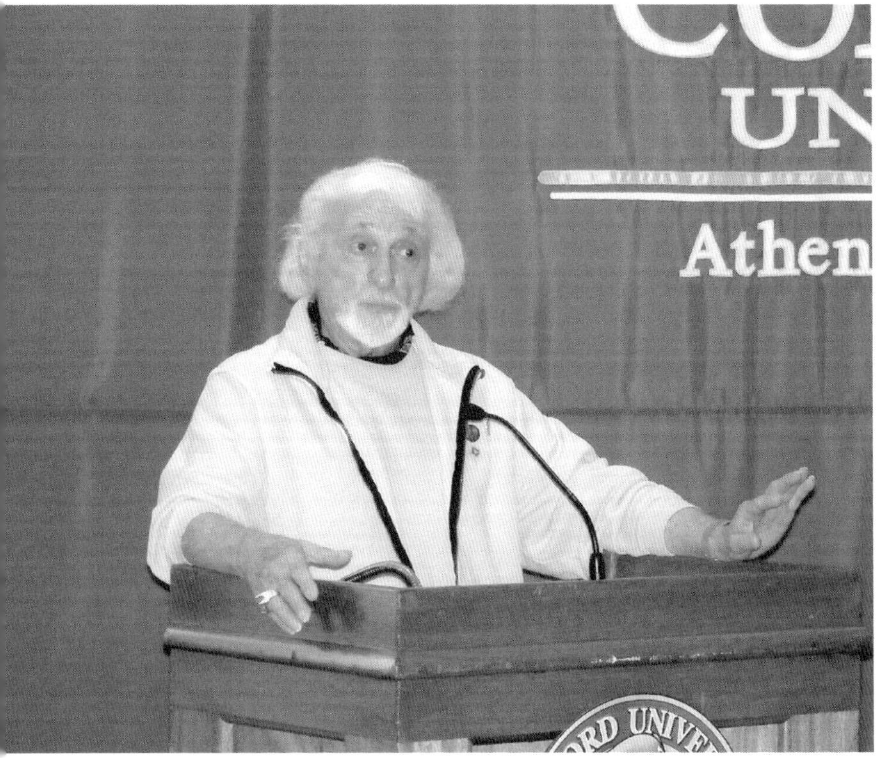

Be Brilliant
Welch native Pete Ballard is shown here being honored on February 2, 2012, as the "Great Groundhog Watcher" during Concord University's Groundhog Day Breakfast. An accomplished artist, Ballard made an impact in the international art and entertainment world through the many colleagues, associations, and abiding friendships he nurtured through the years. (Photograph by the author.)

McDowell Political Leader
State senator John Pat Fanning of Iaeger was appointed to the West Virginia State Senate in 1968 and served in nonconsecutive terms until 2012, when he chose not to seek reelection. The Fannings have served McDowell County families through Fanning Funeral Home for many years. His brother, the late Bob Fanning of Welch, was famous for the line, "I'll be the last guy to let you down." (Photograph by the author.)

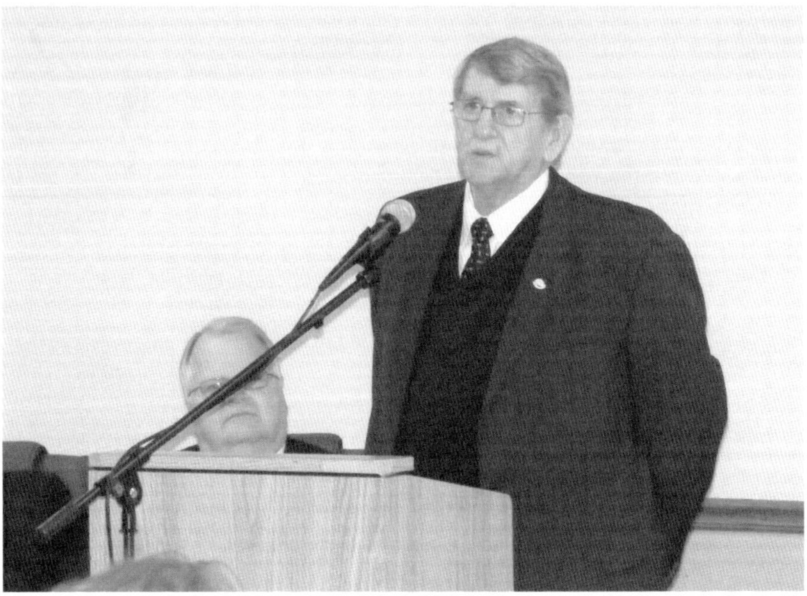

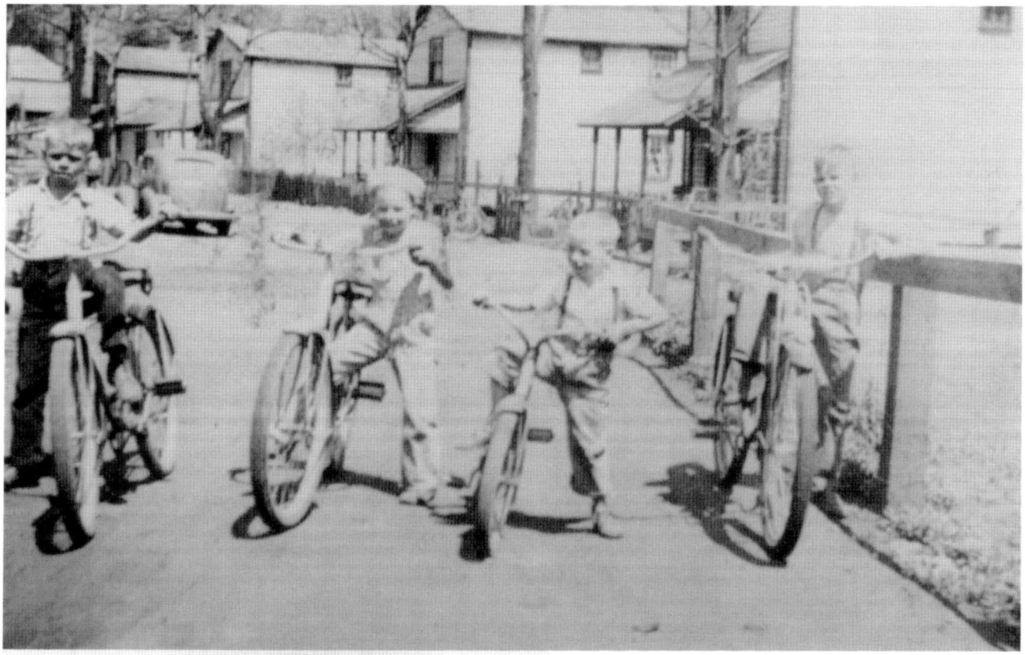

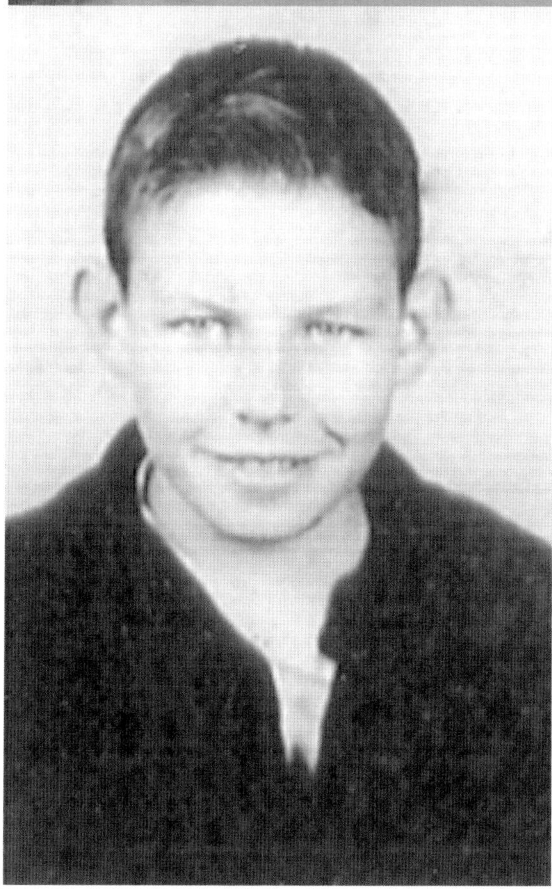

Bikers
Four young lads from Havaco, West Virginia, are riding their bicycles in the town's main street. The boys are, from left to right, Richard Stroupe, Rick Tolley, Bob Stroupe, and Bill Tolley (Rick Tolley's first cousin). One of Rick Tolley's distant relatives, Luther Tolley, was killed in the January 1946 Havaco Mine explosion. (Courtesy of Bob Stroupe.)

Child is Father to the Man
Rick Tolley is shown here in his Havaco fifth-sixth grade class picture. Tolley's family moved to Wyoming County, West Virginia, where he excelled in baseball, basketball, and football at Mullens High School. Tolley played center and linebacker at Virginia Tech, and started his coaching career in 1962. He became head coach of the Marshall University Thundering Herd football team in December 1969. He died on November 14, 1970, when the plane carrying the MU football team, several college officials, and MU boosters crashed near the Huntington, West Virginia, airport. Everyone aboard the plane died in the crash. (Courtesy of Bob Stroupe.)

Country Crooner

Although he was born and raised in Buchanan County, Virginia, the family of King Malachi "Mel" Street moved to Welch in 1948 or 1949. It was there that, in 1951, Cecil Surratt of Coalwood, West Virginia, gave him an opportunity to play guitar and sing on Welch radio station WELC. At the time, Street was working for the West Virginia State Highway Department along with his father, Alden Street. Mel never attended high school, according to his brother, Elbert Street. Street had his own Saturday morning show on WOVE Radio in Welch. He joined Surrat and became a member of the Bluefield, West Virginia–based Swing Kings, and left the area to work at a power plant in Niagara Falls, New York, but returned home in 1963 to open an auto-body repair shop in Bluewell and to continue his pursuit of music.

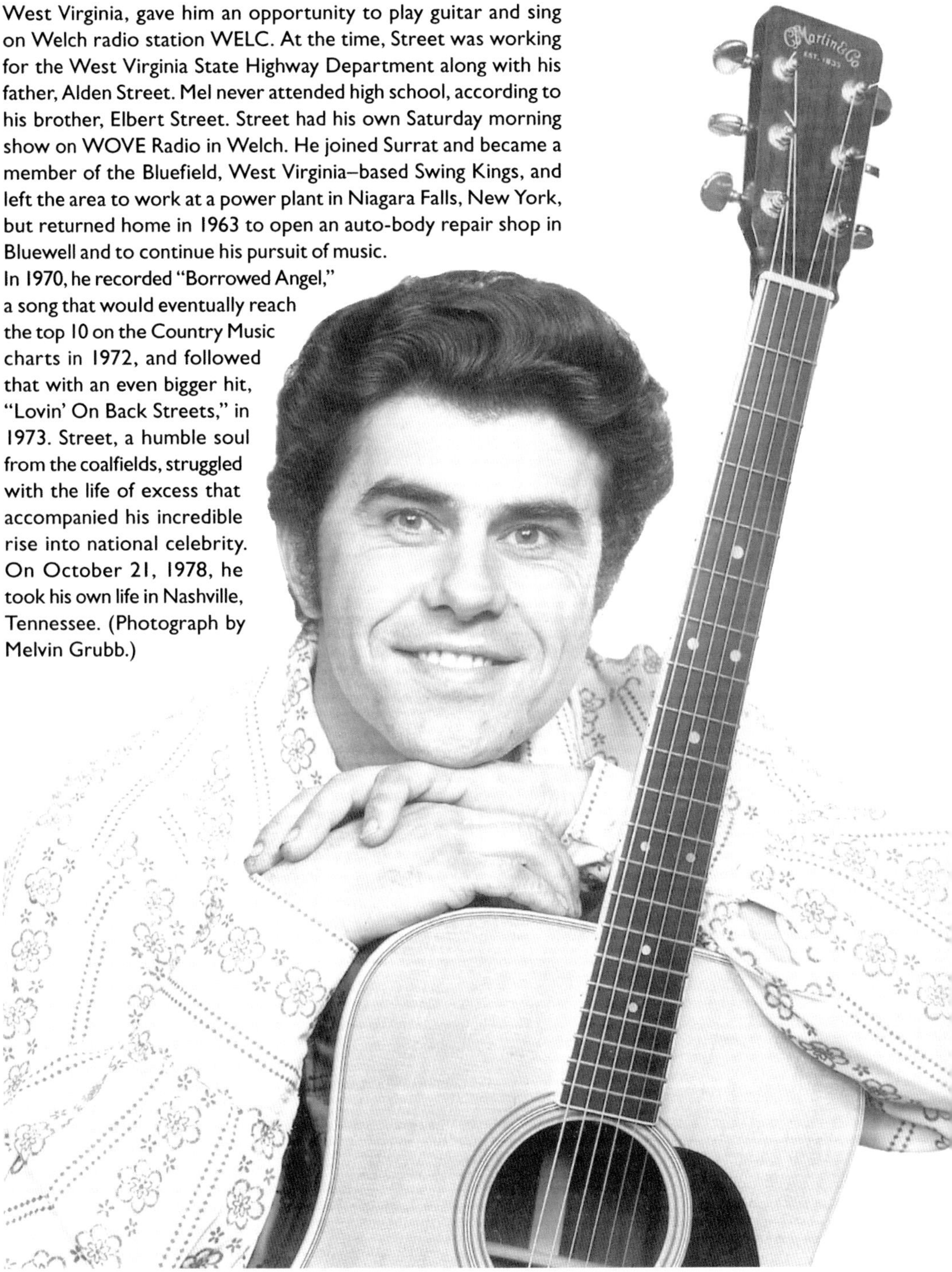

In 1970, he recorded "Borrowed Angel," a song that would eventually reach the top 10 on the Country Music charts in 1972, and followed that with an even bigger hit, "Lovin' On Back Streets," in 1973. Street, a humble soul from the coalfields, struggled with the life of excess that accompanied his incredible rise into national celebrity. On October 21, 1978, he took his own life in Nashville, Tennessee. (Photograph by Melvin Grubb.)

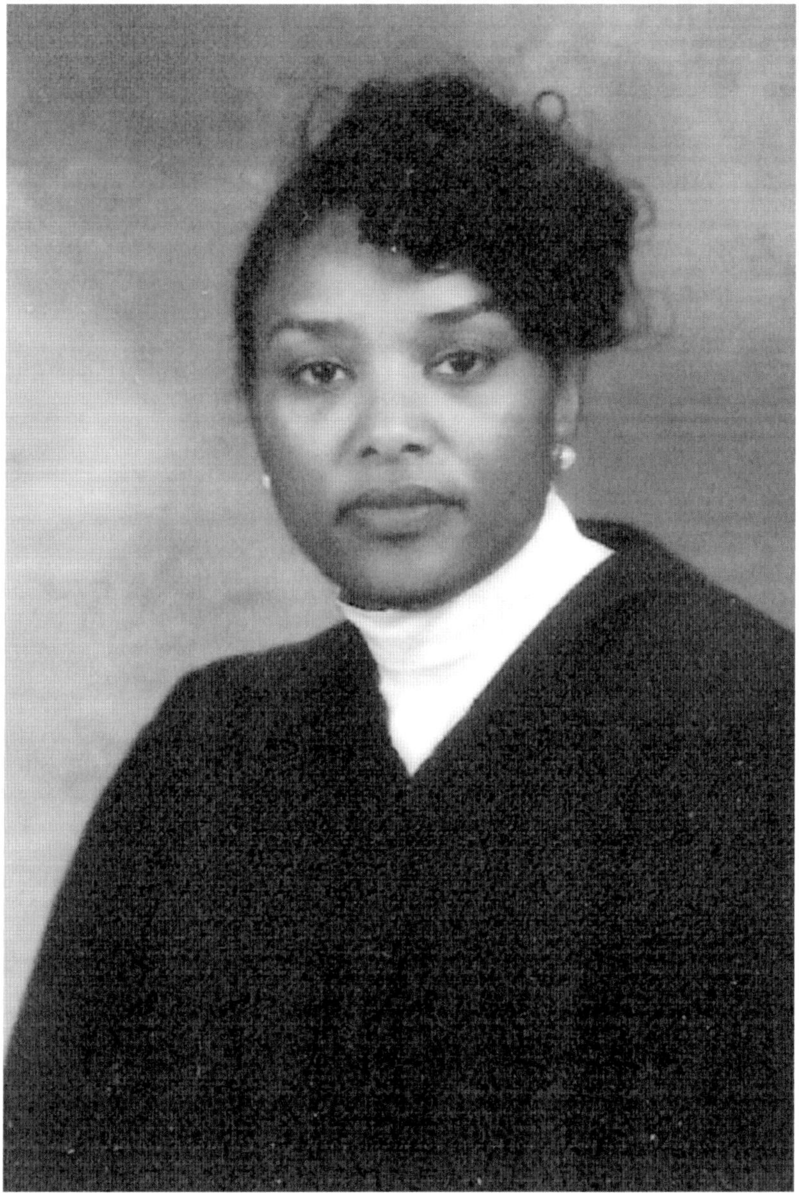

Best and Brightest

On July 8, 2009, Pres. Barack Obama appointed Irene C. Berger of Berwind, West Virginia, to serve as US district judge for the Southern District of West Virginia. On October 27, 2009, the US Senate approved Berger's appointment by a 97-0 vote, and she became the first African American female to serve as a federal judge in West Virginia. Prior to her appointment, Judge Berger had established a remarkable career in the legal community. She earned her undergraduate degree in mathematics from West Virginia University in 1979, and her law degree in 1979 from the WVU College of Law. From 1979 to 1982, she worked as a staff attorney for the Charleston, West Virginia, Legal Aid Society, and in 1982, she became assistant prosecuting attorney for Kanawha County, West Virginia. In 1994, Judge Berger served as an assistant US attorney for the Southern District of West Virginia, and in that same year, governor Gaston Caperton appointed her to be a circuit court judge in Kanawha County. (Courtesy of Karen Sword.)

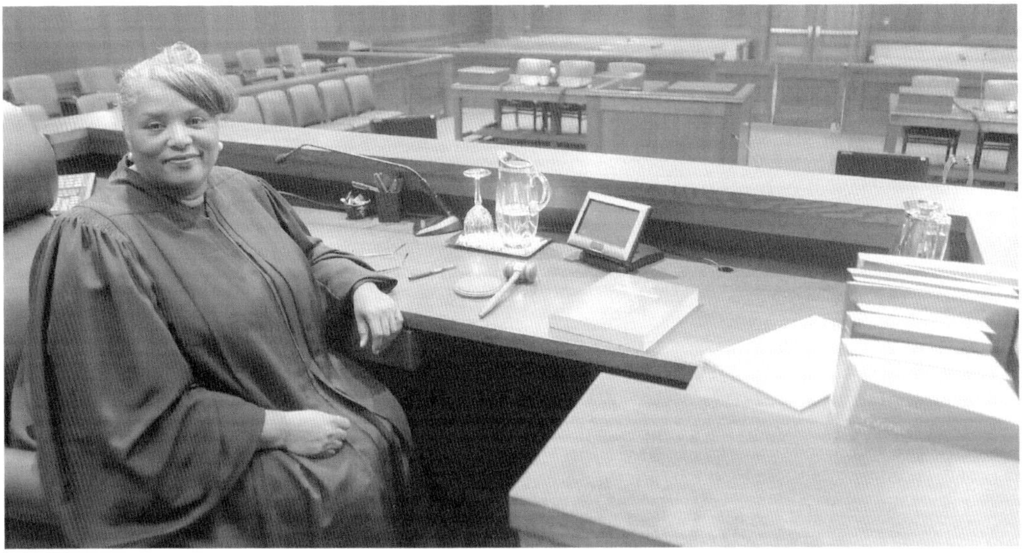

On the Bench

District Judge Irene C. Berger of the Southern District of West Virginia is shown here in her courtroom in the Robert C. Byrd Federal Building in Beckley. Senators Robert Byrd and John D. "Jay" Rockefeller IV recommended Berger to serve on the federal bench in 2004 during the administration of Pres. George W. Bush, but the appointment was not made at that time. (Photograph by Rick Barbero.)

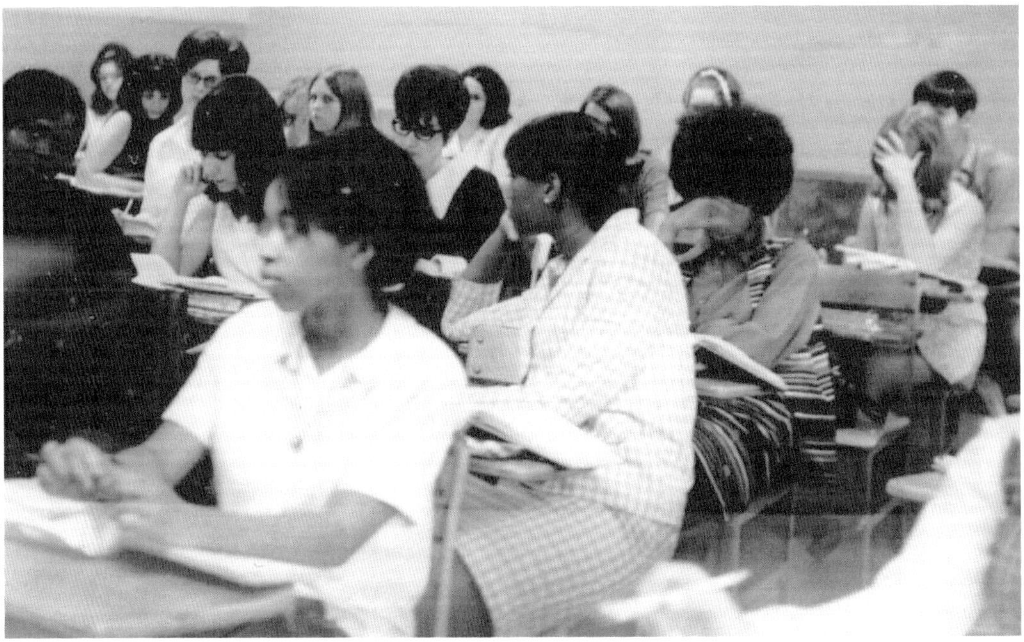

School Days

Irene C. Berger (center, in houndstooth, checked suit) is seen with other students of her seventh-grade class at Big Creek Junior High School. Judge Berger credited her family, the people of the Berwind community, her teachers, and her church for encouraging her to reach for her dreams. (Courtesy of Anita Moody.)

The Champ and the Banker

Heavyweight boxing champion Billy Conn (left) is shown here with John Knox McConnell Jr., president of the First National Bank of Keystone, West Virginia, in a November 1981 photograph taken during a dinner in Bluewell. McConnell authored a self-published book about his relationship with Conn, *The Boxer and the Banker*, and built First National Bank of Keystone, transforming approximately $17 million in assets in 1977 into a $500-million bank at the time of his death on October 26, 1997. (Author's collection.)

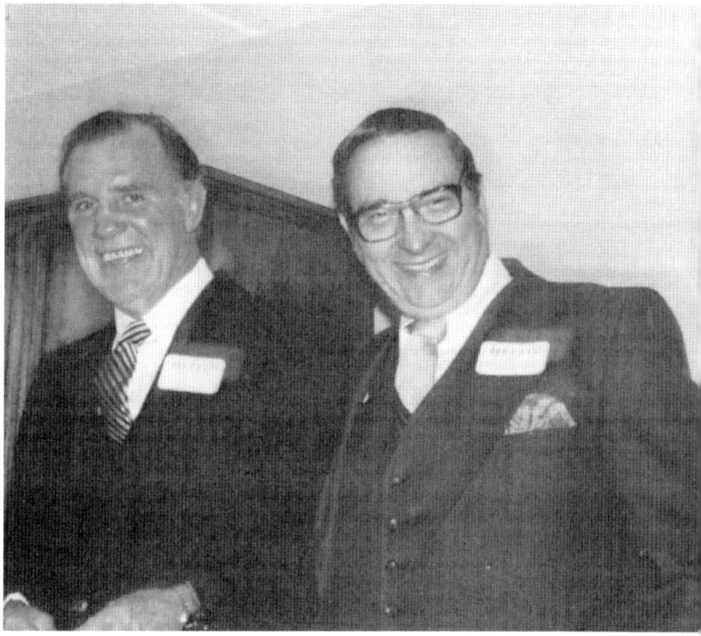

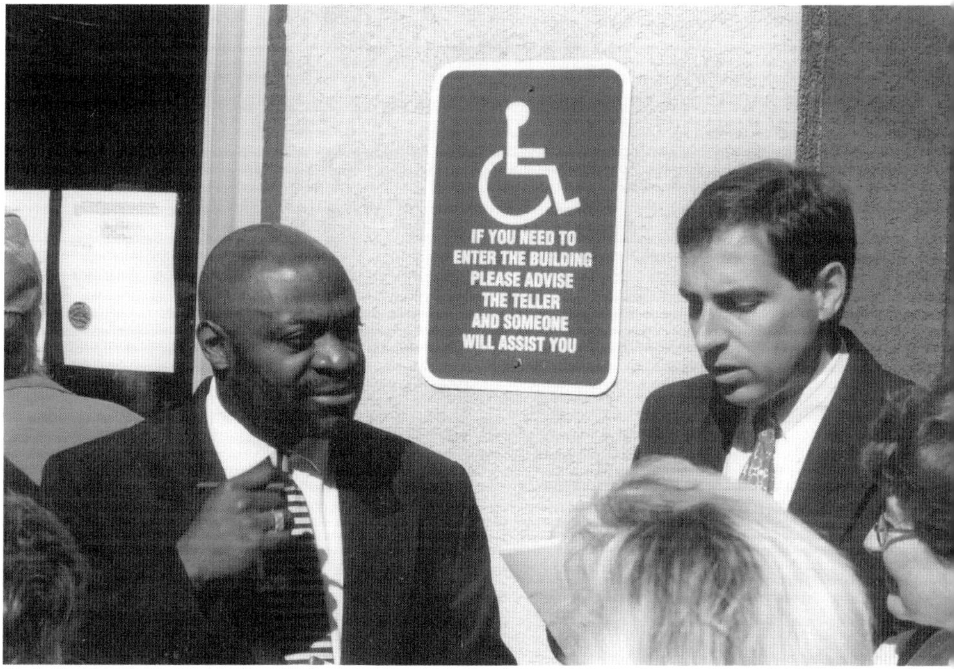

The Day the Bank Stood Still

Rickie L. McCullough (left) and David Barr of the Federal Deposit Insurance Corporation are shown on September 1, 1999, standing in front of the First National Bank of Keystone after the Office of the Comptroller of the Currency (OCC) declared the bank insolvent due to apparent fraud and $515 million in loans being carried on the books illegally. McCullough and Barr explained the bank failure to scores of confused bank customers. The OCC appointed the FDIC to serve as receiver of the bank's $1.1 billion in assets. (Photograph by the author.)

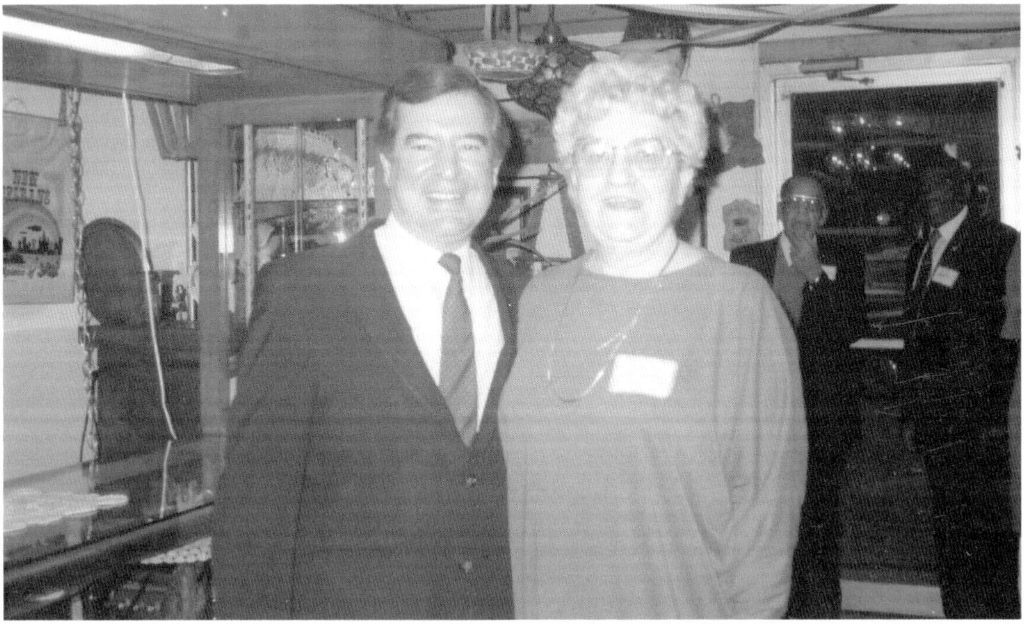

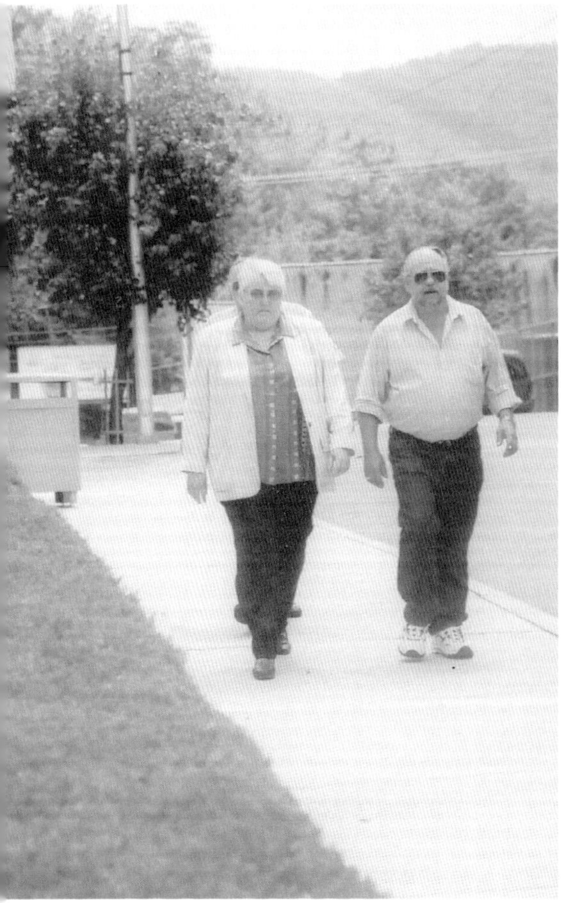

Happier Times
Billie Cherry (right) is shown here with US representative Nick Rahall at a party in Keystone, West Virginia. Cherry came to Keystone in 1977 to help John Knox McConnell Jr. at the First National Bank of Keystone, and was serving as chairperson of the bank's board of directors when the bank failed. Cherry was convicted of bank fraud in October 2001, sentenced to 16-plus years in prison, and died at the University of Kentucky Medical Center at age 82 while serving as an inmate at the federal prison camp in Lexington. (Author's collection.)

Bank Shot
Terry Church, shown here with her husband, Hermie Church, arrives at the Elizabeth Kee Federal Building in Bluefield, West Virginia, during her 2000 trial on federal conspiracy and obstruction charges. Church was convicted in two separate trials and sentenced to 27-plus years in prison, but her sentence was later reduced after she agreed to help government investigators unravel the massive fraud at the bank. She was senior vice president of the First National Bank of Keystone when the bank failed. (Photograph by Eric DiNovo.)

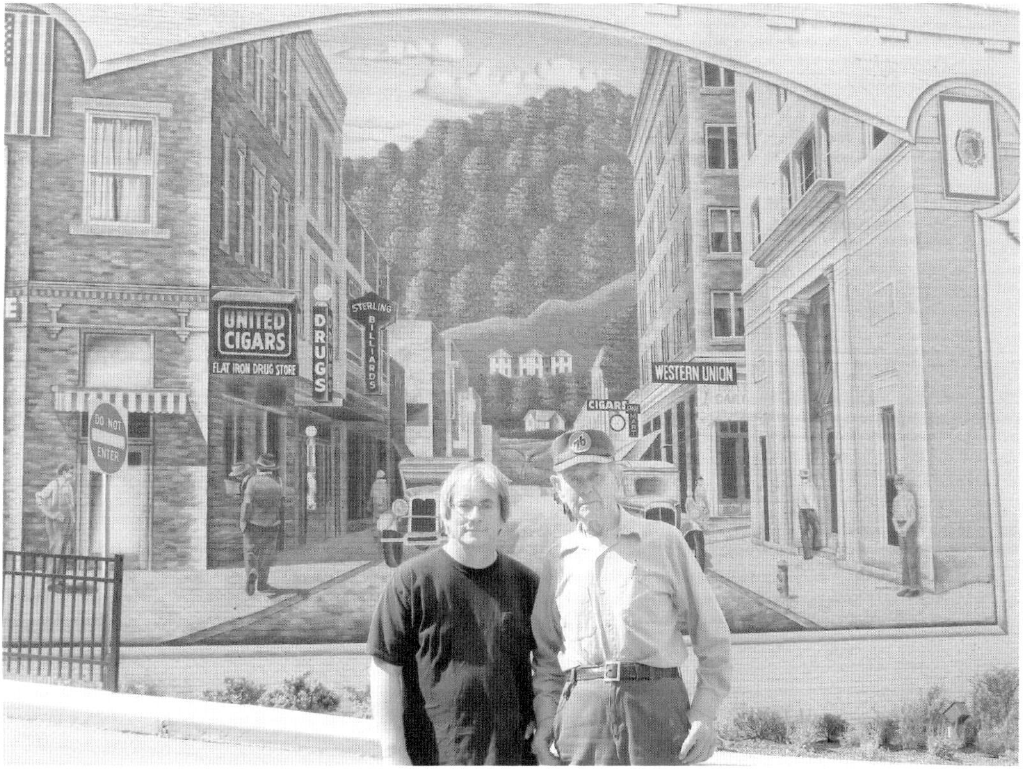

On the Street Where You Live
Noted McDowell County artist Tom Acosta (left) poses with Ed Shepard at the intersection of Wyoming and McDowell Streets in Welch. Acosta's mural of a McDowell Street scene includes a likeness of Shepard at the far right. (Photograph by the author.)

Things of the Past
James Ellwood Jones is shown here enjoying breakfast on the porch of his mansion in Switchback, West Virginia, as his unidentified servant serves him coffee. The life that Jones and other coal barons enjoyed in the early 20th century disappeared as a result of the changes taking shape in the coalfields. (Courtesy of Judy McDaniel.)

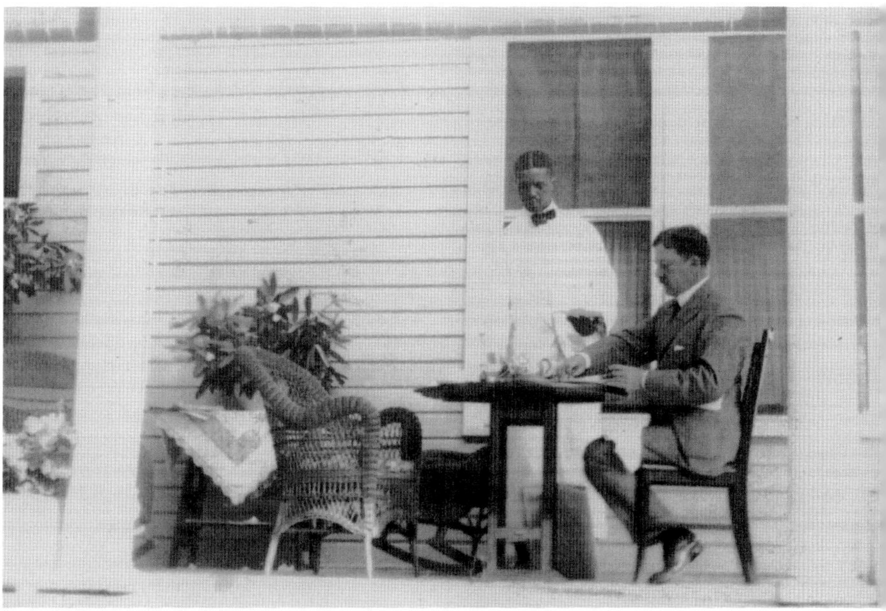

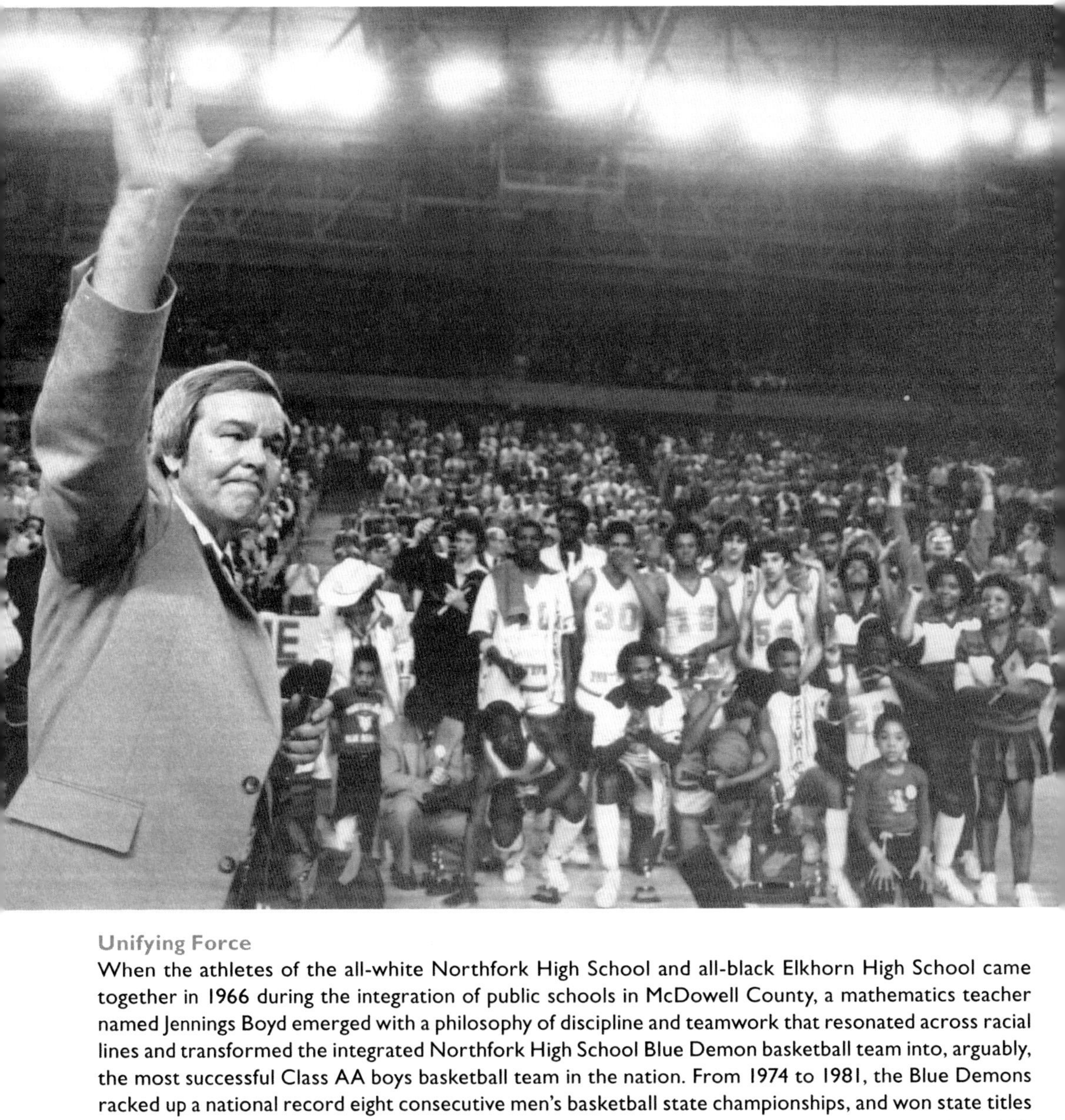

Unifying Force

When the athletes of the all-white Northfork High School and all-black Elkhorn High School came together in 1966 during the integration of public schools in McDowell County, a mathematics teacher named Jennings Boyd emerged with a philosophy of discipline and teamwork that resonated across racial lines and transformed the integrated Northfork High School Blue Demon basketball team into, arguably, the most successful Class AA boys basketball team in the nation. From 1974 to 1981, the Blue Demons racked up a national record eight consecutive men's basketball state championships, and won state titles in 1971 and 1984. The Northfork Lady Blue Demons also earned state girls' basketball titles in 1976, 1977, and 1979. While many schools in previously segregated parts of the country faced difficult challenges during the early years of integration, Coach Boyd helped the students of Northfork High School achieve balance through basketball. (Courtesy of Michael Boyd.)

CHAPTER FIVE

Free State Melting Pot

Emma Lazarus could have been speaking directly to the people of McDowell County when she penned the lines "Give me your tired, your poor, / Your huddled masses yearning to breathe free, / The wretched refuse of your teeming shore. / Send these, the homeless tempest-tossed to me, / I lift the lamp beside the golden door," in her famous poem "The New Colossus," about the Statue of Liberty. A few timber, coal, and railroad entrepreneurs came to McDowell County to expand their fortunes, but most of the people who were included in the 1950 census of more than 95,000 souls were the ancestors of Russian, Greek, and Italian workers, the sons and daughters of Polish, Hungarian, and Slovakian laborers, the daughters and sons of African American slaves who earned their freedom through the American Civil War, and the ancestors of Scottish, Irish, French, Spanish, and Welsh mountain people who settled in this rugged territory to escape the encroaching civilization from the eastern United States.

Through most of the 19th century, there were only a few farms in McDowell County before the timber and coal developers came to harvest the hidden natural bounty of the woods and the minerals buried beneath the surface. In order to entertain the coal miners and their families and to keep workers close to home, coal operators constructed company houses and stores, bowling alleys, theaters, churches, and schools. But the various races, creeds, and nationalities that escaped the bondage of their former lives to come to the coalfields in search of opportunity brought the foods, traditions, and cultures of their ancestral homes and made them part of the Free State of McDowell. Even the Lazarus family came to the Flat Top coalfields and operated general merchandise and liquor stores.

The story of McDowell County, West Virginia, is a story of how people from diverse backgrounds and cultures came together and carved a civilization out of an unforgiving land and, in so doing, provided the chance for future generations to succeed and make their mark on the world in myriad ways.

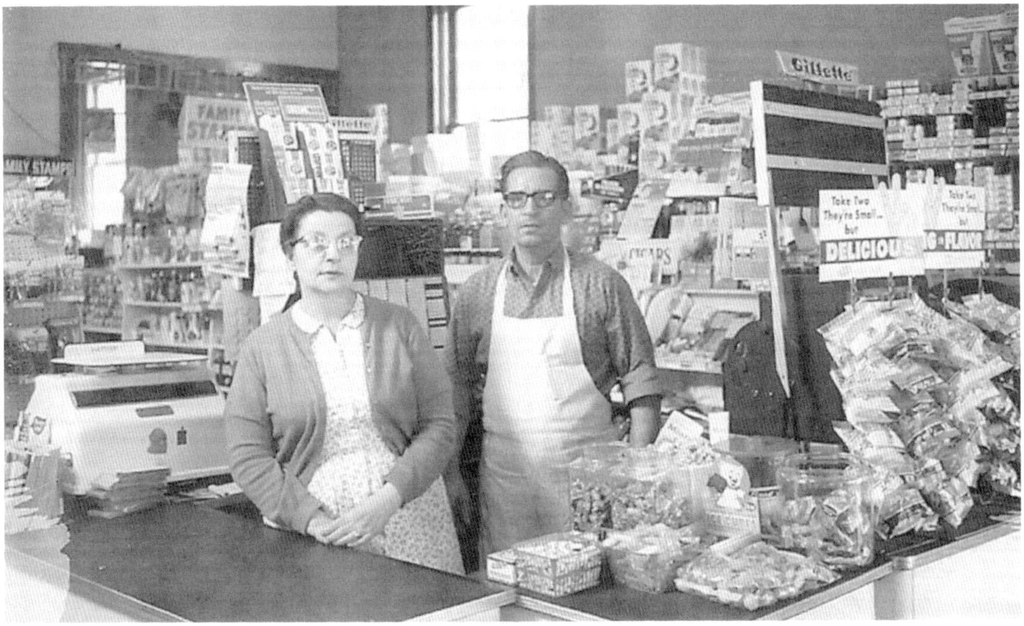

Friendly Faces
Mary (Genadopoulos) Balasis and her husband, Adamantios Balasis, owned and operated the West Virginia Grocery in the heart of Kimball after Adamantios and Mary's father purchased the store from A.P. Wood. Adamantios escaped death by refusing to reboard a cargo ship for the return trip to Europe. The ship was sunk by a German U-boat, and all aboard died. Mary's father was blinded in the mines, but the two families managed to survive. The story of how they came to the New World and made it into the coalfields of southern West Virginia is a testament to strength and will. (Courtesy of Markella Gianato.)

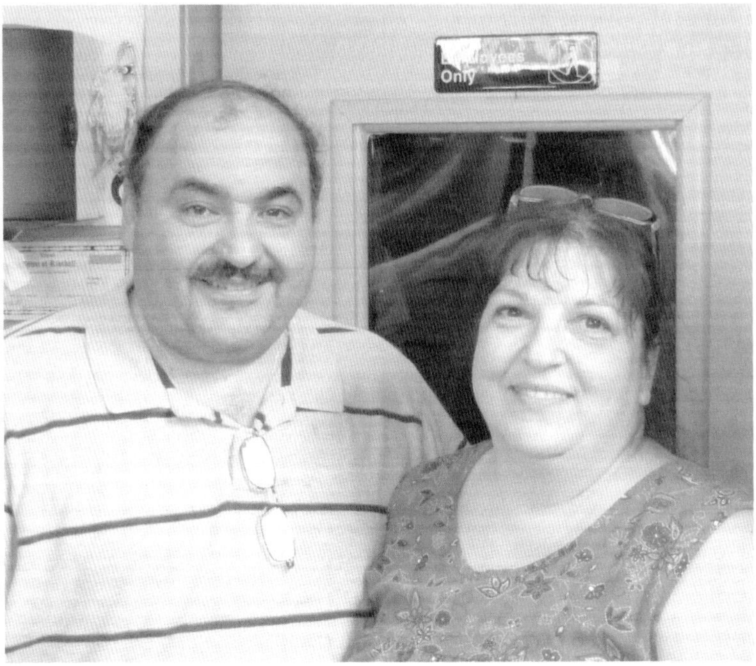

Best of Two Worlds
Jimmy Joe Gianato, the director of Homeland Security and Emergency services for West Virginia, and his wife, Markella (Balasis) Gianato, are shown here in the doorway to the kitchen of the Ya'sou Restaurant in the West Virginia Grocery. The Gianato family maintains the traditions of two cultures while working to keep their community and state safe. (Photograph by the author.)

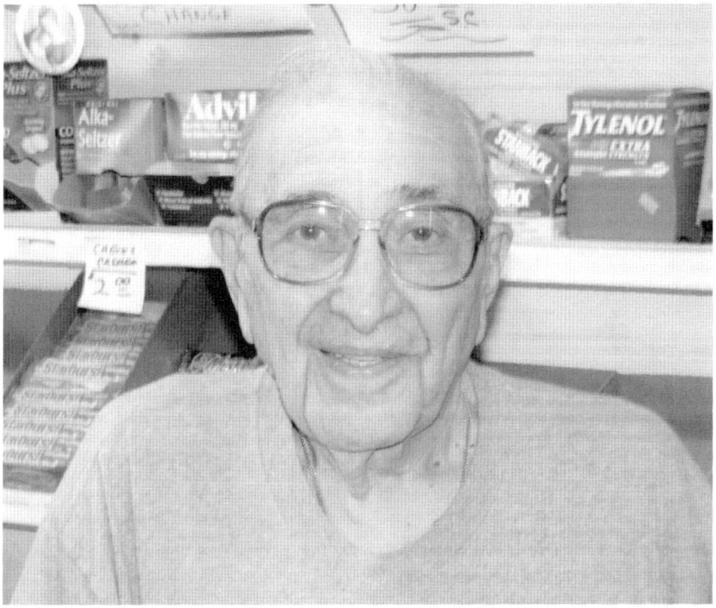

A Man You've Known for All These Years
Jimmy Gianato is shown here at the counter of the Gianato Grocery Store, which has been a fixture in Kimball, West Virginia, since 1924. After his parents were unable to operate the store, Jimmy and his two brothers, Johnny and Mike, both now deceased, ran it. Although inundated by floods in 2001 and 2002, the store is still open. (Photograph by the author.)

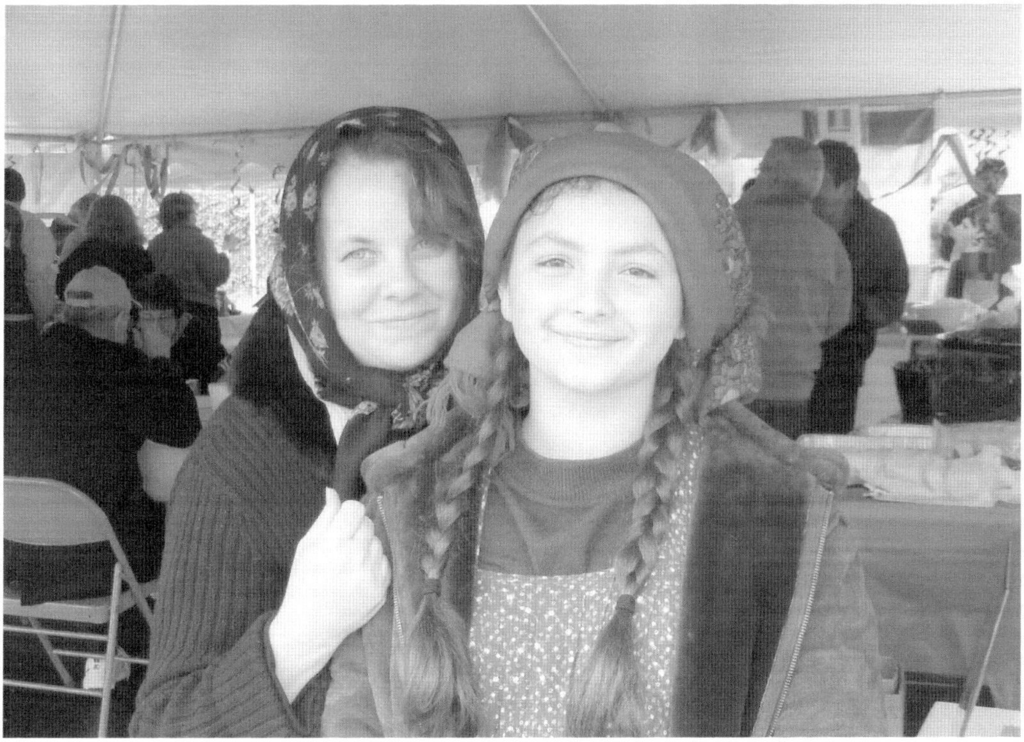

Old World Charm
Lisa Tyson (left) the wife of Fr. Mark Tyson, rector of St. Mary's Orthodox Church, and their daughter, Catherine Tyson, are shown here at the church's first ethnic food festival on October 1, 2011. Although the church is now physically located in Bluefield, West Virginia, its early-20th-century roots were in Crozer Bottom, McDowell County. (Photograph by the author.)

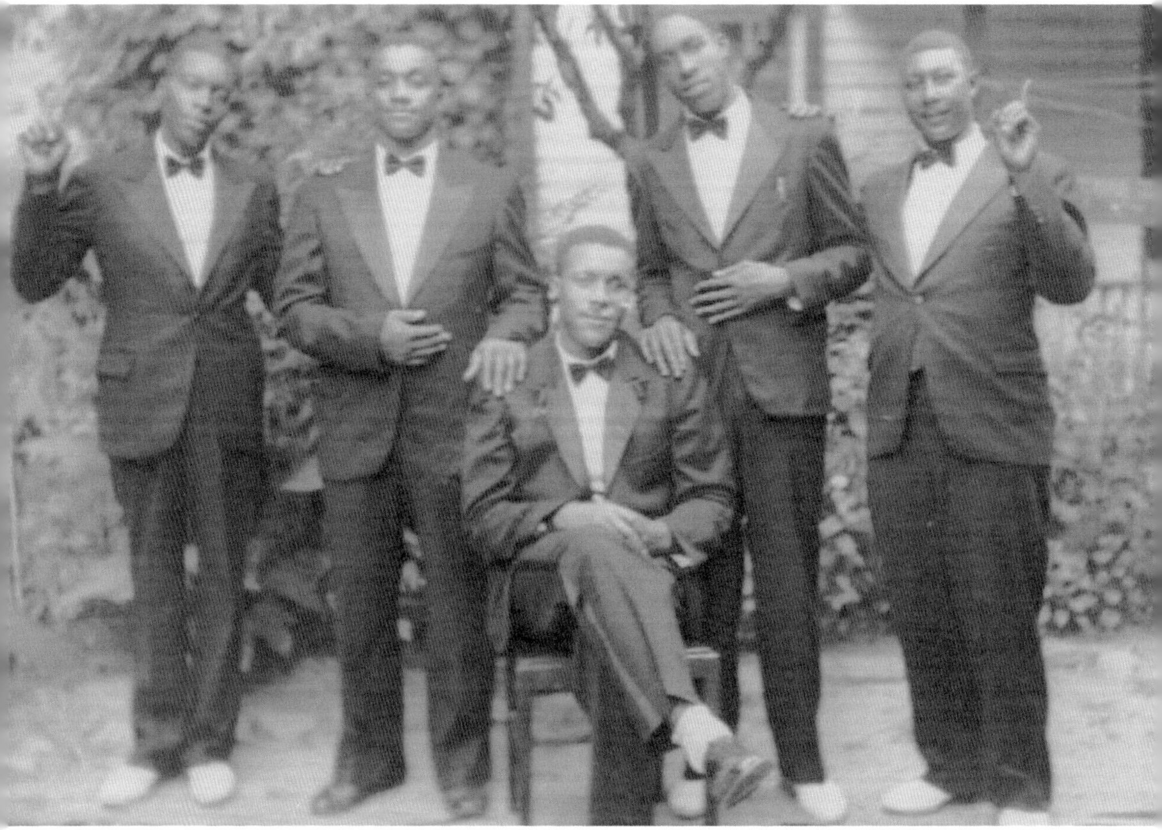

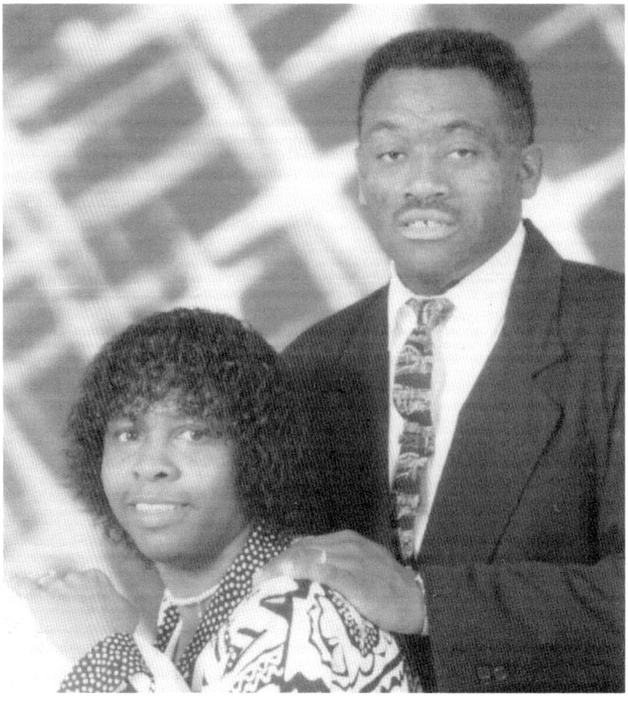

Music in the Melodies
The Caples Evening Quartet is all dressed up and ready for the show. Group members included Haywood Perry and W.E. Lewis, but the other three members, and Perry's and Lewis's place in the photograph, are unknown. (Courtesy of the Eastern Regional Coal Archives.)

Gospel in their Soul
Evangelist Gloria Miller and her husband, Deacon Karl Miller, perform at churches throughout West Virginia. Karl Miller is the pianist for the Flat Top Missionary Baptist Association. Karl and Gloria reside in Northfork, West Virginia, and carry the gospel to church congregations and concert venues wherever they are called to perform. (Courtesy of Karl Miller.)

The Soul of McDowell County

The musical Womack family traveled a great deal, but about 20 years ago, Curtis Womack, shown here, returned to McDowell County to help his mother, Naomi Womack, who had moved back to Northfork from the West Coast. "I was born in Charleston, West Virginia, and Bobby was born in Cleveland, Ohio, but our grandmother always lived in Maybeury, West Virginia," Curtis Womack said. Curtis's uncle Solomon Womack was the first member of the family to make it big in the music world, singing with Claude Jeter and the Swan Silvertones. But it was Bobby Womack, younger than Curtis by less than a year, who emerged as a star out of the family band, called the Womack Brothers and later the Valentinos. Popular music fans recall that a line from a Claude Jeter song inspired Paul Simon's song, "Bridge Over Troubled Water." Bobby Womack's song "But it's All Over Now" helped the Rolling Stones get their first hit in the United Kingdom. Bobby's friendship helped advance the careers of folks like Jimi Hendrix and Janis Joplin, and his guitar playing put the funk in the music of artists like Wilson Pickett and Sly & the Family Stone. But the singing Womack family weren't the only ones who made a mark in the R&B world. Garnett Mimms of Ashland, Northfork Hollow, had a big hit with "Cry Baby." He returned to his gospel roots early in his career, and continues to make a joyful noise unto the Lord. (Photograph by the author.)

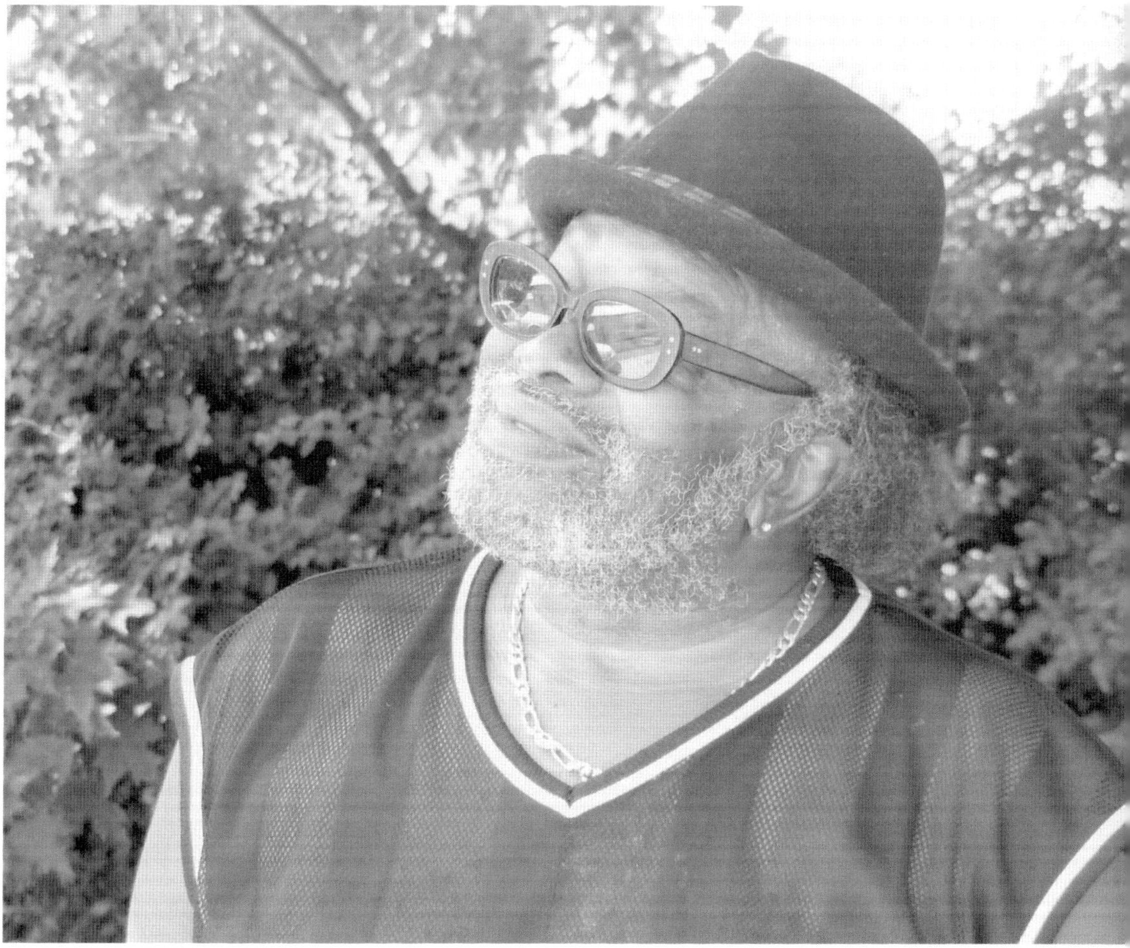

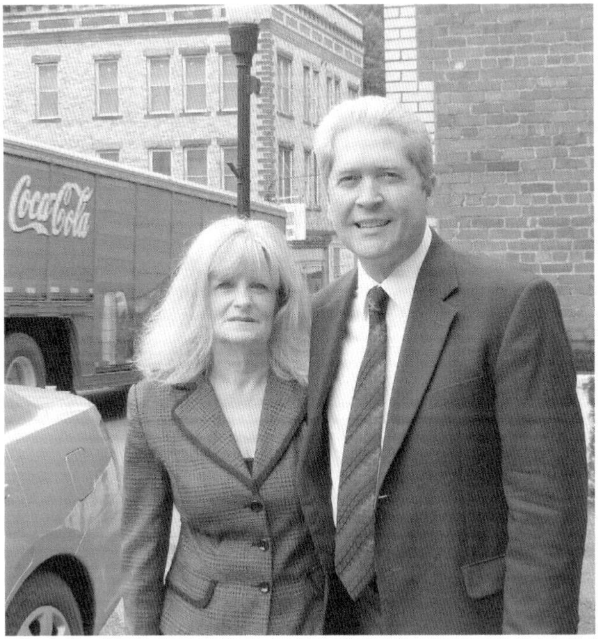

Service to Community
Longtime McDowell County prosecuting attorney Sid Bell and his wife, Drema, are shown here on Wyoming Street in Welch. The Bells met when they were both working at the *Welch Daily News*. At the suggestion of former McDowell prosecutor Wade Watson, and out of a desire to serve the county, Bell went to the West Virginia University College of Law, earned his law degree, and, after serving a term on the county board of education, was elected prosecutor. (Photograph by the author.)

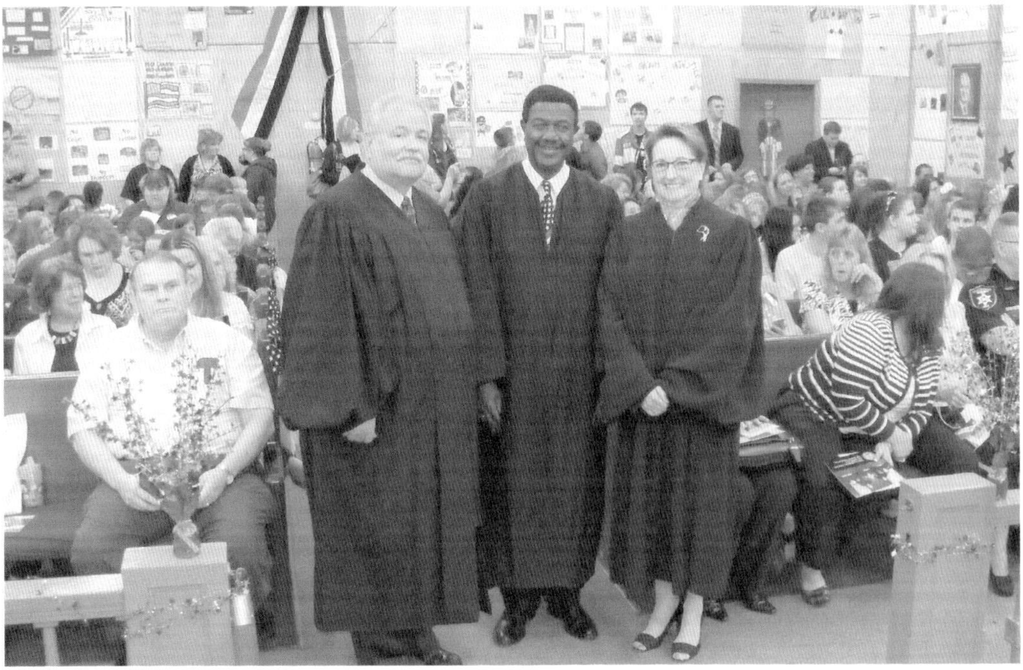

Law Day Observed
The McDowell County circuit courts have been celebrating Law Day for several years, bringing well-known state and national speakers to the court to talk with public school students on topics related to the importance of the rule of law. Justice Robin Davis of the West Virginia Supreme Court of Appeals was the keynote speaker at the May 1, 2012, Law Day celebration. The McDowell County circuit court judges shown here are, from left to right, Rudolph J. "Rick" Murensky II, Booker T. Stevens, and Robin Davis. (Photograph by the author.)

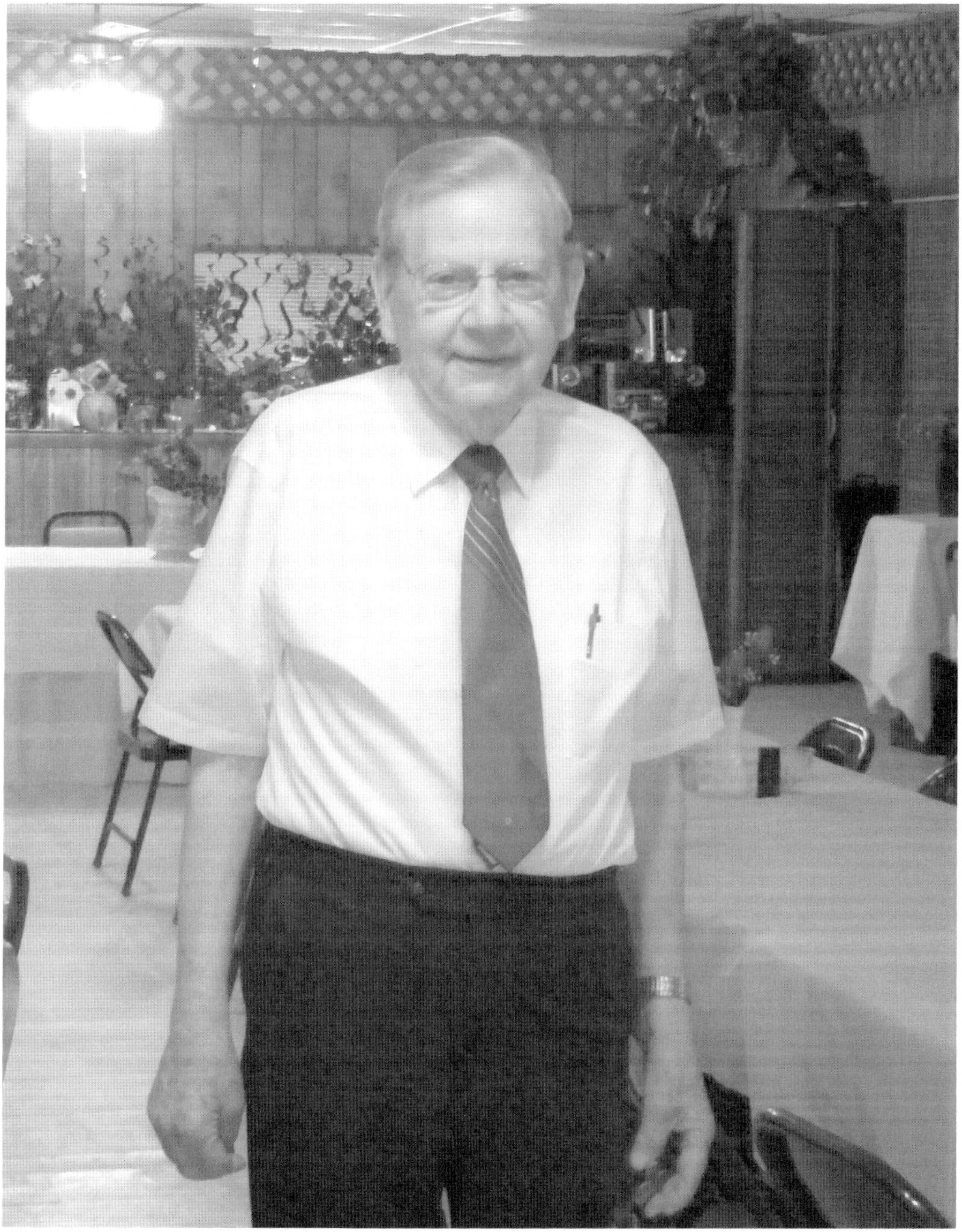

Today's Special

Raymond Bean, owner and operator of Raymond's Restaurant on McDowell Street in Welch, has been serving the public since opening his business in the 1960s. Bean opened a grocery store at the same location, beside the Temple Theater and across the street from the Pocahontas Theater, but coal miners stopping in the store asked Bean to make them sandwiches. He eventually added a deli, and soon transformed his business into a restaurant, and now has a successful catering business as well. (Photograph by the author.)

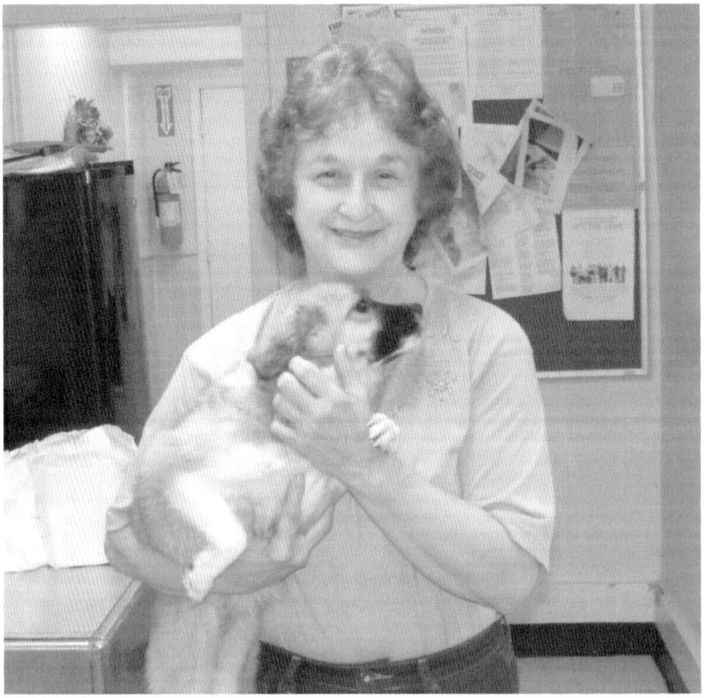

Precious Moments

Sharon Sagety, shown here in the McDowell County Animal Shelter with four-month-old Precious, has worked as a volunteer with the McDowell County Humane Society for 37 years, and operates a no-kill shelter in Superior, West Virginia. The shelter is located in the former Cannelton Coal Company Store, and was donated to the Humane Society by the Pocahontas Land Company. The shelter features a cat deck, several isolation rooms, and plenty of exercise space for the animals that are housed in the shelter. (Photograph by the author.)

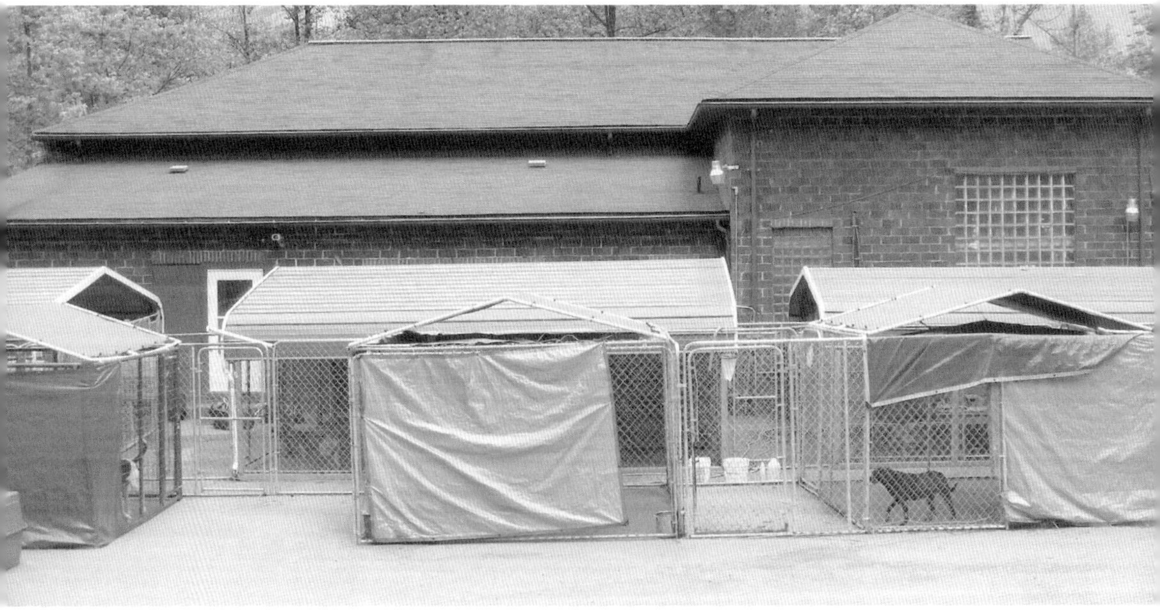

Shelter from the Storm

The former Cannelton Coal Company Store has ample room to store donations of pet food, kitty litter, and cleaning supplies for the animals. Sharon Sagety, whose family immigrated to the coalfields from Budapest, Hungary, works with pet adoption agencies nationwide to place abandoned pets with good homes, after they have gone through a thorough medical screening process and have regained their strength. (Photograph by the author.)

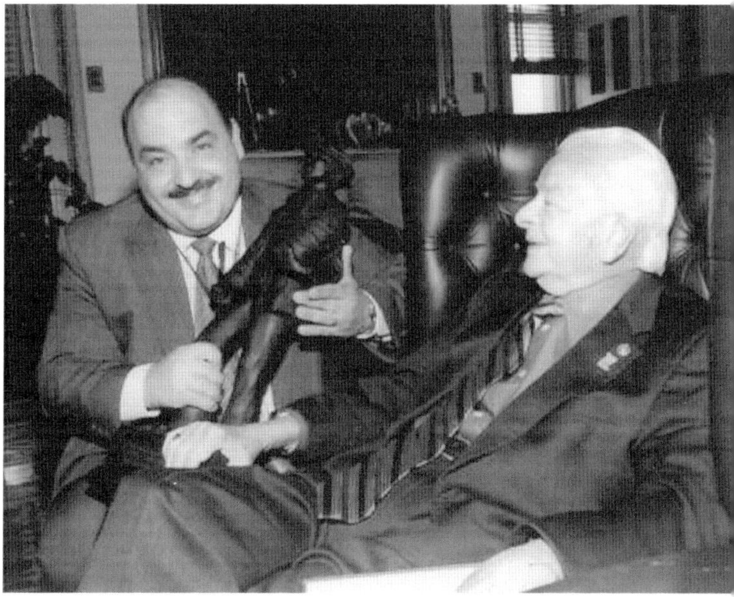

For the Coal Miners

Kimball native Jimmy Joe Gianato (left), West Virginia director of Homeland Security and Emergency Services, is shown here presenting a statue of a coal miner made of coal to Sen. Robert C. Byrd. Through the years, Byrd remained one of the most steadfast supporters of coal miners and their families. He died in office on June 28, 2010, with 51 years of service in the Senate, the longest in US history. (Courtesy of Jimmy Gianato.)

Importance of Education

After he returned from military service during World War II, Ellis Ray Williams worked to help students improve themselves through education. Williams (left) is shown here with five students at the county's vocational education center. During the last decade of Sen. Robert C. Byrd's life, the senator worked with Williams and other members of the McDowell Museum Commission to restore the World War I Memorial in Kimball, West Virginia, that honored black veterans of that war. (Courtesy of Ellis Ray Williams.)

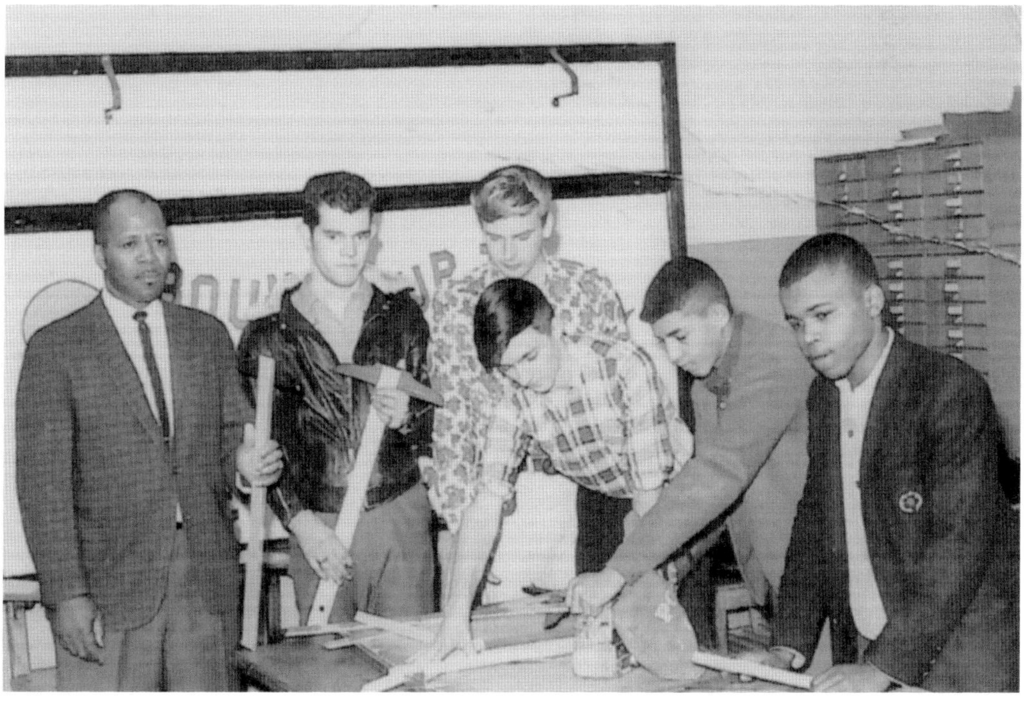

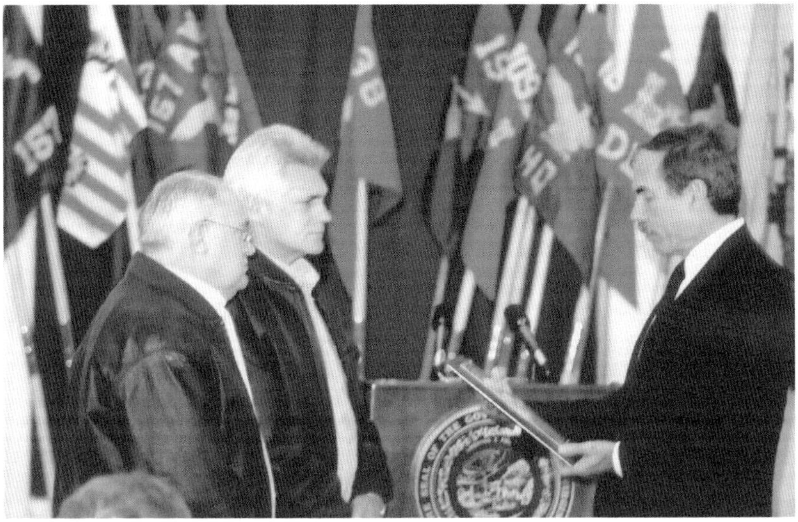

Remembering Coal Miners

West Virginia governor Bob Wise (right) presents a Governor's Citation for Heroism to Bobby Riggs (far left) and Jack Riggs, the brothers of Joe Riggs, one of three McDowell County coal miners among 13 killed in the September 23, 2001, mine explosion in Brookwood, Alabama. Joe Riggs, 51, of Roderfield; Joseph P. Sorah, 46, of Welch; and David Blevins, 52, of Anawalt went back into the Jim Walters Resources Blue Creek No. 5 Mine to save others, and were killed in a second blast. (Photograph by the author.)

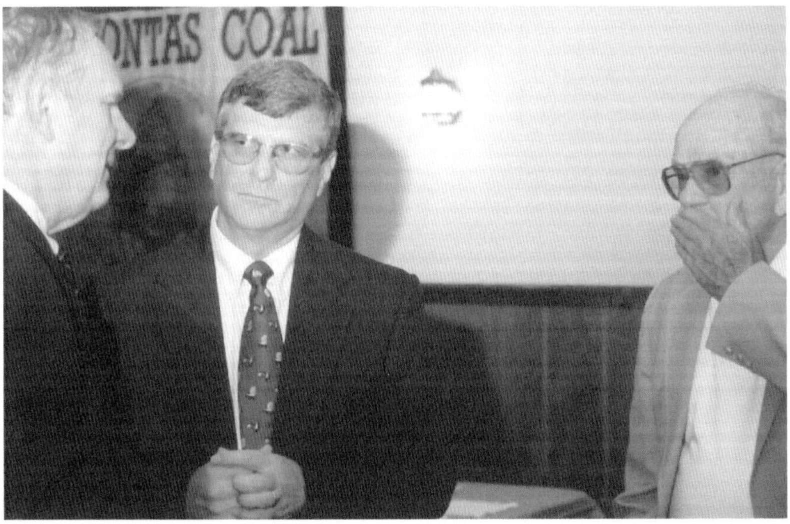

McDowell Coal Leadership

State delegate Eustace Frederick (left), a native of Delta Hollow, talks with Mike Miano (center), a native of Gary, and Jack Caffrey, of Welch, at a Pocahontas Coal Association meeting in 1998. Before he retired, Frederick was senior vice president of Consol's Southern Appalachian Region. Miano and Caffrey served as directors of the state Division of Environmental Protection. (Photograph by the author.)

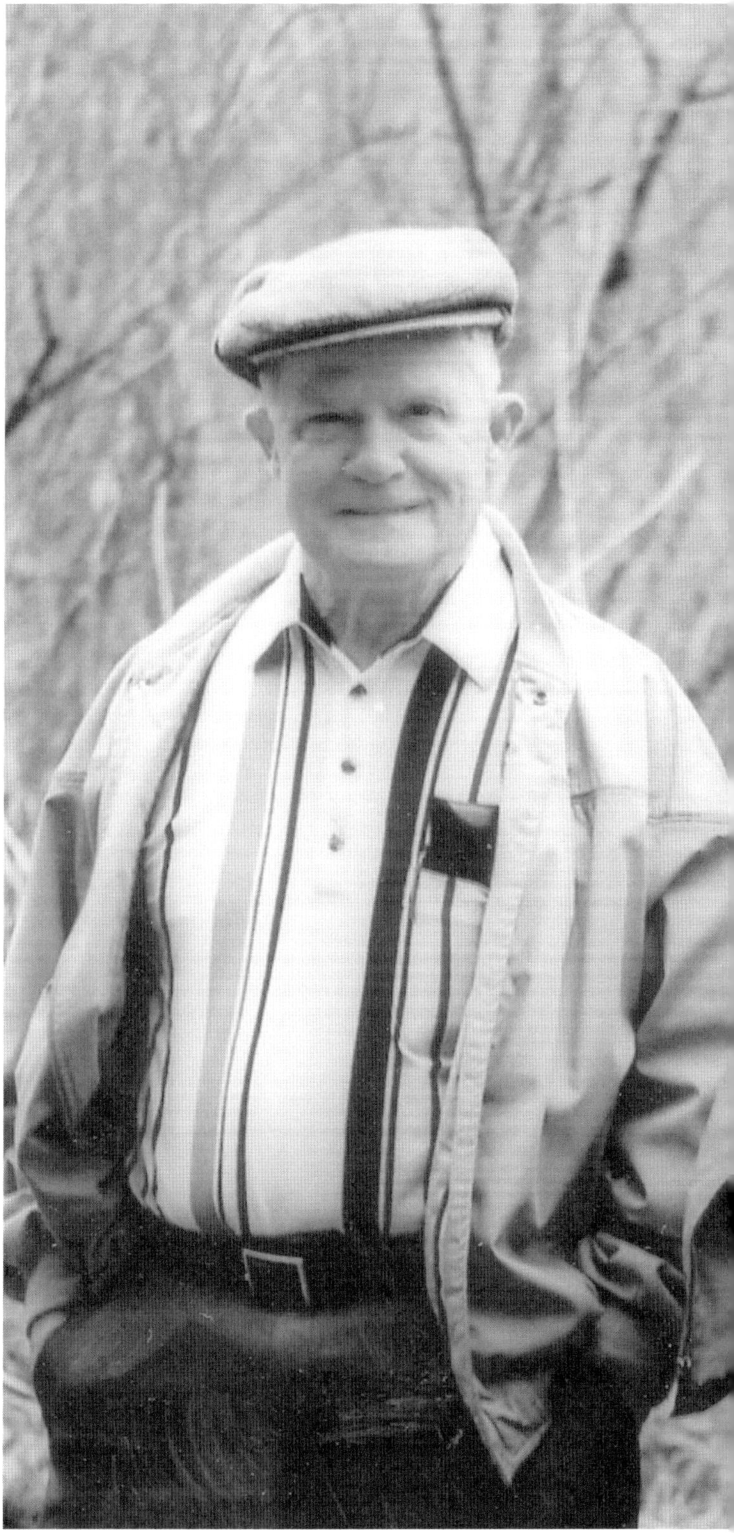

Dedicated to Remembering the Past

Early Henry Smith worked as the fire boss at the Olga Coal Company's Coalwood Mine from 1947 to 1960. During that time, he worked closely with mine superintendent Homer Hickam Sr. to ensure the safety of the coal miners. He also worked with the youth of the community as the local Cub Scouts scoutmaster. When many teenage boys in the country were fascinated with the Russian launch of *Sputnik* on October 4, 1957, Smith considered experimental rocketry to be a worthwhile activity for the scouts in his troop. Of course, the more famous of the rocketry clubs from the Cub Scout troop was headed by Homer Hickam Jr. and included Billy Rose, Jimmy Carroll, Quenton Wilson, and Sherman Siers. But another group, led by Early Smith's son, Grant F. Smith, which included Jackie Likens, Norman Hatmaker, Ronnie Farris, and Jimmy Seirs, was also in the Coalwood space race. Sadly, Grant Smith and his wife, Cynthia, were killed in a car wreck on September 29, 2009, as they were on their way to visit Grant's mother, Cathleen (Justice) Smith, at her home in Falls Mills, Virginia. Early Smith's family was among the Carroll County, Virginia, families recruited by George L. Carter when he came to McDowell County to open the mines at Coalwood and Caretta. The descendants of those families still gather in Hillsville, Virginia, in the fall of each year for an annual West Virginia Reunion. In addition to his work with the scouts, Early Smith assembled an incredible collection of artifacts related to coal-mine history, and had just opened his own coal-mining museum prior to his death on November 11, 2002. (Photograph by the author.)

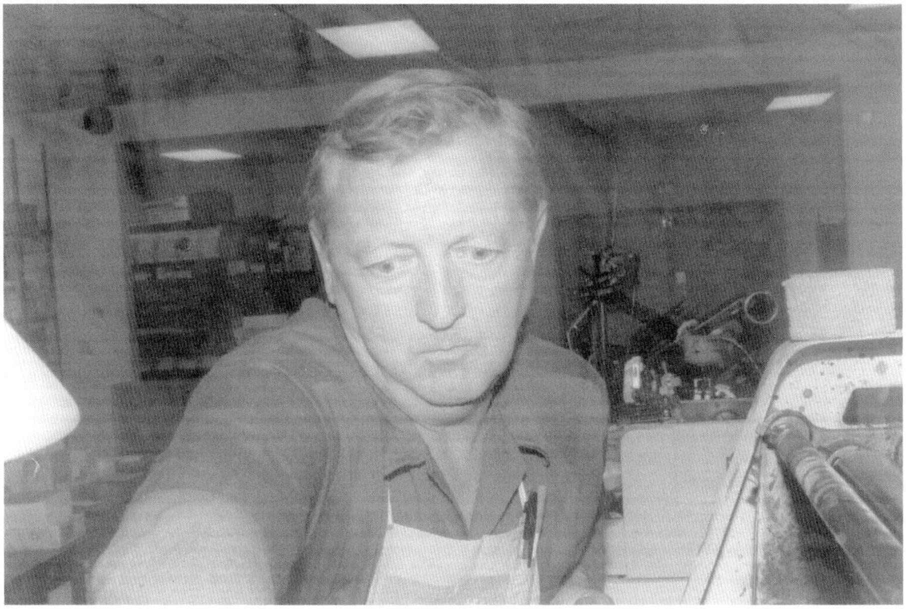

Positive Impressions
Kenneth Davidson, a printer by trade, grew up in McDowell County and graduated from Elkhorn High School. An avid historian, Davidson has worked to preserve the history of the coalfields, and, with his brother Roger Davidson, has worked to locate, identify, and, if possible, clear many abandoned family cemeteries of the coalfields. (Photograph by the author.)

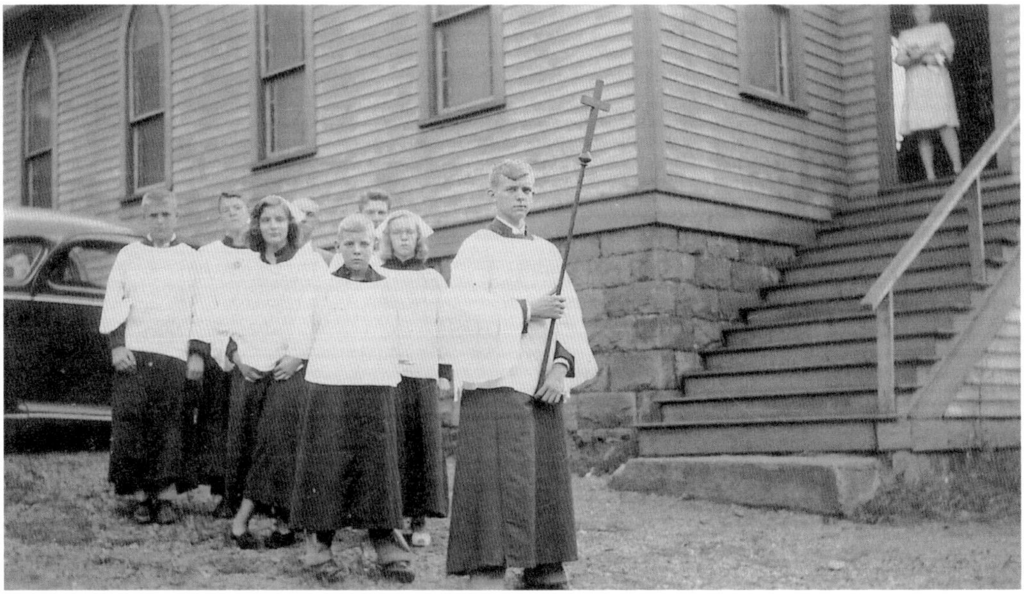

Procession
The choir of Grace Episcopal Church in Eckman, West Virginia, is shown here preparing to enter the church. Bill Norris is in the foreground, holding the staff. He is flanked by, from left to right, Bill Barksdale, Curtis Cowell, Shirley Norris, W.J. Openshire, Bob Norris, unidentified, and Molly Cowell. (Courtesy of Shirley Ofsa.)

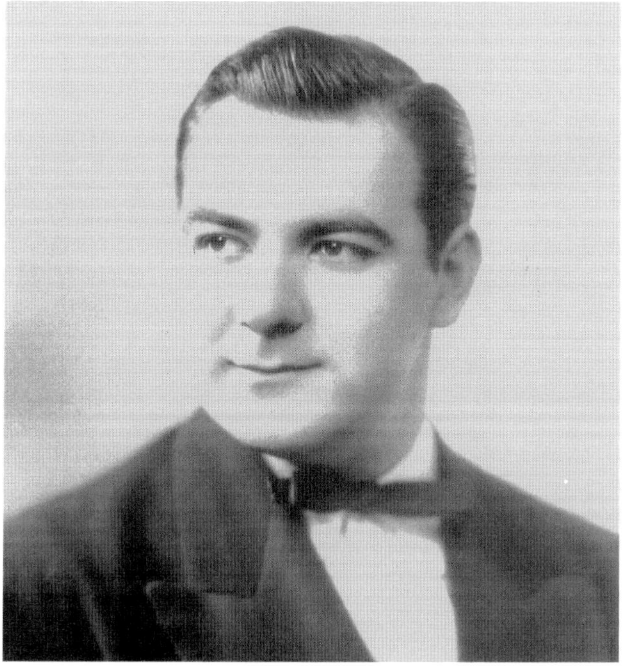

A Star From Afar

Jack Bradley Budnik was a featured performer with Van Keys and his orchestra for a time, but made his mark as a sports announcer, according to Shirley Ofsa. (Courtesy of Shirley Ofsa.)

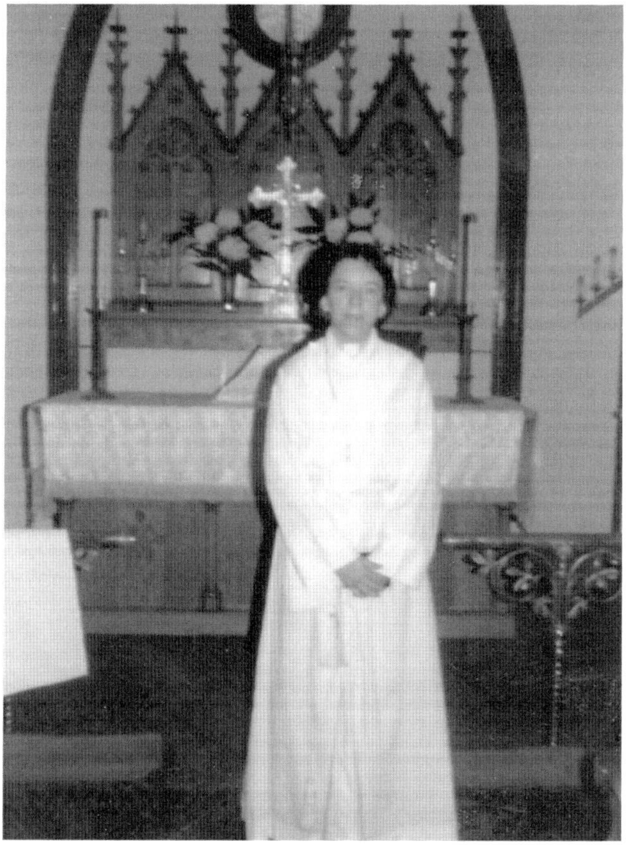

Stormy McDowell

Before pursuing a career as an author/activist, Denise Giardina served as an ordained deacon at Grace Episcopal Church after the church was moved from Eckman to Keystone, West Virginia. A native of Bluefield, she grew up in Black Wolf, McDowell County. Her highly acclaimed novel *Stormy Heaven* draws heavily on her experiences of growing up in a McDowell County coal-mining community. (Courtesy of Shirley Ofsa.)

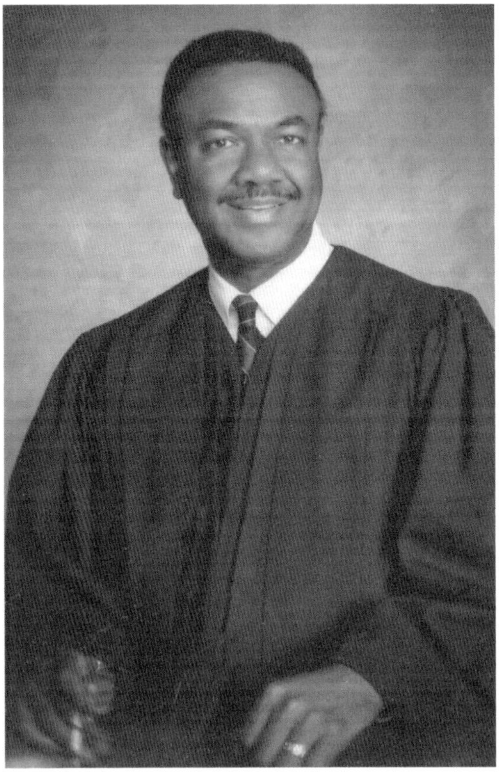

Here Comes the Judge

McDowell County circuit court judge Booker T. Stephens grew up at Warriormines, West Virginia, graduated from Excelsior High School during the segregation era, earned a bachelor's degree from West Virginia State University, and earned his law degree from Howard University. He served two terms in the House of Delegates from McDowell County and was first elected as a circuit court judge in 1984, and he continues to serve in that position. He received the Living the Dream award from West Virginia governor Bob Wise on January 18, 2003. (Courtesy of Booker T. Stephens.)

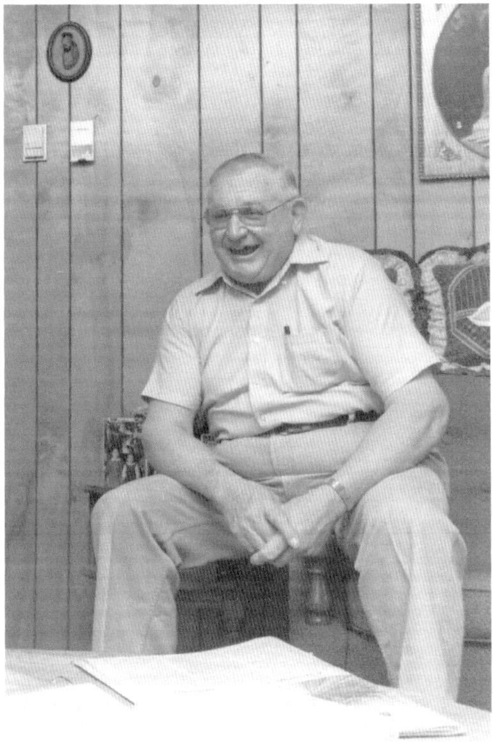

Gary Historian

Mike Hornick spent his career working in the US Steel mines at Gary, West Virginia. His encyclopedic memory of life in the coalfields made him an incredible resource for historians trying to learn about McDowell County. Both of his parents immigrated to the United States from Czechoslovakia, and the coal company changed his father's name from Vazily Hornyak to Wash Hornick to make it easier for the payroll clerk. Hornick shared some of his insights with the West Virginia History Film Project in 1992 before his death. (Photograph by Phil Farmer.)

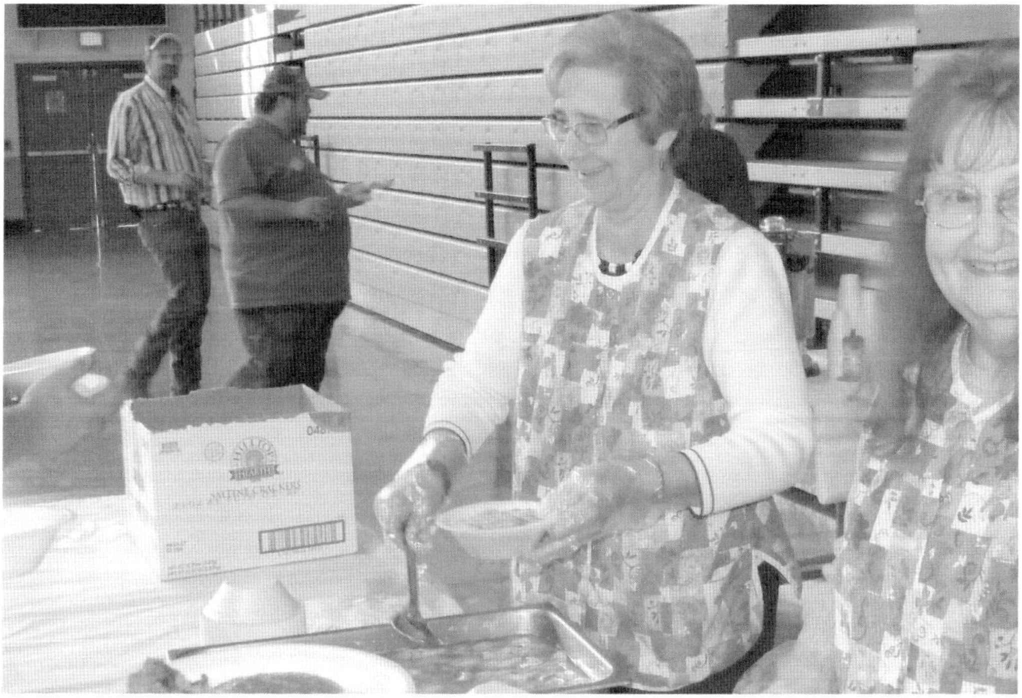

Oyster Dinner

Welch mayor Reba Honaker works in the food service line during the 2012 Welch 40 & 8 Oyster Dinner, an annual event that traditionally draws a huge crowd, especially in an election year. For many years, the dinners were "stag," or men only, events, but Republican congressional candidate Maryanne Brewster shook things up in 1990, and the dinners have been coed ever since. (Photograph by the author.)

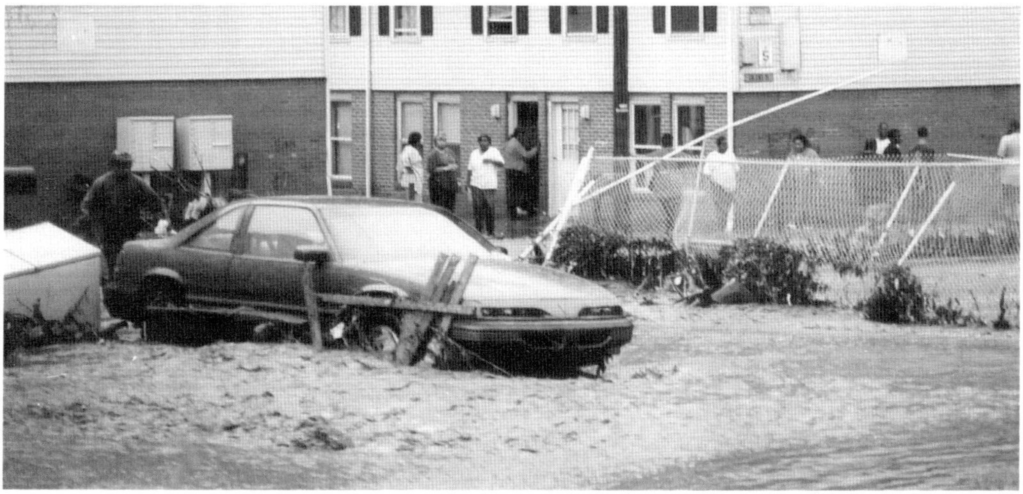

Under Water

The housing development in the Midletown Section of Keystone is shown here during the July 8, 2001, flood that ravaged much of McDowell County. The flood severely reduced the supply of available community housing. The development above had replaced several dilapidated structures in the area of Keystone that was better known as Cinder Bottom. (Photograph by the author.)

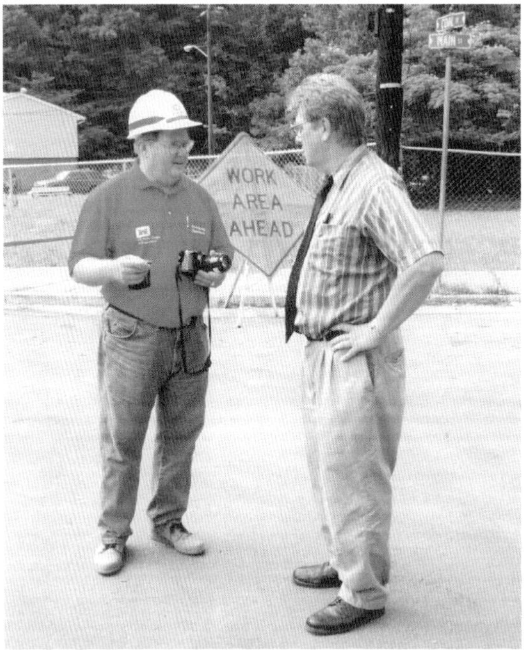

Wright Man for the Job

Steve Wright, a spokesman for the US Army Corps of Engineers (left), talks with the author about the corps' plan to remove dilapidated structures throughout McDowell County following the May 2, 2002, floods that claimed seven lives in the county and caused widespread property damage. This photograph also shows the section of Keystone known as Cinder Bottom. (Courtesy of Tim Hairston.)

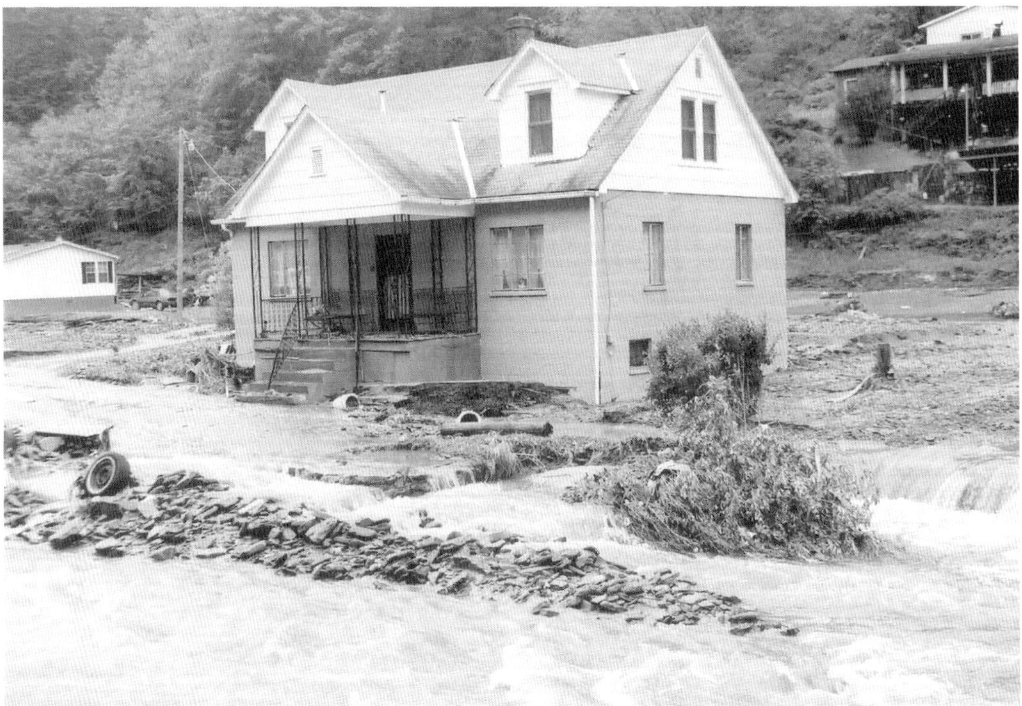

High-water Mark

This home on the northern slope of Premier Mountain was surrounded by water during the May 2, 2002, floods that ravaged McDowell County. While several communities did not experience significant flood damage in the 2001 flood, most McDowell County communities suffered great losses the following year. (Photograph by the author.)

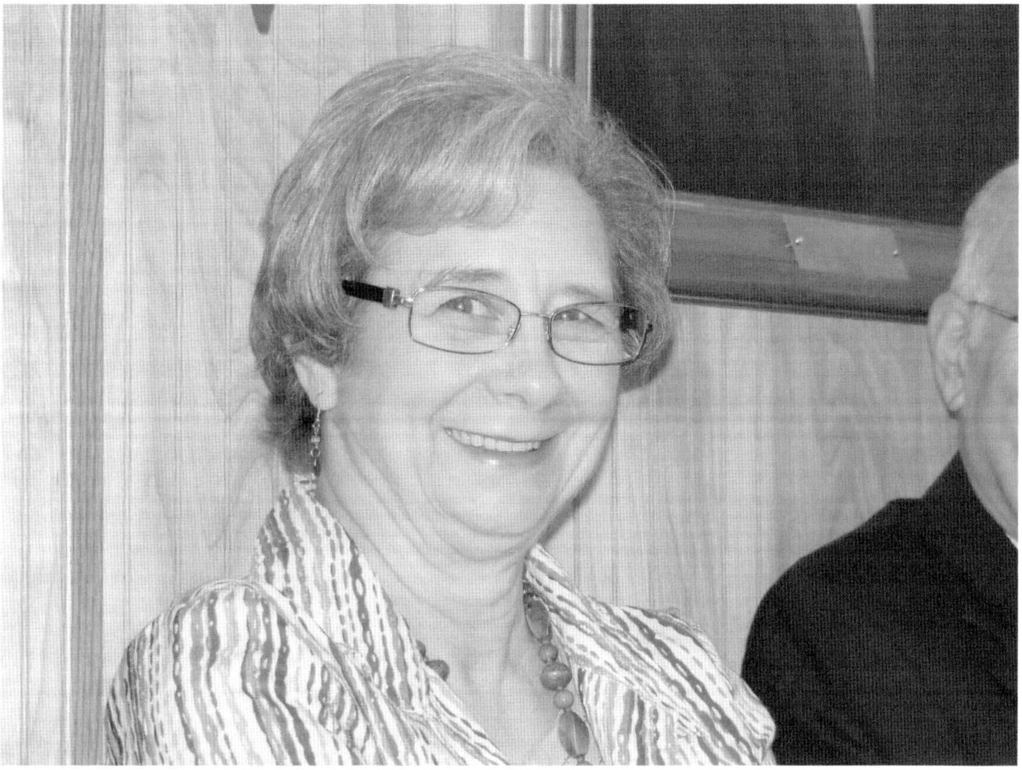

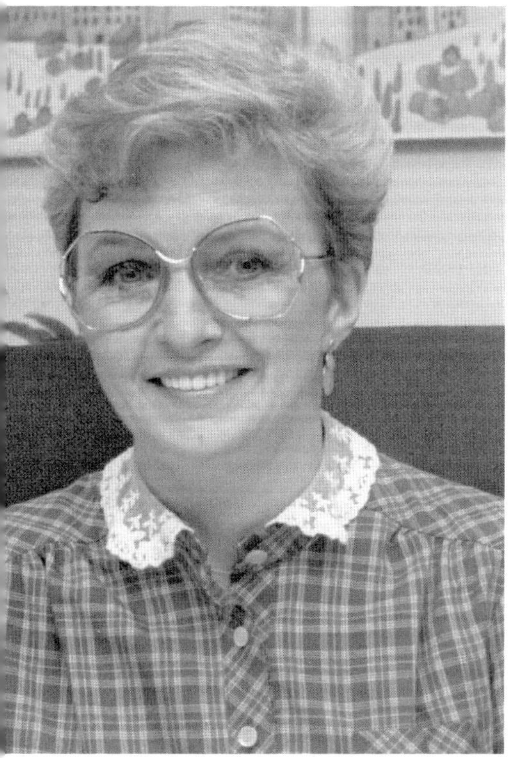

Greeting Adversity with a Smile
Welch mayor Reba Honaker worked as an educator in the McDowell County Public Schools, and later opened a flower shop, Flowers by Reba, on McDowell Street in Welch, where she delivered smiles to her customers. During her time operating a business, she and former Welch mayor Martha Moore worked together to improve the community. Honaker accepted the position of mayor after the death of her friend. (Photograph by the author.)

Longest-serving Mayor
Martha Ann (Hurt) Moore was elected to the Welch City Council in 1984, and within four months was appointed city clerk. She served in that position until 1986, when she was elected mayor—a post she held until her death on October 19, 2010. In 1990, she was selected "Mayor of the Year" by the West Virginia Municipal League, and launched a citywide beautification project that continues to serve as a reminder of her passion for the city she loved. In 2011, the city dedicated the Martha H. Moore Riverside Park on McDowell Street in her memory. (Photograph by the author.)

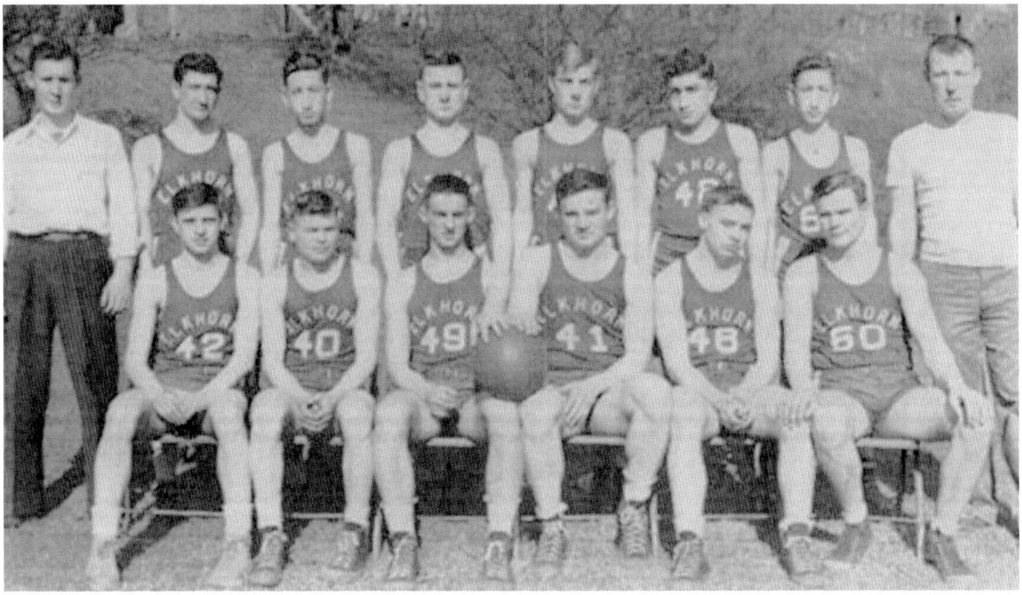

On the Warpath

The 1948 Elkhorn High School Indians basketball team poses for a team photograph. Shown here are, from left to right, (first row) Perry Cunningham, John Baraa, Mike Junip, Eustace Frederick, Allen Coleman, and Burr Musick; (second row) Stan Sharp (manager), Dan LaFon, Raymond Mosko, Buster Hicks, Andy Labosky, David LaFon, unidentified, and Jack Owens (coach). (Courtesy of Gary Dove.)

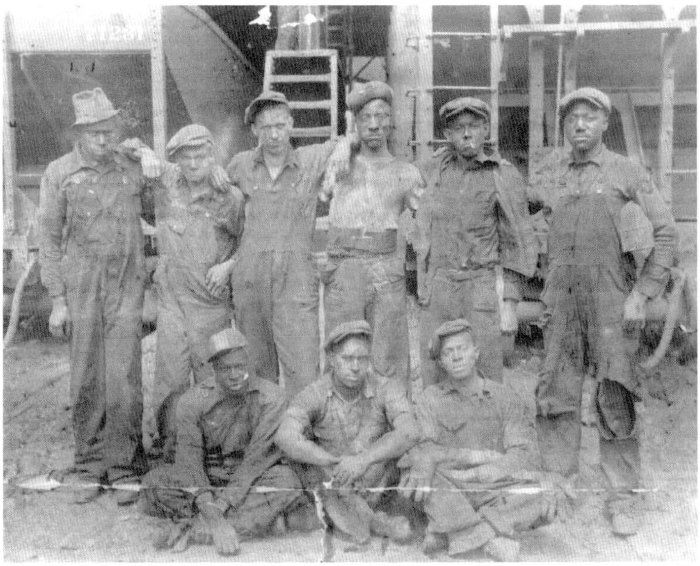

Ready to Work

The "Melting Pot of Nations" came together in McDowell County to form a great workforce and fuel the growth of many cities at home and overseas. Members of the Algoma Coal & Coke Company tipple crew shown here are, from left to right, (first row) Bill Davis, John W. "Jack" Wright, and Otis Pennington; (second row) Bury "Tokie" Thomas, Junior Green, Maynard Pike, Theodore Hale, Hamp Glover, and Herbert Hale. (Courtesy of Randal Wright.)

CHAPTER SIX

Today's Topics

During the first half of the 20th century, McDowell County grew faster than any other county in West Virginia, eventually reaching a population of more than 95,000 residents and ranking among the top five counties in terms of population in 1950. Those lofty figures would not last. Coal-mine mechanization, the end of coal as the fuel of choice for steam locomotives, and big coal companies seeking out new coal seams that were easier to mine, all combined to ignite a massive loss of jobs and a dramatic decline in population, which is now roughly a quarter of what it was at mid-century.

For a time, it seemed as though McDowell County had been absolutely forgotten, as many of her native sons and daughters took the "Hillbilly Highway" into the Carolinas to find work. Employers worldwide soon learned that workers from the Free State of McDowell were dependable, honest, and willing to put in a good day's work for fair pay, and, as a result, people who left the county started new lives elsewhere. Still, the beauty of the mountains and the open, friendly people continued to draw them back.

At the dawn of the 21st century, some subtle changes started taking shape that may soon lead to better times ahead for the county. First, a central core of independent coal operators who knew the industry and understood the coal seams kept working to develop new markets for metallurgical coal and provide jobs for coal miners and support industries. Eventually, the whole world caught on to the special steel-making properties of coal from McDowell County, and foreign countries, including Russia and India, have a major presence in McDowell County, as do several major US corporations.

But coal is only one side of the growth potential for the county. The late US senator Robert C. Byrd spent a great deal of effort to bring the Federal Prison Camp McDowell to Welch, West Virginia. At the same time, four-wheeler riders had already found the trails of McDowell County to their liking. And now, the Hatfield-McCoy Trail System has an extensive presence in McDowell County, with budding entrepreneurs starting to redefine success in a changing recreational activity environment.

Even with the positive potential on the horizon, there is a great deal of history yet to be uncovered around every bend in the road and through every hollow. As mining companies repair the scars of the past, new legends are being born as people work to redefine the future of McDowell County.

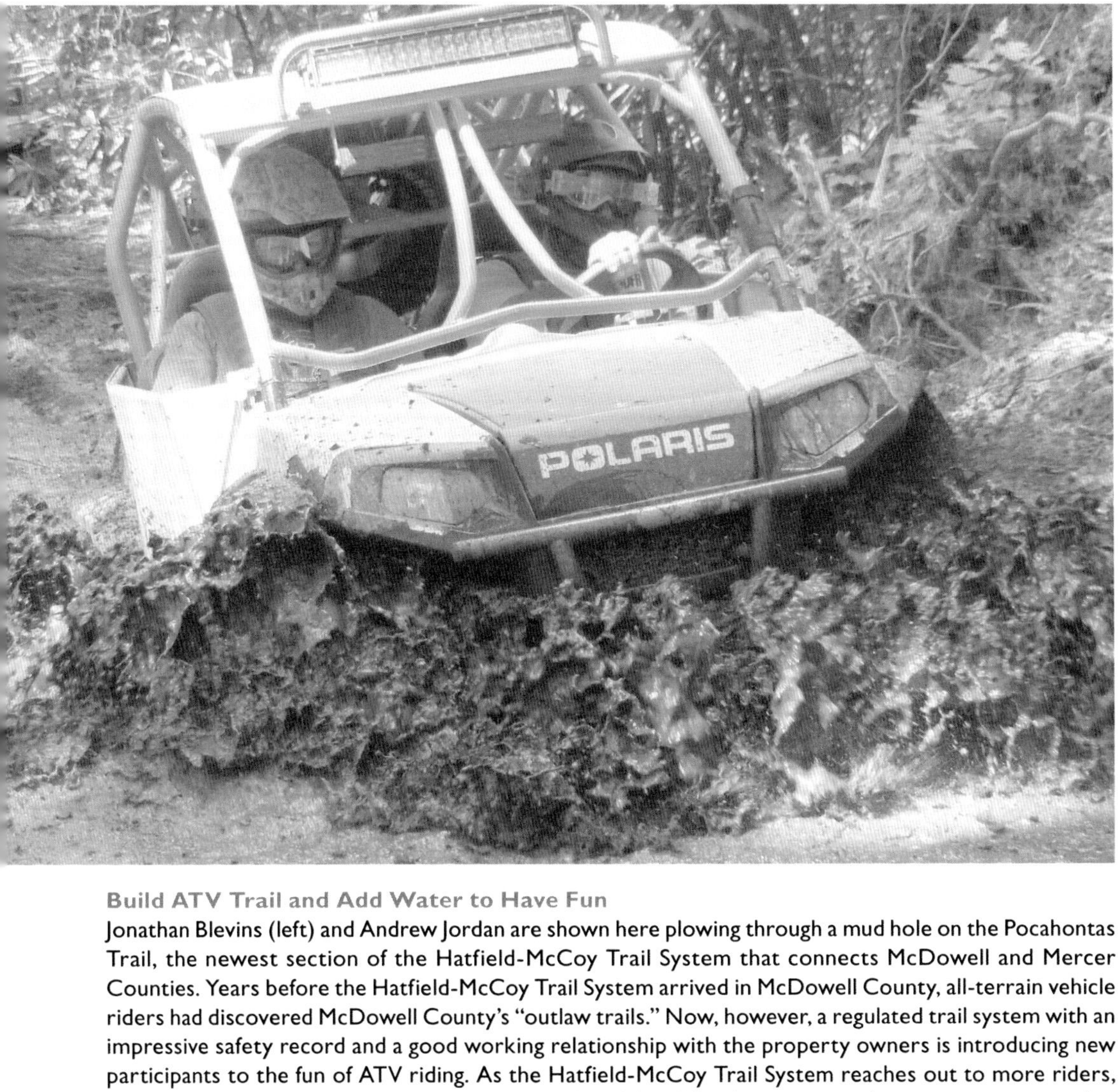

Build ATV Trail and Add Water to Have Fun

Jonathan Blevins (left) and Andrew Jordan are shown here plowing through a mud hole on the Pocahontas Trail, the newest section of the Hatfield-McCoy Trail System that connects McDowell and Mercer Counties. Years before the Hatfield-McCoy Trail System arrived in McDowell County, all-terrain vehicle riders had discovered McDowell County's "outlaw trails." Now, however, a regulated trail system with an impressive safety record and a good working relationship with the property owners is introducing new participants to the fun of ATV riding. As the Hatfield-McCoy Trail System reaches out to more riders, the state encourages local residents to open bed-and-breakfast businesses and convenience stores that cater to ATV riders. In addition, investors are opening new lodging areas to serve the riding public. As John Fekete, assistant director of the Hatfield-McCoy Trail System, said, build the trail, "and just add water" to watch the riders come to a new trail site. (Photograph by the author.)

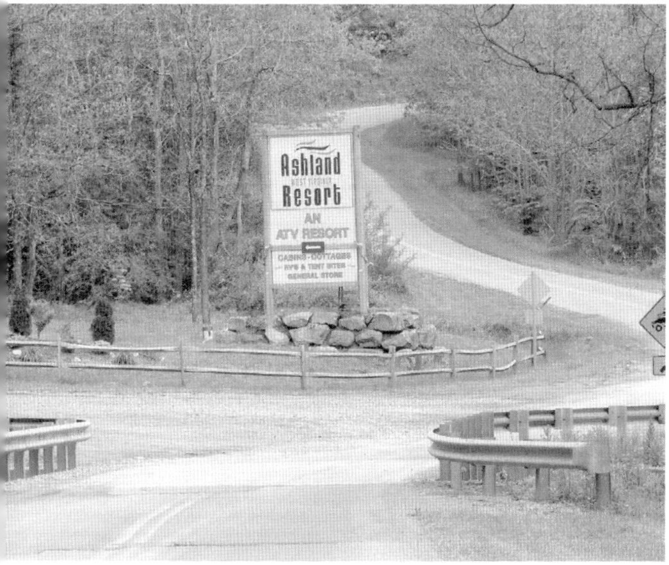

The First Resort

Even before the arrival of the Hatfield-McCoy Trail System, developer Ken Bazzle started working with Sharon Walden of SAFE Housing and Economic Development to develop a site on the trail system that could provide lodging and necessities for the hundreds of visitors to McDowell County. The Ashland Resort combines a rustic exterior with modern conveniences to serve the ATV-riding public. (Photograph by the author.)

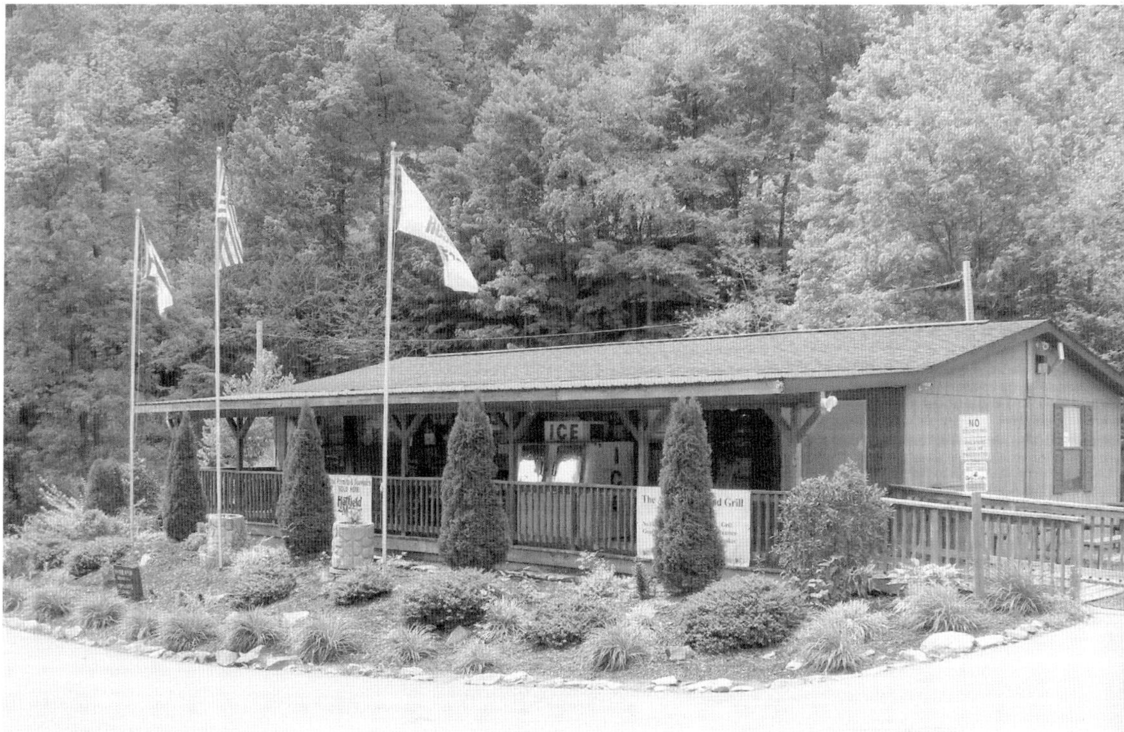

Communitywide Impact

The Ashland Resort operates a convenience store that meets the needs of the ATV riders. Along with bringing jobs into McDowell County, the Ashland Resort worked with the residents of Ashland, as well as several local, state, and federal government agencies to develop a creative sewage waste water system that purifies the waste water by pumping it 357 feet up a mountain, into three settling ponds on a reclaimed surface mine site. In this way, an artificial wetlands is created that further purifies the water. (Photograph by the author.)

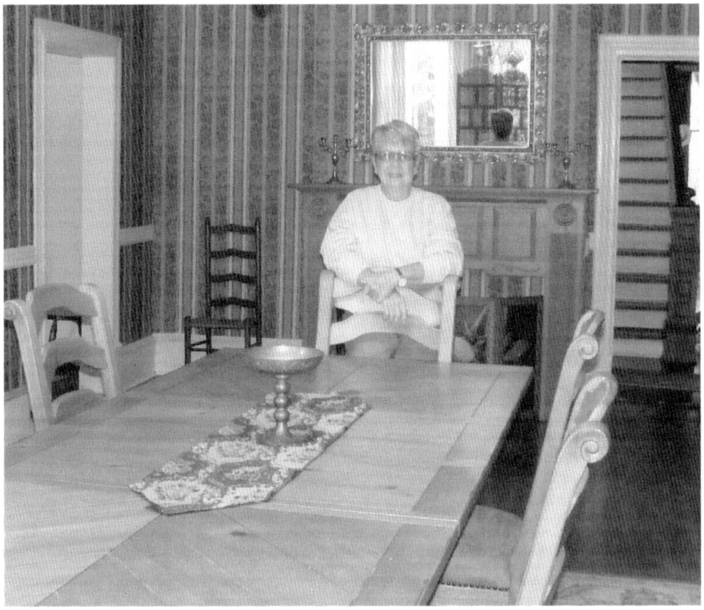

Me and Mister Jones
Judy McDaniel is shown here in the formal dining room of her bed-and-breakfast, located in the James Ellwood Jones mansion on Powerhouse Hill in Switchback, West Virginia. McDaniel's mother, Grace Haynes, bought the mansion at a McDowell County sheriff's sale in the mid-1950s. McDaniel has also transformed the former gardener's residence into a bunkhouse for ATV riders. The bed-and-breakfast is called Me and Mr. Jones. (Photograph by the author.)

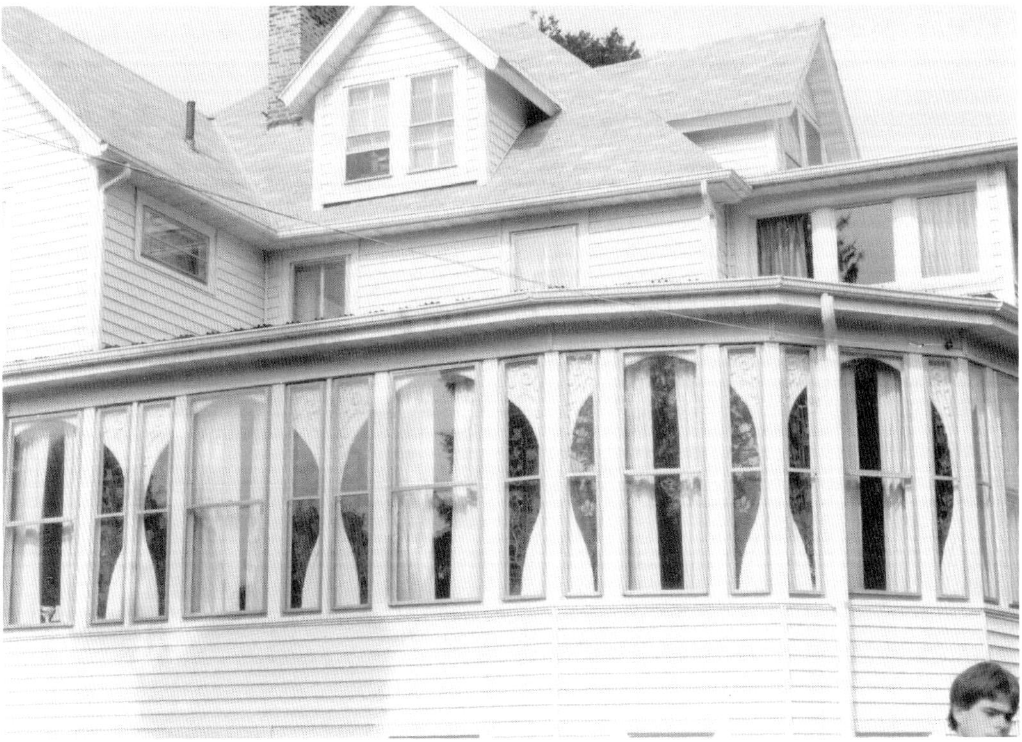

A Home on the Hill
The James Ellwood Jones home on Powerhouse Hill in Switchback includes a C-shaped main room with tongue-and-groove ceilings and floors and 66 stained-glass windows imported from Scotland. Jones, the last and most powerful coal baron of the southern West Virginia coalfields, had 25 coal mines under his supervision and five mining operations that he could see from his backyard. (Photograph by Evonda Archer.)

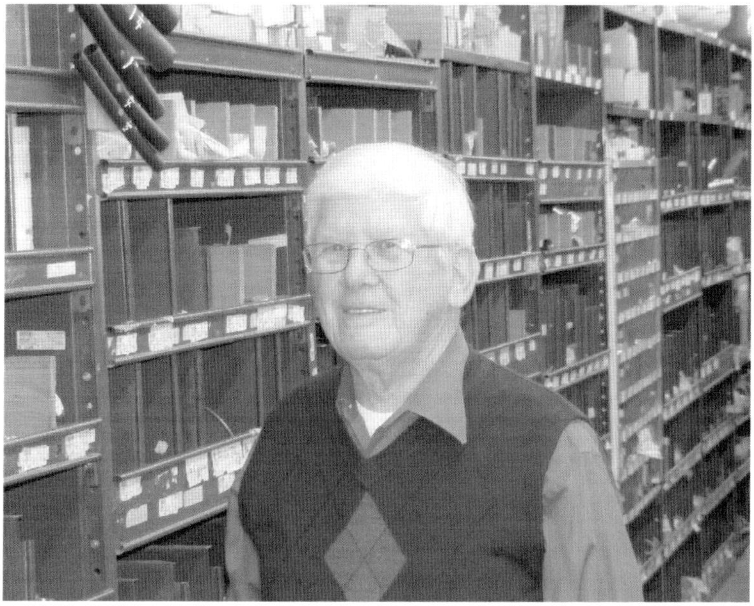

Jimmy's Hardware
Jimmy Hampton operated a grocery store in McDowell County for a time, but his business eventually evolved, and he opened Jimmy's Hardware in Roderfield in 1993. Hampton graduated from Welch High School in 1952. (Photograph by the author.)

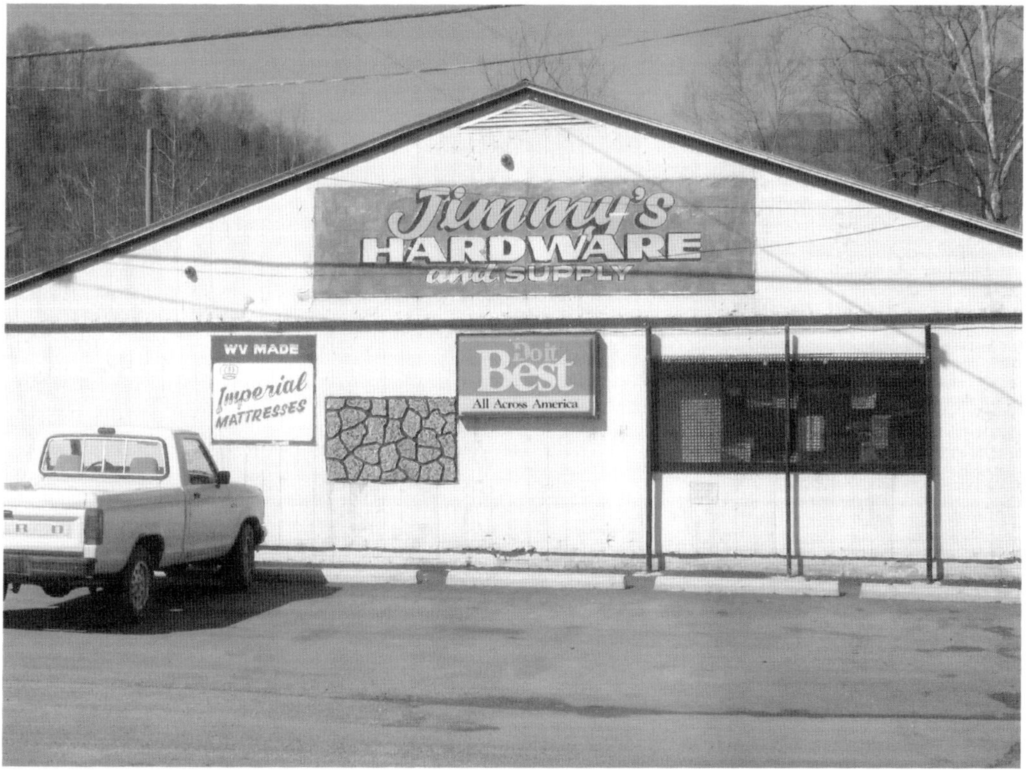

The Store You've Known for All These Years
After he closed his grocery store to concentrate on the hardware business, Jimmy Hampton also started carrying appliances. The store is strategically located on US Route 52 between Welch and Iaeger, West Virginia, and always seems to stay busy. (Photograph by the author.)

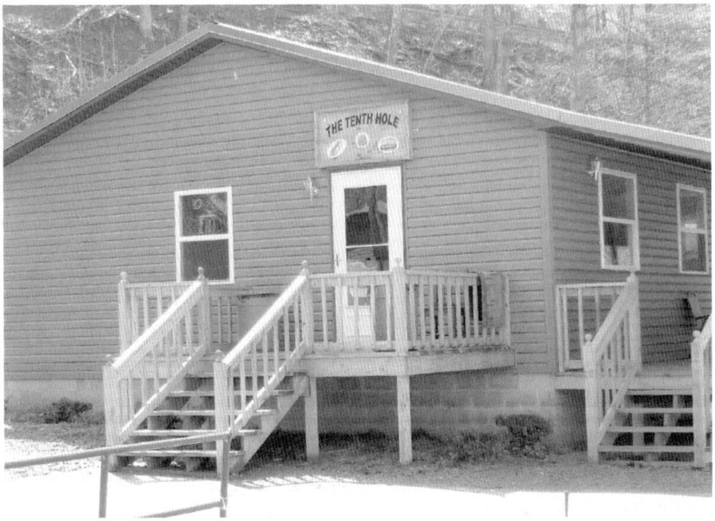

Economic Development Project
The McDowell County Economic Development Authority (EDA) built and provided the appliances and furnishings for the Tenth Hole Restaurant as a way to encourage more activity around the EDA's Black Wolf Golf Course in Skygusty, West Virginia. (Photograph by the author.)

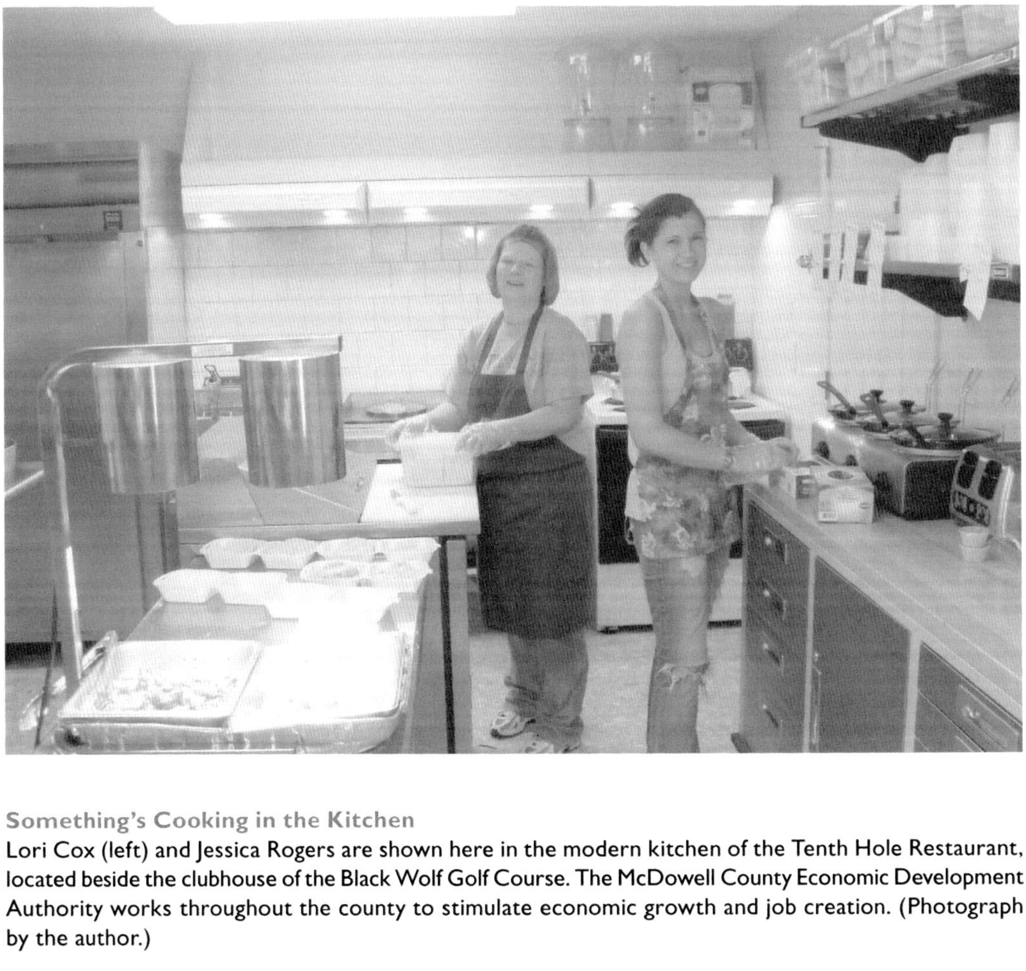

Something's Cooking in the Kitchen
Lori Cox (left) and Jessica Rogers are shown here in the modern kitchen of the Tenth Hole Restaurant, located beside the clubhouse of the Black Wolf Golf Course. The McDowell County Economic Development Authority works throughout the county to stimulate economic growth and job creation. (Photograph by the author.)

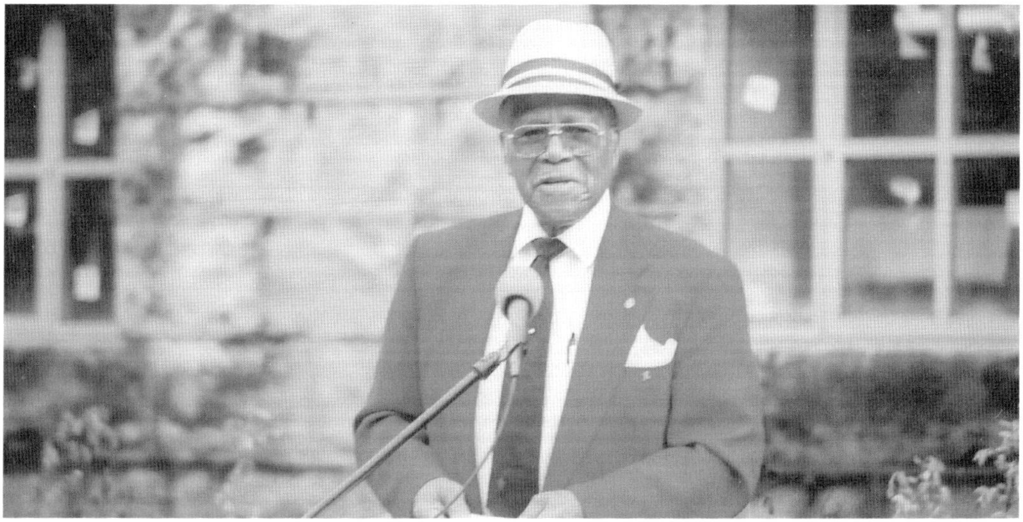

Lifelong Commitment to Veterans
Ellis Ray Williams is shown here in front of the Kimball War Memorial building before reconstruction of the memorial got under way. The McDowell County Museum Commission started working to restore the structure in 1980, but the job didn't really take flight until Sen. Robert C. Byrd took a personal interest in the project. (Photograph by the author.)

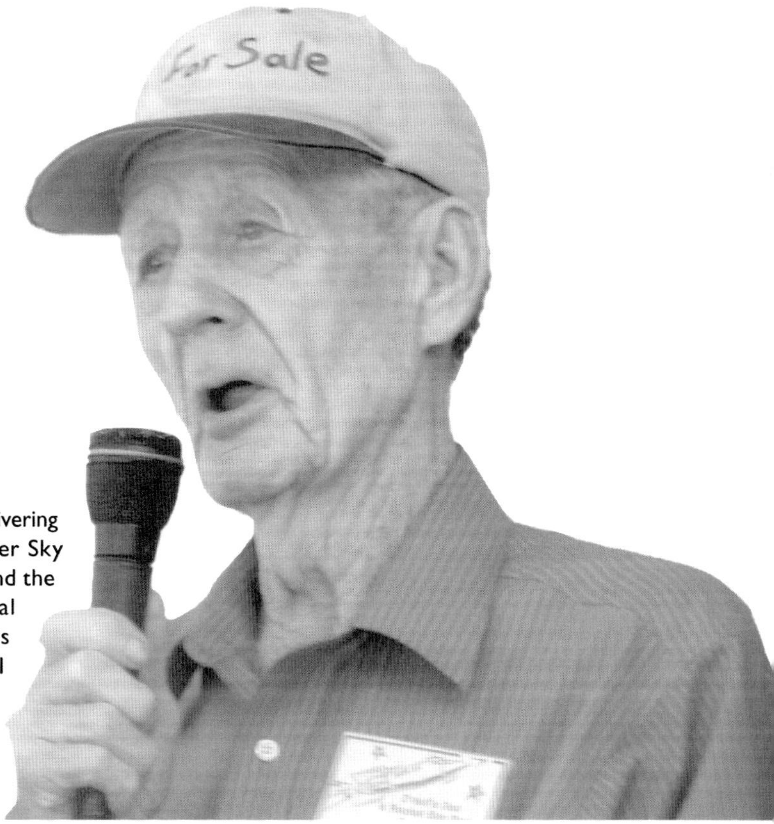

Red
Ernest "Red" Carroll, shown here delivering a prayer to open the 2010 October Sky Festival, was the driving force behind the Coalwood, West Virginia, festival from its inception in 1999 until his death on January 8, 2011. The 2011 festival went on in Coalwood as planned, but early in 2012, Homer Hickam announced that the 2012 festival would be held in Beckley. (Photograph by the author.)

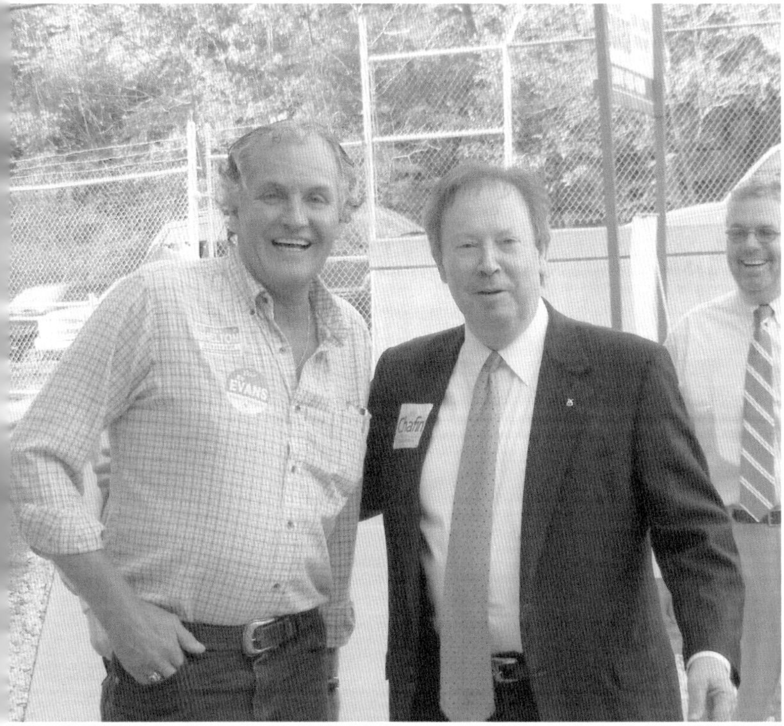

Celebration at the Welch Armory

McDowell coal man Eddie Asbury (left) and state senator H. Truman Chafin are shown here walking into the National Guard Armory in Welch for the annual 40 & 8 Oyster Dinner. Asbury, from Anawalt, West Virginia, is a highly respected coal operator. Chafin is from Mingo County and has served in the state senate since 1982. He was the senate majority leader from 1998 to 2010. Harold McBride, a member of the McDowell County Commission, is in the background. (Photograph by the author.)

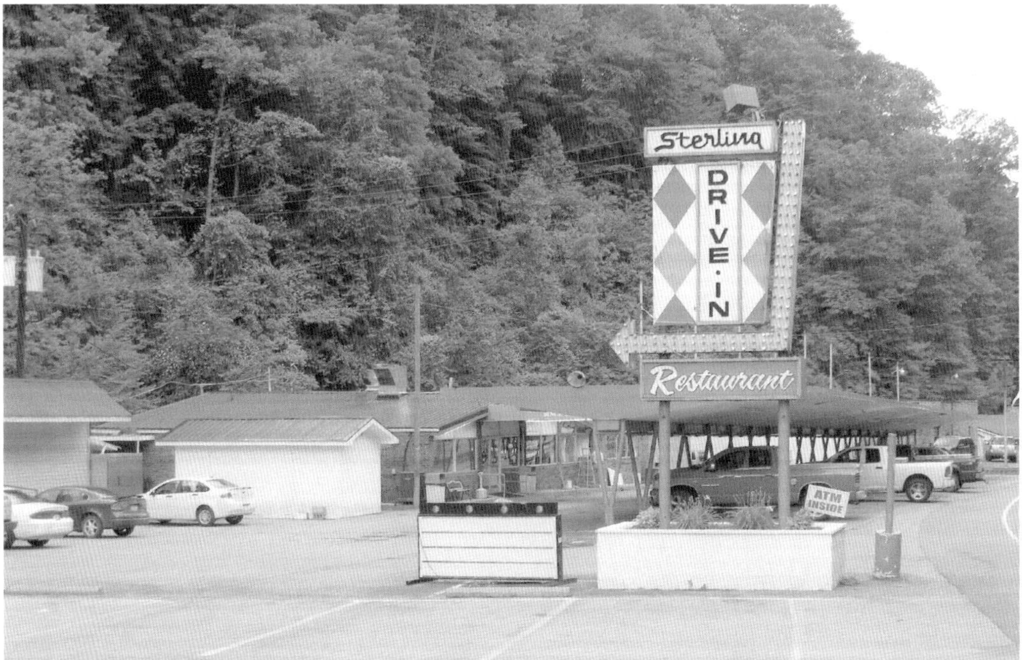

Sterling Drive-In

The Sterling Drive-In, located on Stewart Street in Welch, is one of the region's oldest continuously operating drive-in restaurants. Commissioner Harold McBride recently acquired the restaurant and is in the process of a modernization project. However, the curb service remains. (Photograph by the author.)

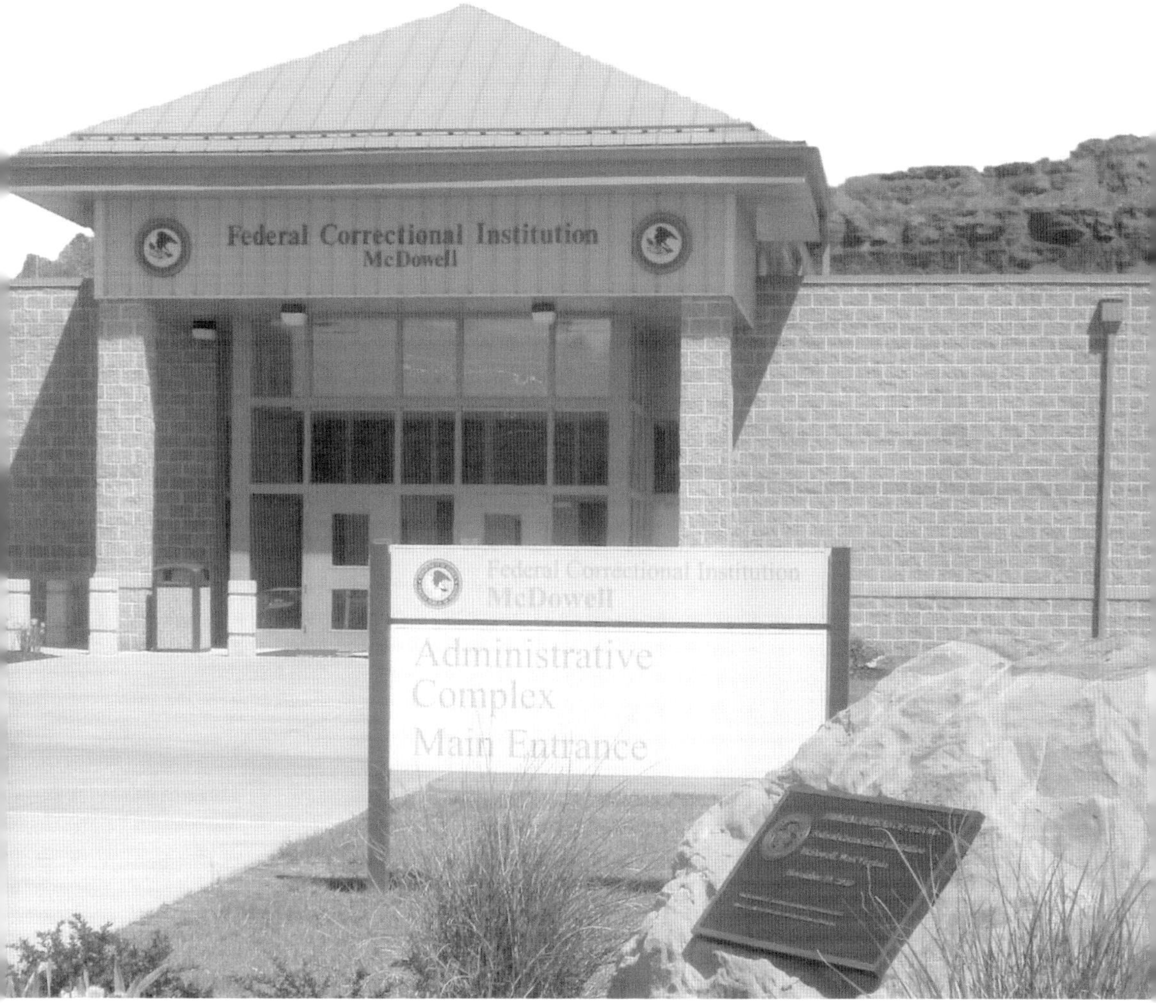

The Big House

The Federal Correctional Institution McDowell was brought to reality with the steadfast support of the late US senator Robert C. Byrd, along with many other individuals and organizations committed to McDowell County. Helping to secure the institution's establishment were state senator Richard Browning, executive director of the Coalfields Expressway Authority; the McDowell County Commission; local coal operators; Jack Caffrey of Welch; the late Welch mayor Martha Moore; and other like-minded community leaders. The medium-security federal prison, which houses male offenders, is located about four miles north of the city of Welch and has brought hundreds of jobs into the coalfields of southern West Virginia. The immediate benefits of new jobs and the expansion of the community's tax base are impressive, but other, longer-term benefits, such as the potential growth in housing for federal employees, motel-style facilities for inmate visitors, and a boost to local restaurants and other service-related businesses, is starting to make a difference. City water service and sewer infrastructure has improved as well. Most important, the Federal Bureau of Prisons staff has been searching for ways that inmates can make a positive contribution to the region through programs supporting the McDowell County Humane Society. (Courtesy of FCI McDowell.)

Ready to Rock 'n Roll

David Cline, shown here on the four-wheeler he rides between his home, shop, and coal mine operations in Bull Creek, West Virginia, started Rock-N-Roll Coal with a credit card and a dream. He has built the business into a very successful, environmentally sensitive, and safe underground coal-mining company that provides jobs in western McDowell County. (Photograph by the author.)

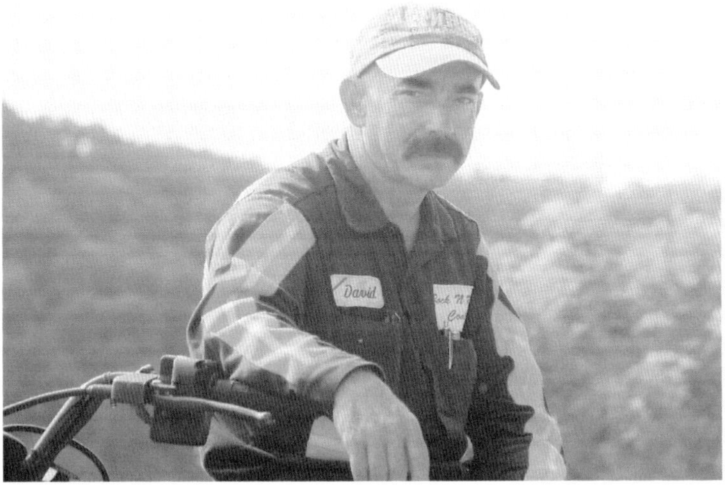

In it for the Long Haul

Dewayne Dotson of Bradshaw, West Virginia, is one of a group of 20-something entrepreneurs who see opportunities in the coal industry that others may have overlooked. After completing a degree in mining engineering and working in underground coal mines, Dotson saw the potential for building a trucking business to haul coal from small mines to preparation plants. He made his first million dollars before his 26th birthday. He is also a certified safety instructor for coal miners. (Photograph by the author.)

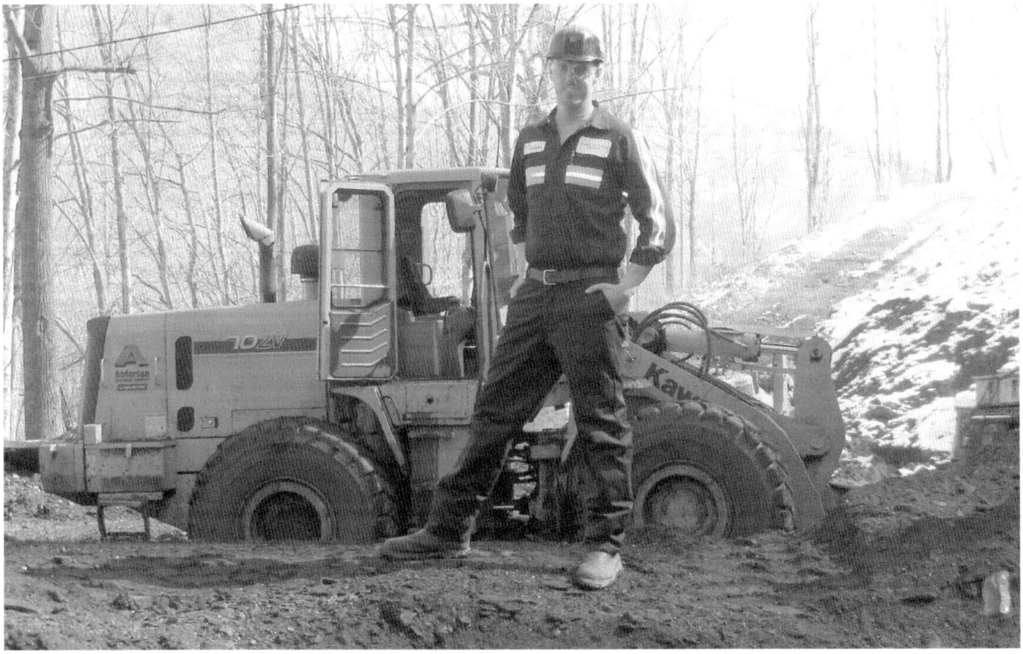

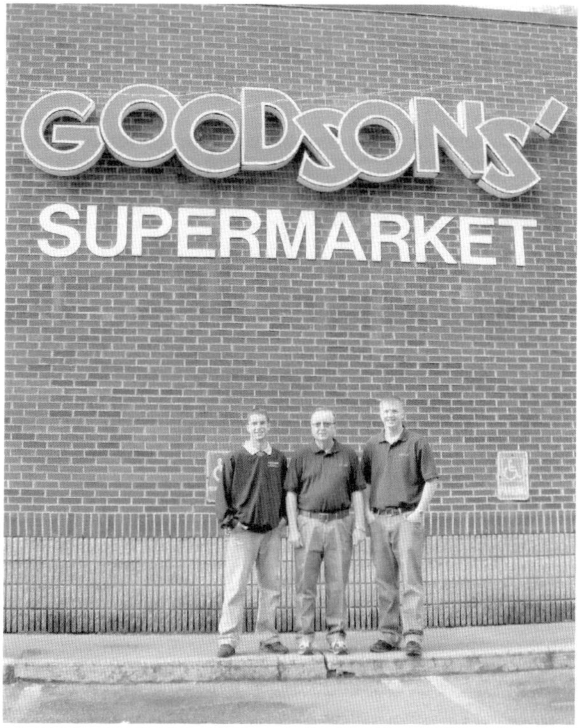

Three to Make Ready

The Goodsons' Supermarket in Junior Poca, near Welch, has been one of McDowell County's most successful businesses since it opened its first store in Davy, West Virginia, in 1904. Jeff Goodson (center) is shown here with his sons, Kevin (left) and Jerry at the store on US Route 52, about two miles north of Welch. (Photograph by the author.)

All in the Family

The Goodson family continues to meet the region's grocery needs. The business started in Davy, West Virginia, moved to a location on Wyoming Street in Welch, and is now in Junior Poca, West Virginia. Shown here are, from left to right, (seated) Margaret "Birdie" Goodson and Wanless Goodson; (standing) Jerry, Kevin, Jeff, Todd, Don, and Paul Goodson. (Courtesy of Goodson's Supermarket.)

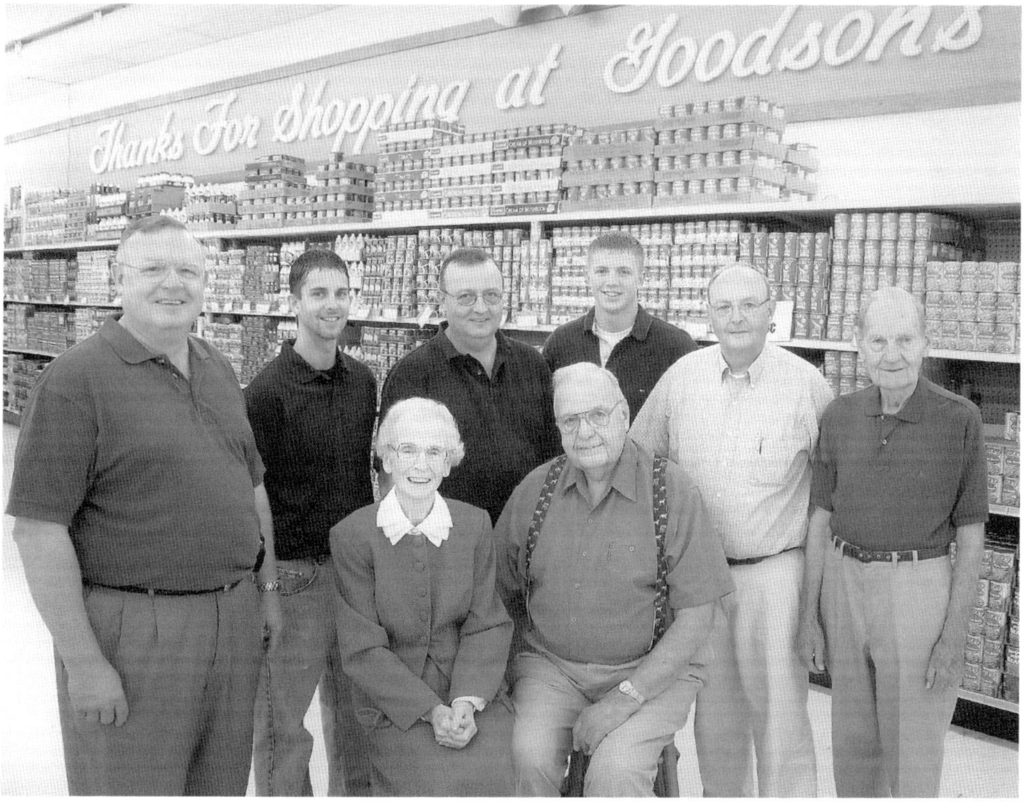

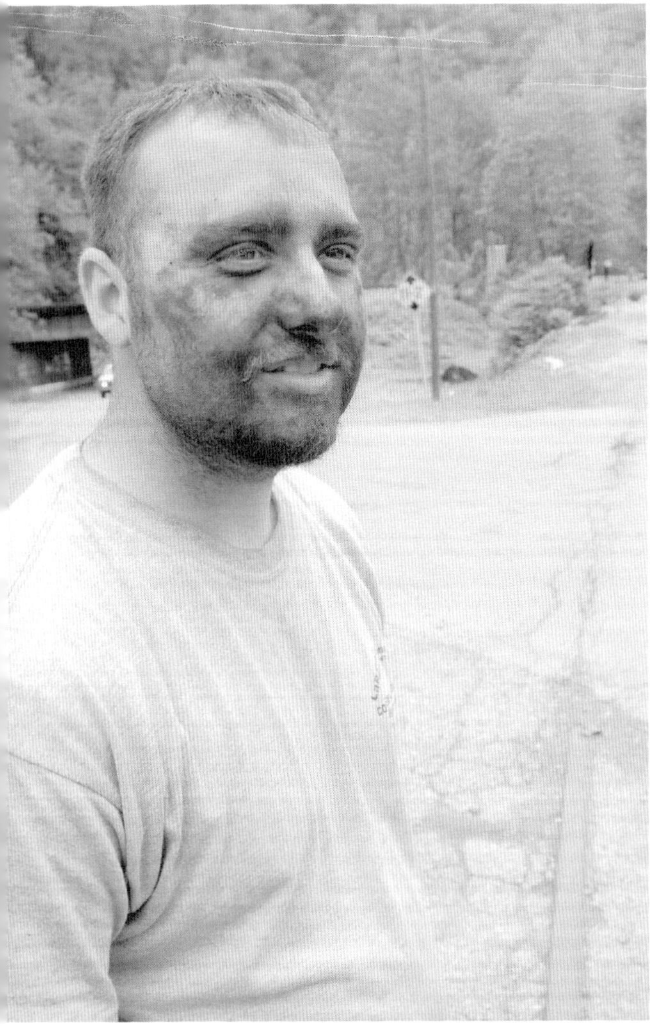

The Face of Coal

Jonathan Dotson is shown here after finishing his shift in Cobalt Coal's Westchester Mine near Big Sandy, West Virginia. Dotson works as a roof bolter at the mine, which became nationally known when Thom Beers and his Original Productions team filmed the operations for a ten-part series on Spike TV called *Coal*. (Photograph by Eric DiNovo.)

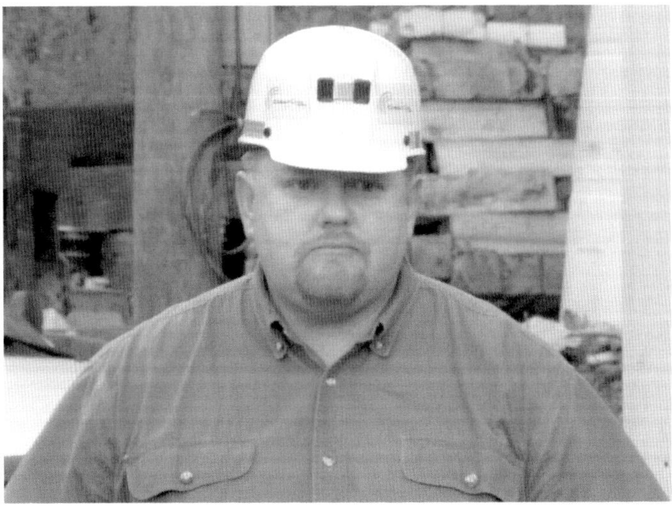

Coal Man

Mike Crowder, chief executive officer of Cobalt Coal, learned a great deal about coal mining during his experiences working to start a coal mine from scratch and from the exposure—good and bad—that came with being seen every week on national television. Spike TV did not pick up *Coal* for a second season, but Cobalt Coal is still mining Sewell Seam coal. (Photograph by the author.)

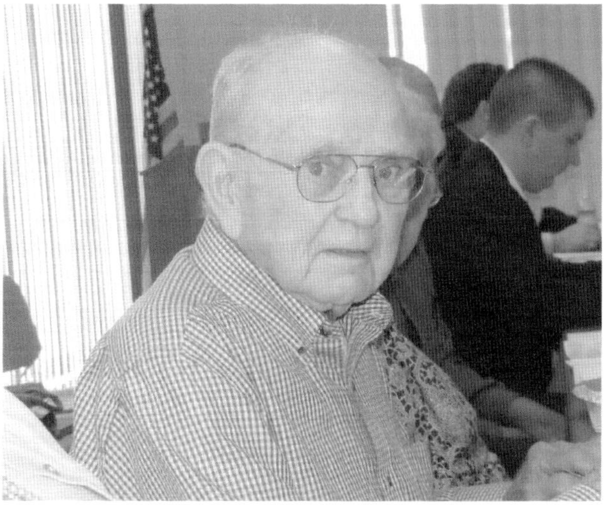

Dedicated to McDowell County
Jack Caffrey came to work for US Steel Coal Company as a coal-mining engineer and helped usher in a new age of regional coal mining through his work to start the Pinnacle Mine, now owned and operated by Cleveland-Cliffs, near the McDowell-Wyoming county border in Pineville, West Virginia. After he retired, Caffrey jumped into community service work and continues to serve McDowell County. (Photograph by the author.)

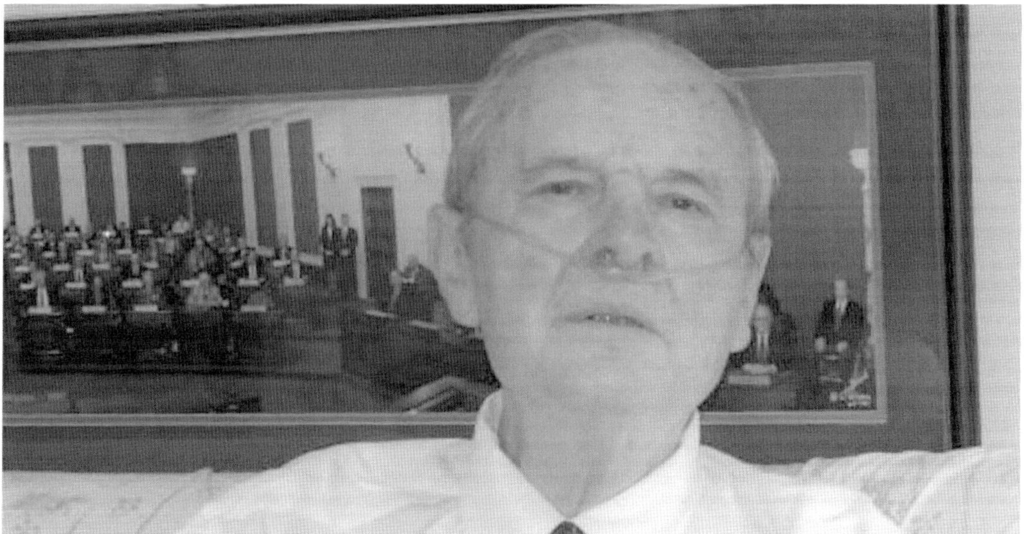

Champion of the Coal Industry
State delegate Eustace Frederick, shown here during an interview a few months before his death on November 6, 2008, was dedicated to coal-mine safety. His career in the coal industry began when he was a student at Virginia Tech in the 1950s, and continued through his 40-year career with Consol. That same commitment to coal-mine safety didn't stop during his 15 years of service in the West Virginia House of Delegates. Frederick was 78 when he died of a respiratory-related disease. (Photograph by the author.)

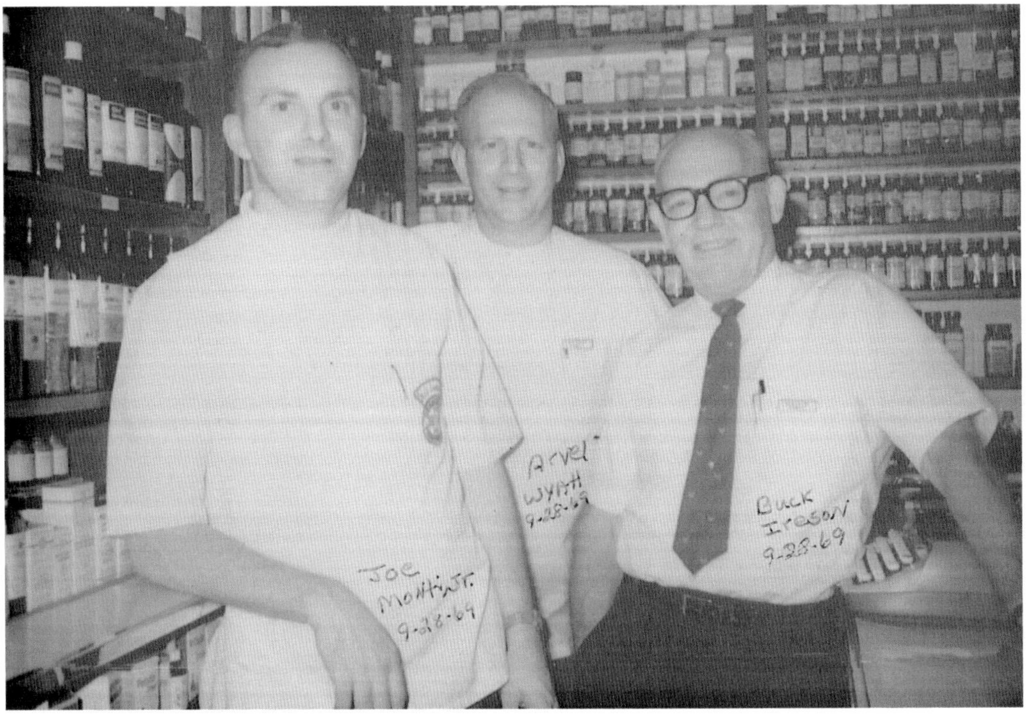

Here to Serve

Joe Monti Jr. (left), Arvel Wyatt (center), and Buck Ireson pose for a photograph on September 28, 1969, in the Flat Iron Drug Store on McDowell Street in downtown Welch. The old Flat Iron building had served as a saloon before it was transformed into a drug store. (Courtesy of Joe Monti.)

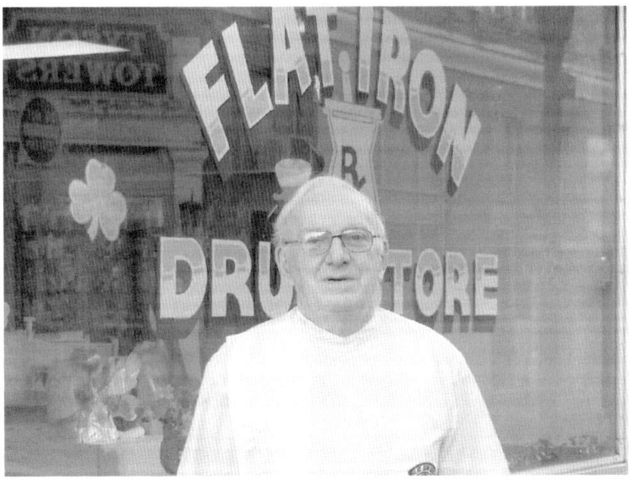

Still the One

Joe Monti poses in front of his business in downtown Welch, West Virginia. Like all of the McDowell Street businesses, the Flat Iron Drug Store was swamped by water, mud, and debris during floods on July 8, 2001, and May 2, 2002. Monti and his staff, however, didn't throw in the towel and quit. Faithful West Virginia University Mountaineer fans, Monti, his staff, family, and friends kept the business going through hard times, and it remains a busy and important business in the community. (Photograph by the author.)

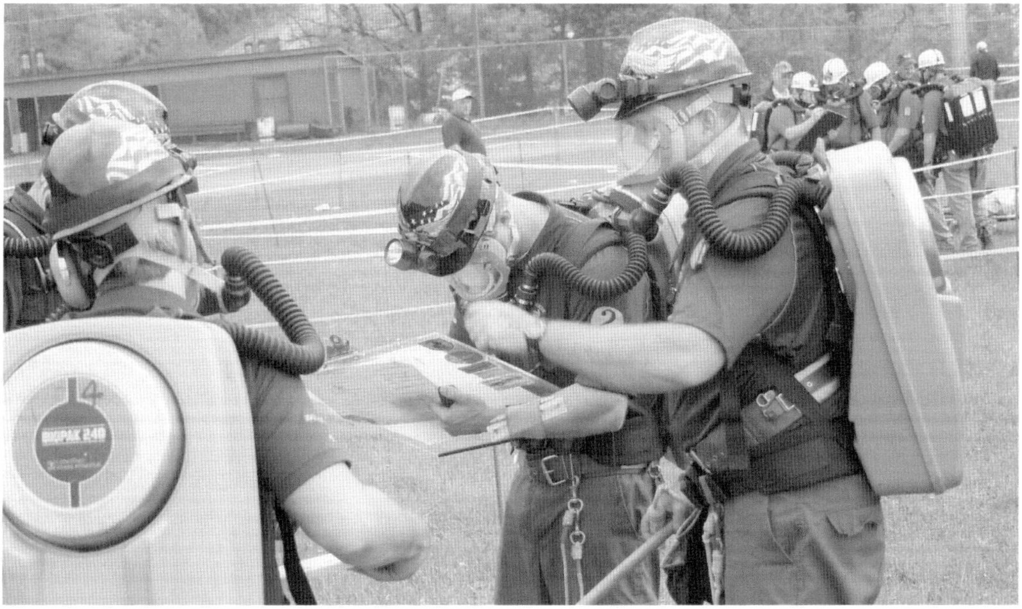

Coal Miners to the Rescue
Welch is home to the Smoke Eaters, Post No. 1 of the National Mine Rescue Association. The Smoke Eaters host an annual mine rescue team competition on the Bluefield State College campus in Bluefield, West Virginia. A mine rescue team from Consol Energy is shown here participating in the competition in 2011. (Photograph by Eric DiNovo.)

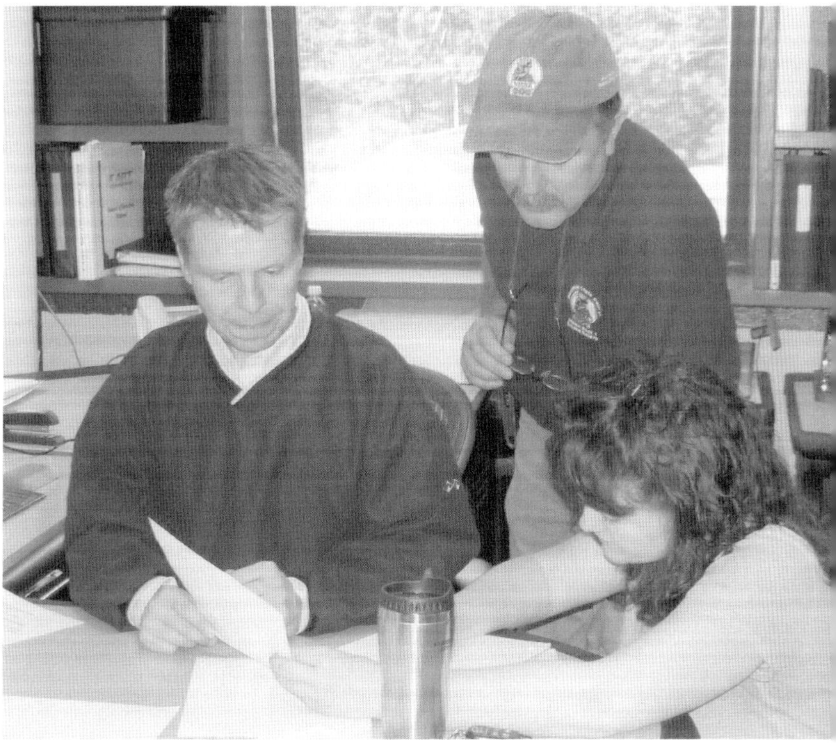

Work Detail
Mike Plumley (standing), director of the Welch Post No. 1 mine rescue competition, is shown here going over the problems the miners will encounter with Bruce Mutter (left) and Heather Williams of the Bluefield State College Center for Applied Research and Technology. The competitions help keep mine rescue teams sharp in the event of a mine explosion anywhere in the coalfields. (Photograph by the author.)

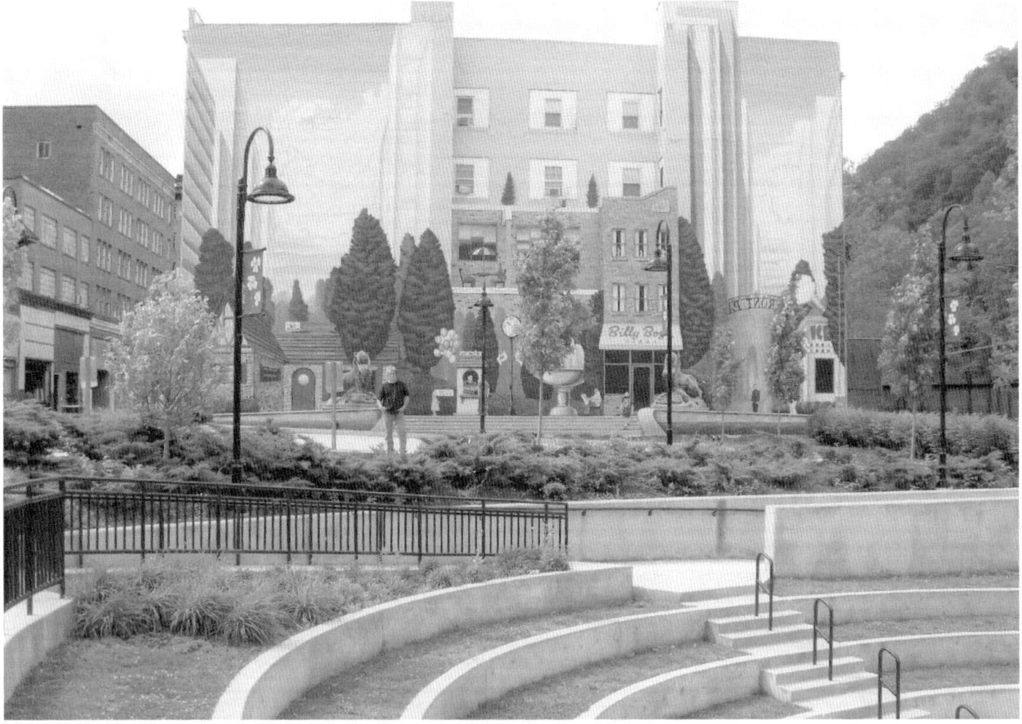

Work of Art

Tom Acosta stands in front of another of his murals—this one on McDowell Street in Welch, West Virginia. The theater in the foreground is part of the Martha H. Moore Riverside Park complex, named in honor of longtime Welch mayor Martha Moore. (Photograph by the author.)

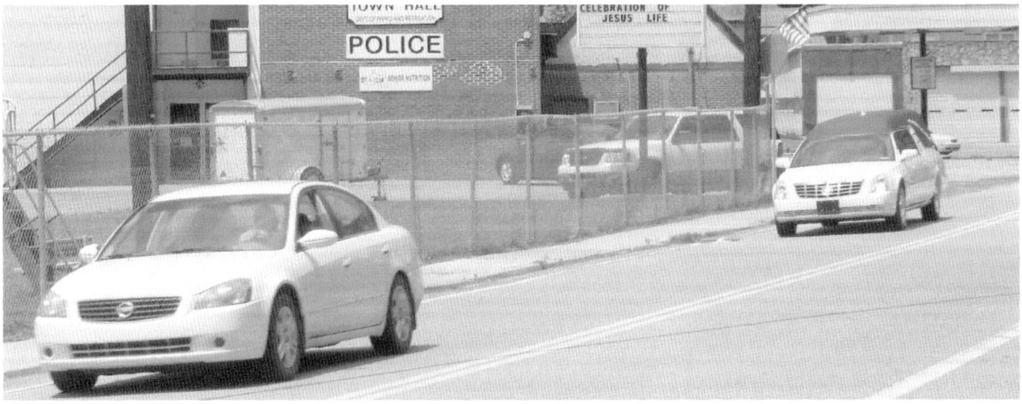

Home Going

A hearse transported Pastor Mark Randall Wolford from his funeral service at the Apostolic House of the Lord Jesus in Matoaka, West Virginia, to the Wolford family cemetery in Pike County, Kentucky, on June 2, 2012. Pastor Wolford died after suffering a rattlesnake bite during a religious service at Panther State Park on May 27, 2012. His father, Mack Wolford, also died after receiving a rattlesnake bite, on August 28, 1983, at the Lord Jesus Temple in Mile Branch near Iaeger, West Virginia. The Wolfords were members of a church that thinks true believers can handle poisonous snakes and get bitten without being harmed. (Photograph by the author.)

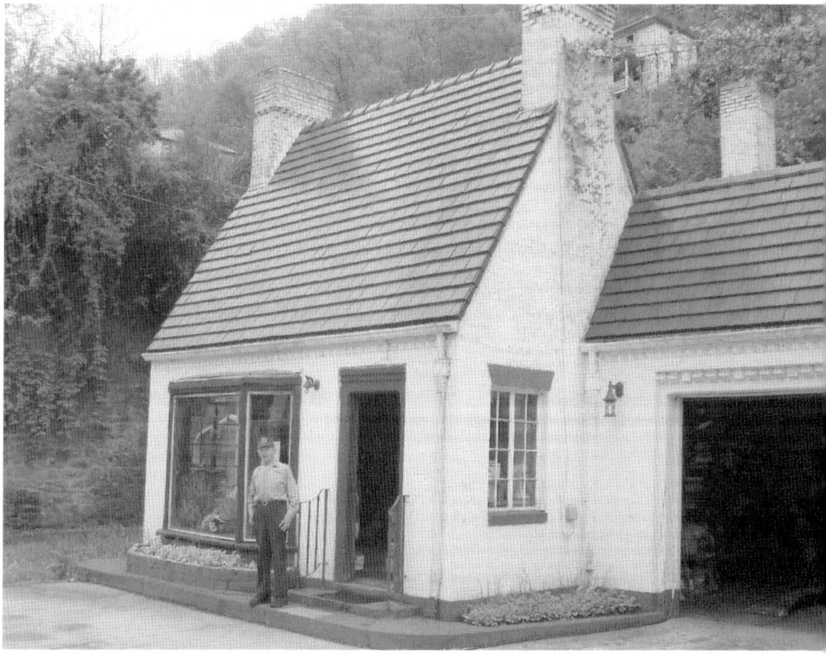

Dedicated to Business
Ed Shepard is shown standing in front of the service station where he has worked every day since he bought it in the 1950s. Pure Oil gave the station its look in 1953, and Union 76 continued that look when it acquired Pure Oil. Shepard hasn't sold gas at the station for years, but he continues to serve customers. (Photograph by the author.)

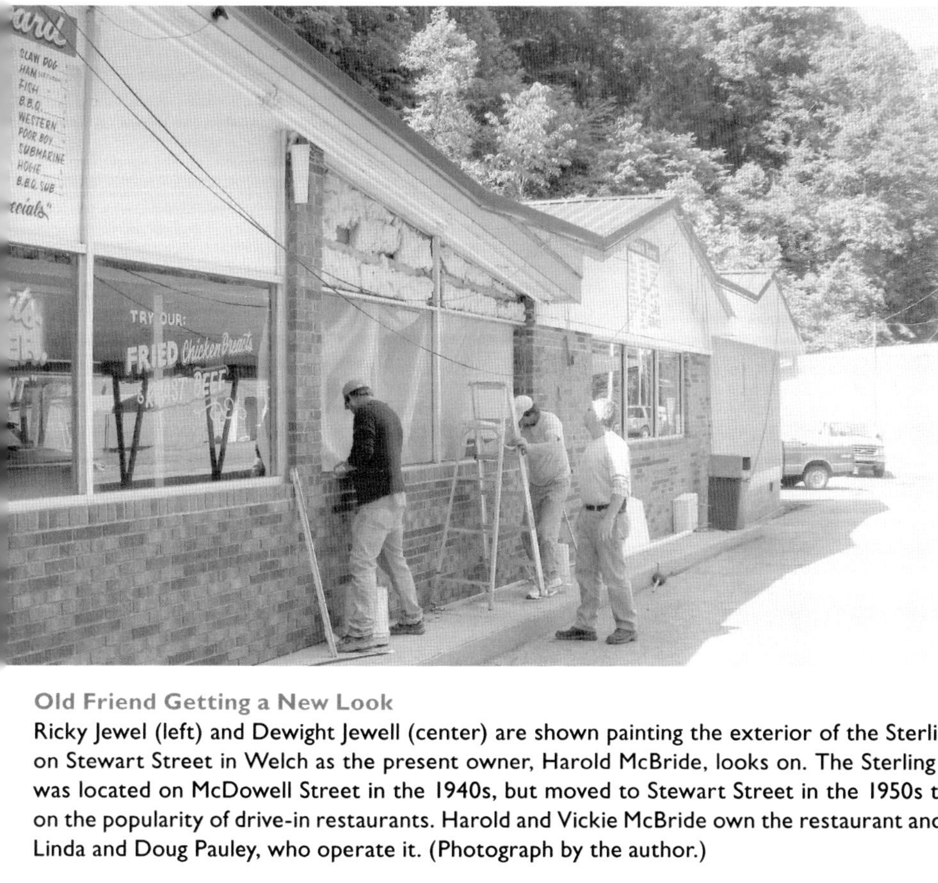

Old Friend Getting a New Look
Ricky Jewel (left) and Dewight Jewell (center) are shown painting the exterior of the Sterling Drive-In on Stewart Street in Welch as the present owner, Harold McBride, looks on. The Sterling Restaurant was located on McDowell Street in the 1940s, but moved to Stewart Street in the 1950s to capitalize on the popularity of drive-in restaurants. Harold and Vickie McBride own the restaurant and work with Linda and Doug Pauley, who operate it. (Photograph by the author.)

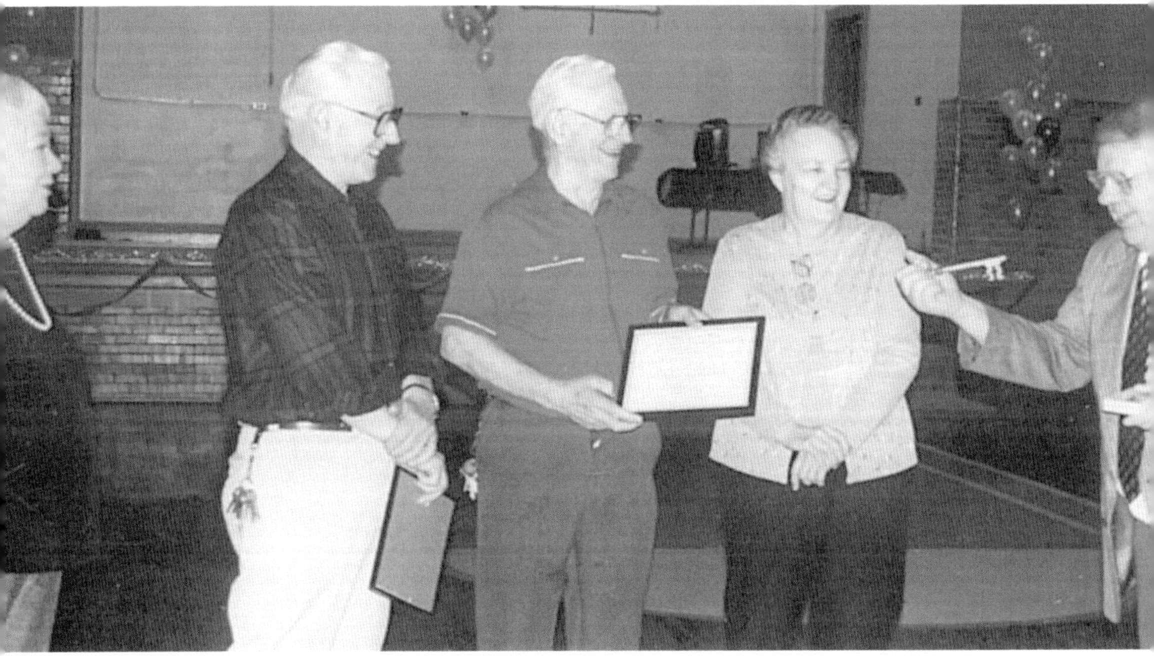

For the Good of McDowell County

Dr. Thomas Clark Hatcher, mayor of War, West Virginia, is shown presenting the key to the city of War to twins Rush Justice and Riley Justice as their wives look on during a surprise birthday party the town held for the twins in April 2000. Shown here are, from left to right, Delores Justice, Riley Justice, Rush Justice, Mary Ann Justice, and Hatcher. The brothers operated the Justice Twins Barber Shop in War for 55 years. Mayor Hatcher was a son of the late Beatrice Hatcher and former state senator Glenn Hatcher. After a successful career in national and international education, Dr. Hatcher returned to War in 1991 to teach. He also founded the McDowell County Historical Society; served as president of the Tazewell County, Virginia, Historical Society; was active in the Clinch Mountain Militia of the Sons of the American Revolution; and actively promoted War and McDowell County wherever he went. As mayor of War, he was active in the fight against the scourge of prescription drug abuse in the region at the time of his death on July 17, 2012. (Courtesy of Anita Moody.)

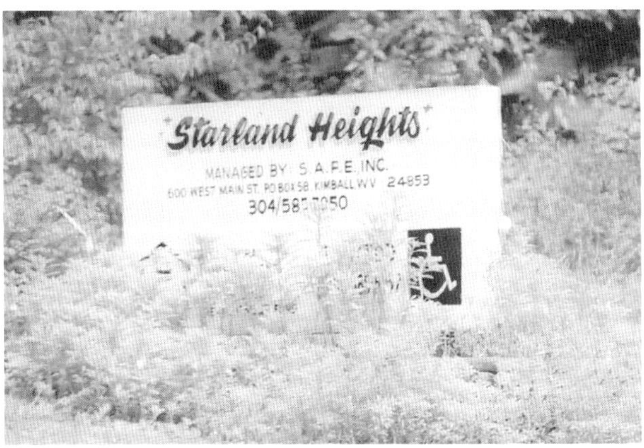

New Developments in the Stars

Former SAFE executive director Sharon Waldron was already working to bring new affordable housing to McDowell County when the floods of 2001 and 2002 left hundreds of families homeless. The transformation of the old Starland Drive-In Theater property into affordable housing was one of the first steps in accomplishing that goal. (Photograph by the author.)

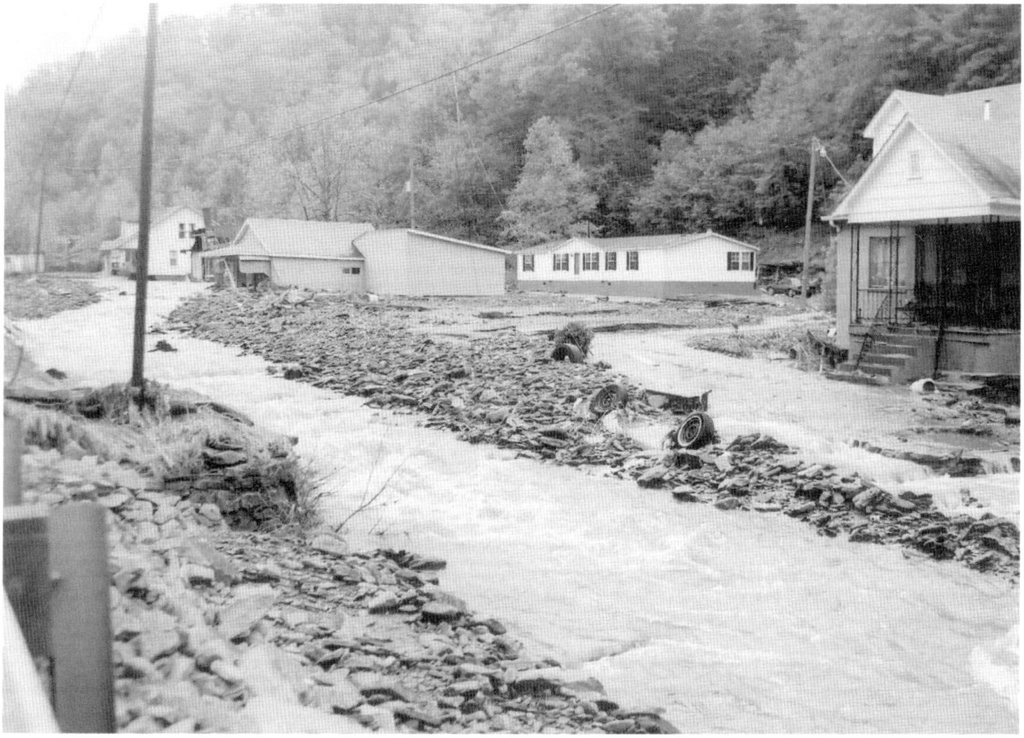

Water, Water Everywhere

The steep mountain slopes of McDowell County have always presented a major challenge to the people who call the county home. The May 2, 2002, flash flood, shown here, cut off scores of families from access to the outside world for several days until the National Guard, West Virginia Highway Department workers, and local volunteers could arrive with aid. (Photograph by the author.)

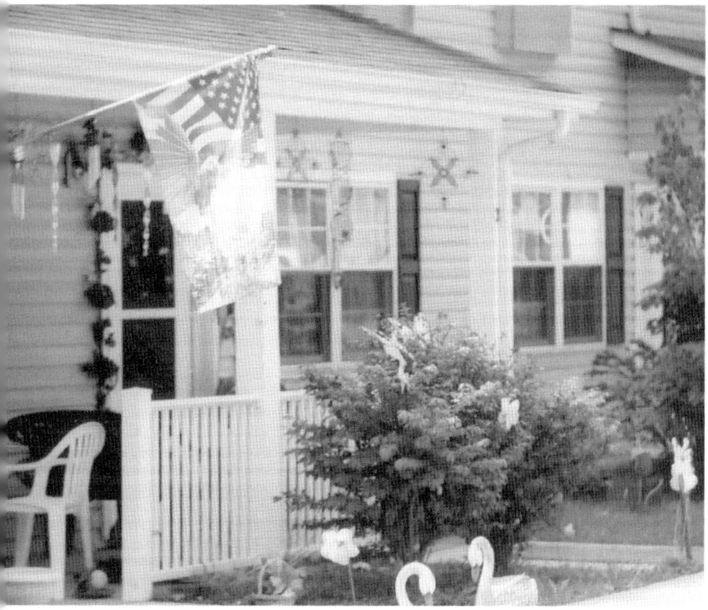

Home in the Hills

SAFE Housing and Economic Development (SHED) built affordable housing for low-income families, like the residences shown here at the Starland Heights Development. In addition to these homes, SHED rehabilitated and flood-proofed existing housing and renovated homes outside of the floodplain to provide housing opportunities. (Photograph by the author.)

He Did it with a Bow

Ryan Matney of Berwind, West Virginia, took up the sport of archery when he was nine years old to help preserve his eyesight, which was slowly being robbed by a birth defect, craniosynostosis. Archery saved his vision, and in seven years of competitive archery, he became a seven-time IBO World Champion in the 18 and under category, and earned a host of other honors. In 2010, his classmates at Big Creek High School in War, West Virginia, voted him "Most Likely to Succeed" and "Easiest to Google." (Courtesy of Karen and Arley Matney.)

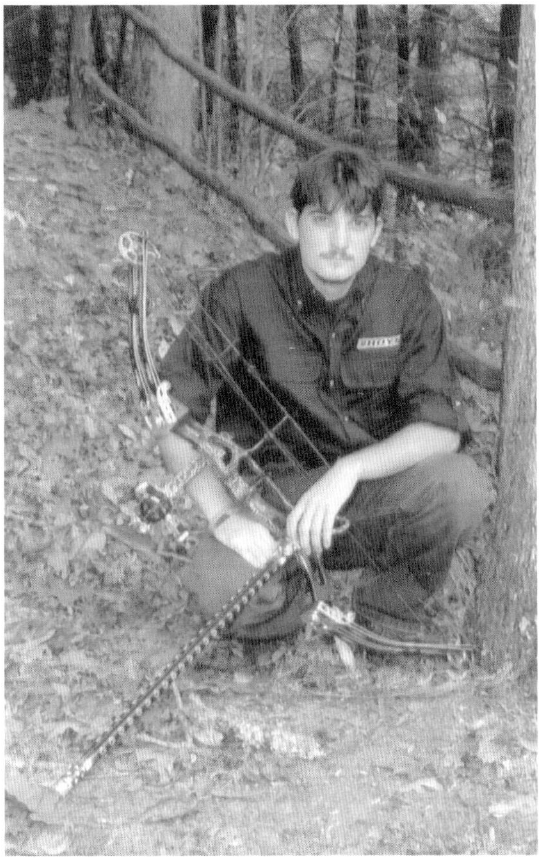

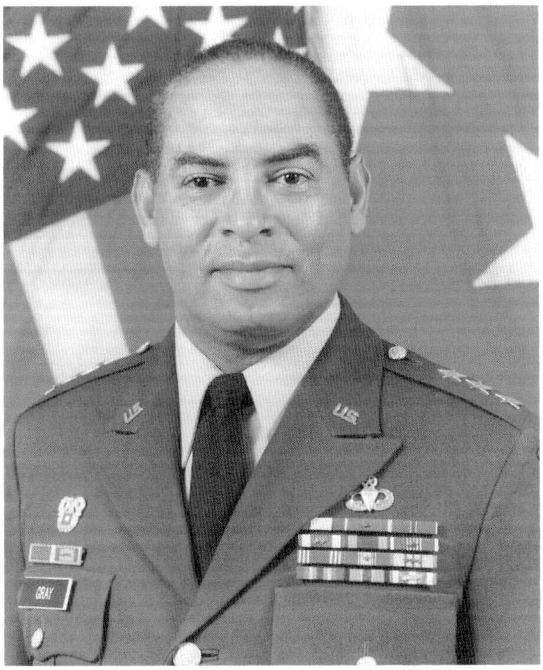

A Farewell to Arms

Lt. Gen. Robert E. "Bob" Gray died as a result of injuries he received in a two-vehicle wreck near Millen, Georgia, on November 23, 2011. Gray was a native of Algoma, West Virginia, a 1959 graduate of Elkhorn High School, and earned his undergraduate degree at Ohio State University and entered a career in the US military. He was one of a few US Army line officers to serve three combat tours in the Vietnam War, and he retired a three-star general in 1997. He returned home on November 11, 2004, to serve as keynote speaker at the McDowell County Veterans Day Parade, and volunteered in the restoration of the Oakgrove Cemetery in Bluewell, West Virginia. (Courtesy of Annie Gray.)

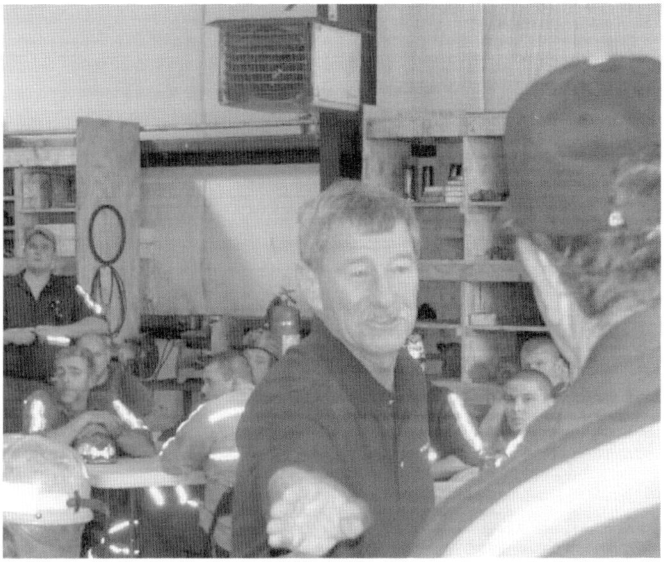

King Coal Still in the News

Mike Quillen, former president and chief operating officer of Alpha Natural Resources, is shown here meeting with employees of the Brooks Run Mining Company's Cucumber Mine in Cucumber, West Virginia. Brooks Run coal miners work the famed Pocahontas No. 3 coal seam at the Cucumber Mine, while Alpha Natural Resources provides hundreds of jobs in the southern West Virginia coalfields. (Photograph by the author.)

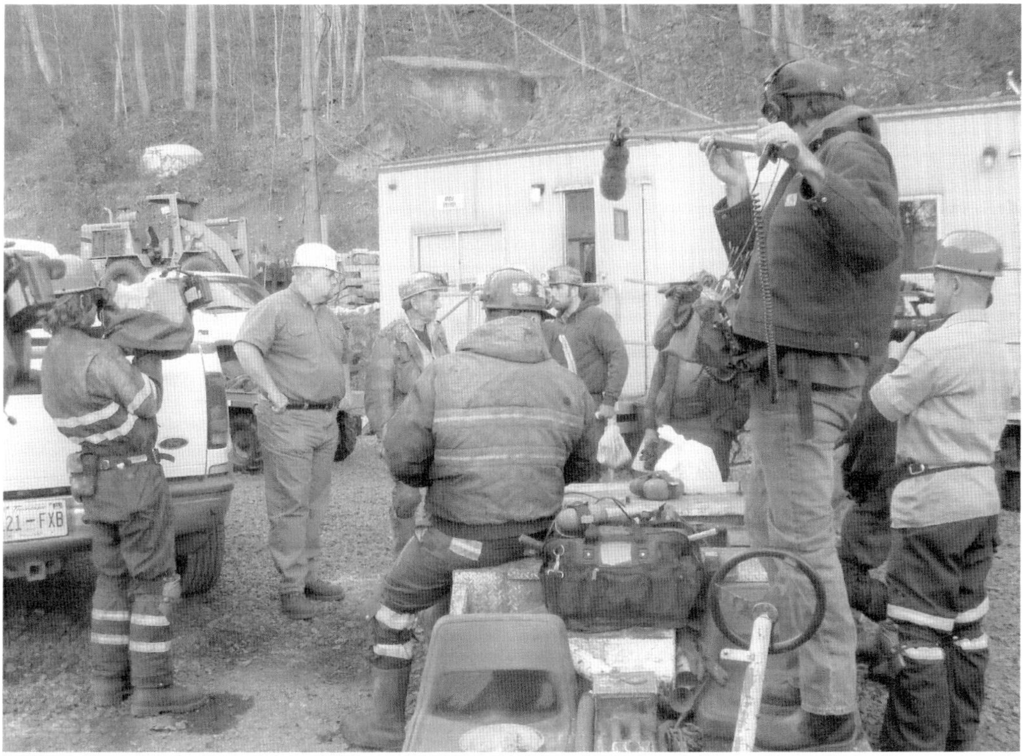

There's No Business like Coal Business

Mike Crowder (at left, in white helmet) is shown here watching Cobalt Coal Company coal miners during their pre-shift meeting before entering the Westchester Mine near Big Sandy, West Virginia. The crew from Thom Beers' Original Productions went through the 80-hour New Miners Training Course before being allowed to go underground with the Cobalt miners to film the series *Coal*, which aired nationally on Spike TV during the spring of 2011. (Photograph by the author.)

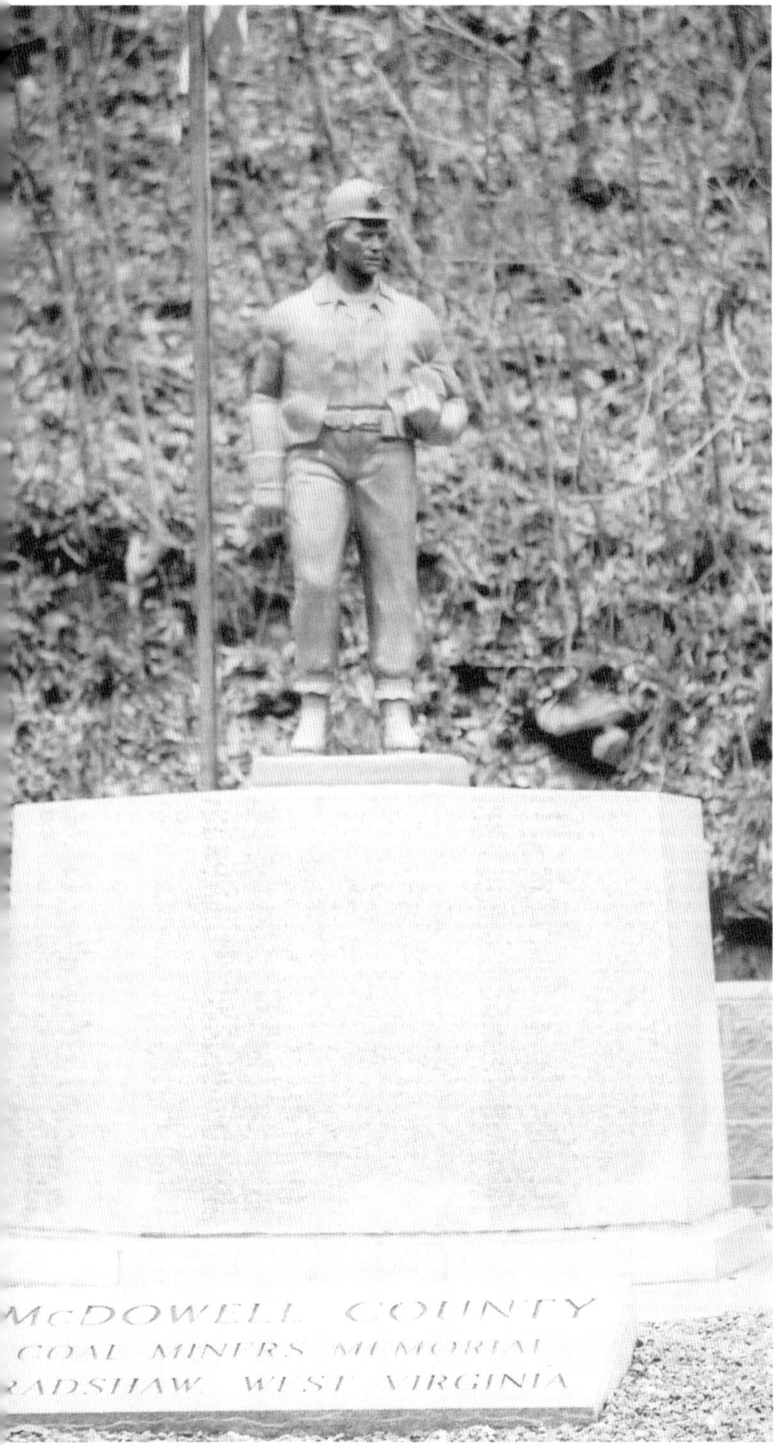

Respect for All Coal Miners
A coal miner affectionately known as "Joe Coal" stands atop the McDowell County Coal Miners' Memorial in Bradshaw, West Virginia. The memorial was developed by the Sandy River District Action Committee, headed up by Geneva Steele, and dedicated in 1992 to honor all coal miners. McDowell County has been the site of many mine tragedies, starting with the explosion at the Algoma Mine on September 15, 1902, which left 17 dead. Other mine disasters include: Lick Branch, December 29, 1908 (49 dead); Second Lick Branch, January 12, 1909 (56 dead); Bottom Creek, November 18, 1911 (14 dead); Jed, March 26, 1912 (81 dead); Yukon, December 15, 1917 (18 dead); Second Yukon, March 28, 1924 (24 dead); Yukon, May 22, 1928 (17 dead); Bartley, January 10, 1940 (91 dead); Havaco, January 15, 1946 (15 dead); Bishop, February 4, 1957 (37 dead); and Second Bishop, October 27, 1958 (22 dead). Countless other coal miners have been killed or injured in roof falls or other accidents, and even more suffer from the lingering effects of coal workers' pneumoconiosis, also known as black lung. (Photograph by the author.)

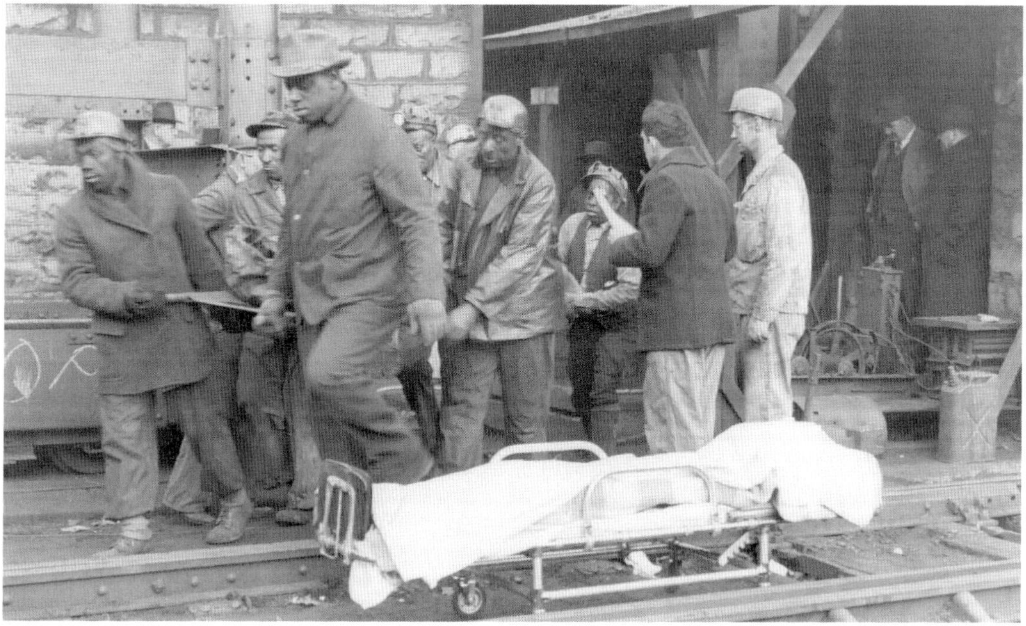

Band of Brothers

The brotherhood of coal miners and coal-mining families transcends traditional racial, ethnic, and religious boundaries that often tear people apart. The coal miners shown here working to rescue victims and remove the dead from the Havaco mine disaster in 1946 worked together when they were each called upon to shoulder a load. (Courtesy of the Eastern Regional Coal Archives.)

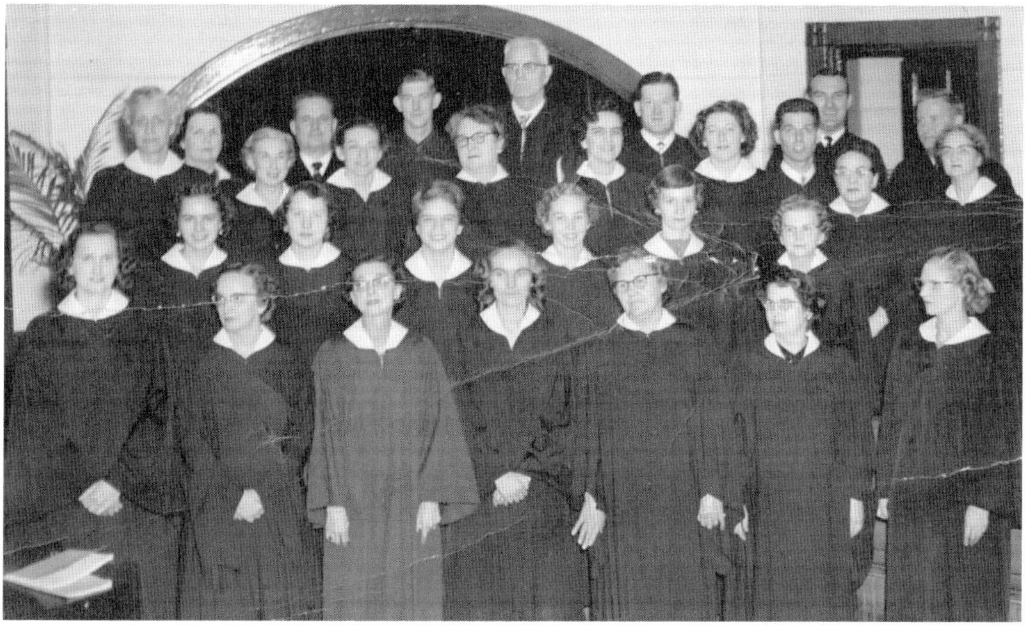

Hallelujah

The First Community Choir of McDowell County is shown in this 1955 photograph. The choir's 29 members came from various Baptist, Methodist, and Episcopalian churches, but the county has been represented by many other faiths through the years. (Courtesy of Shirley Ofsa.)

BIBLIOGRAPHY

Archer, William R. "Bill." *McDowell County.* Charleston, SC: Arcadia Publishing, 2005.

———. *Welch.* Charleston, SC: Arcadia Publishing, 2006.

Cohen, Stan. *King Coal: A Pictorial Heritage of West Virginia Coal Mining.* Charleston, WV: Pictorial Histories Publishing Company, 1984.

Cometti, Elizabeth and Festus P. Summers. *The Thirty-Fifth State.* Morgantown: West Virginia University Library, 1966.

Dillon, Lacy A. *They Died in the Darkness.* Ravencliffe, WV: Lacy A. Dillon, 1976.

Johnston, David E. *History of the Middle New River Settlements and Contiguous Territory.* Bluefield, WV: 1906.

Lambie, Joseph T. *From Mine to Market: The History of Coal Transportation on the Norfolk and Western Railway.* New York: New York University Press, 1954.

MacQueen, David A. *The Crozers of Upland.* Upland, PA: David A. MacQueen, 1982.

Marino, Rose R. *The Story of a Hospital, Welch Emergency 1900–1985.* Welch, WV: Rose R. Marino, 1990.

McConnell, J. Knox. *The Boxer and The Banker.* Keystone, WV: John Knox McConnell Jr., 1984.

McCormick, Kyle. *The Story of Mercer County.* Charleston, WV: Kyle McCormick, 1957.

Miller, William J. *Great Maps of the Civil War.* Nashville, TN: Rutledge Hill Press, 2004.

Schuler, Dennis and Larry J. Delp. *Mel Street: A Country Legend.* Charleston, WV: Dennis R. Schuler & Larry J. Delp, 2002.

Shawkey, M.P. *West Virginia: A Book of Geography, History and Industry.* Boston, MA: Ginn and Company, 1922.

Tams Jr., W.P. *The Smokeless Coal Fields of West Virginia.* Morgantown: West Virginia University Press, 1963.

Tribe, Ivan M. *Mountaineer Jamboree: Country Music in West Virginia.* Lexington, KY: University Press of Kentucky, 1984.

INDEX

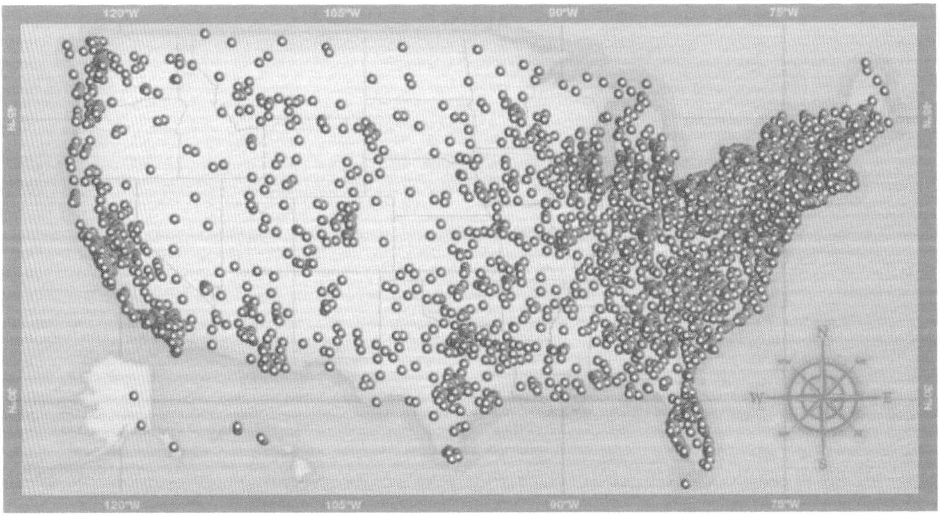

Consistent with our mission to preserve history on a local level, this book was printed in South Carolina on American-made paper and manufactured entirely in the United States. Products carrying the accredited Forest Stewardship Council (FSC) label are printed on 100 percent FSC-certified paper.